GOING THE
DISTANCE

GOING THE
DISTANCE

THE LIFE AND WORKS OF
W.P. KINSELLA

William Steele

Douglas & McIntyre

Douglas and McIntyre (2013) Ltd.
P.O. Box 219, Madeira Park, BC, V0N 2H0
www.douglas-mcintyre.com

Edited by Pam Robertson
Indexed by Emma Skagen
Jacket design by Anna Comfort O'Keeffe
Text design by Mary White
Printed and bound in Canada

Douglas and McIntyre (2013) Ltd. acknowledges the support of the Canada
Council for the Arts, which last year invested $153 million to bring the arts to
Canadians throughout the country. We also gratefully acknowledge financial
support from the Government of Canada and from the Province of British
Columbia through the BC Arts Council and the Book Publishing Tax Credit.

 Canada Council   Conseil des arts
for the Arts   du Canada
 BRITISH COLUMBIA
ARTS COUNCIL
An agency of the Province of British Columbia
Canadä

Library and Archives Canada Cataloguing in Publication

Steele, William, 1973–, author
 Going the distance : the life and works of W.P. Kinsella / William Steele.

Includes bibliographical references and index.
Issued in print and electronic formats.
ISBN 978-1-77162-194-6 (hardcover).—ISBN 978-1-77162-195-3 (HTML)

 1. Kinsella, W. P. 2. Authors, Canadian (English)—20th century—
Biography. I. Title.

PS8571.I57Z86 2018   C813'.54   C2018-902131-4
                                                C2018-902132-2

In memory of John L. Steele III, 1947–2016
He fought the good fight; he finished the race

Dedicated to Al Trabant, whom I am proud to call a friend

Contents

Prologue

Early in the summer of 1989, a group of friends went with my brothers and me to see a matinee at a nearby theatre. My brothers both had an eye on one of the girls in the group, so when she decided she wanted to watch *Indiana Jones and the Last Crusade*, they, and everyone else with us, bought tickets for that show. A few weeks before, however, I had seen a trailer for a movie about a man who heard a voice telling him to build a baseball field on his farm, and plow under his cornfield to do so, and knew I had to see it. So I bought a ticket for that and found myself a seat near the back of the theatre, where I settled in for the next two hours. Once the lights had dimmed and James Horner's music set the stage, I heard Kevin Costner begin narrating, "My father's name was John Kinsella. . ." And I was hooked.

In the opening credits, I learned the movie was based on a novel, *Shoeless Joe*, by some writer named W.P. Kinsella. I soon read and re-read the novel, devouring it for its use of magic realism, though at the time I wasn't aware that the style had a name. When the movie came out on VHS (and later, DVD), I bought a copy and drove my family and friends crazy watching it over and over.

Eight years after I first saw the film, I was completing my coursework for my master's degree in English, and I needed to find a topic for my dissertation. Being told for the first time in my academic career I could write about whatever I wanted, I decided to explore the various father-son relationships in Kinsella's novel and in Phil Alden Robinson's movie. Fully expecting the committee to say my proposal wasn't scholarly enough, I was more than a little surprised when they not only approved the topic but also seemed genuinely interested in the idea. While I was defending the thesis the following spring, one of the committee members became emotional while talking about his own relationship with his father. And in a letter of congratulations, the dean mentioned being reminded as he read it of watching the Brooklyn Dodgers play at Ebbets Field when he was young.

Six years later, I quit my teaching job and moved to Pennsylvania to pursue a doctoral degree in literature and criticism. I found myself having to choose a research topic that would consume my life for the next two years. And once more, I found myself drawn to Kinsella's fiction. By this time, I had read all of his baseball novels and short stories I could find, so I expanded the scope of my research to consider the role the game has in establishing various types of identity in his baseball novels.

During a research trip to the National Baseball Hall of Fame and Museum in Cooperstown, New York, the research librarian became interested in my topic and asked if I had reached out to Kinsella himself. My only interaction with Kinsella had been two years before when I attended a reading he gave in Portland, Oregon, when he looked like he might hit me over the head with my master's thesis when I asked him to sign it. Having later discovered his disdain for academia, specifically for literary theorists, whom he felt spent too much time searching for hidden symbols and their meanings in literature, I had admittedly been reluctant to reach out to him and was unaware of how to contact him. The librarian provided me with Kinsella's address, but my attempt to contact him with a few questions went unanswered.

On the day I graduated with my PhD, the committee member who hooded me during the ceremony, Dr. David Downing, told my wife that it was her job to make sure I pitched my dissertation to a publisher, as it was the first in-depth study of Kinsella's work ever done. I, however, had spent the previous two-plus years immersed in researching and writing about the topic, so I put the manuscript on a shelf for more than three years, until I finally convinced myself to revisit it.

In the fall of 2011, my first book, *A Member of the Local Nine: Baseball and Identity in the Fiction of W.P. Kinsella,* was released just a few weeks after Kinsella's first novel in thirteen years, *Butterfly Winter,* was published. One evening several months later, I received an email from Al Trabant, a man in Canada who introduced himself as a Kinsella fan who was interested in reading anything by or about Kinsella. Though he originally reached out to me to ask about a paper I had presented at a conference, he was happy to hear I had just published a book and requested that I send him a copy.

Some weeks later, Al emailed me again to tell me he was friends with Kinsella and had loaned him my book to read. Although part of me was interested in what Kinsella would think about my critical approach to his work, most of my time was spent thinking about a quote of his I had read somewhere in which he said he kept the heart of a literary critic on his desk. Not long after that, I received an email from Kinsella himself telling me he had just finished the book. "You've done a good job, make some good points, and don't make a fool of yourself as so many academics do, by creating ludicrous interpretations of the books you study," he wrote, and it remains to this day the best compliment anyone has ever given me related to my scholarship. It meant even more coming from someone who had very little to say by way of complimenting people in my line of work.

Two weeks later, Kinsella surprised me even more when he contacted me and asked if I would consider writing his biography. Having turned down multiple offers at the height of his career, he had decided it was time for something to be written while he and the important people in his life were still alive. To Bill's credit, he provided me with hundreds of pages of handwritten autobiographical notes, sent folders full of clippings, and gave me contact information for any of his friends and family I needed for the project. The following summer, we made plans for me to visit him at his home overlooking the Fraser River in British Columbia.

One morning in early August 2013, I was standing outside my hotel in Hope, BC, when a small red car pulled up and an older bearded man waved me over as he unlocked the door.

"Good morning. I'm Bill Kinsella," he said as he shook my hand. "I was thinking of getting some breakfast at Tim Hortons. Will that be alright with you? I figured we would eat and visit a little bit before getting to work."

The next few minutes began what would eventually turn into several hours' worth of conversations, emails and research. When he'd initially approached me about writing his biography, he said, "My life is not that interesting . . . I use my imagination to create interesting stories. But I am a thoroughly unadventurous person, live quietly and confide in virtually no one, which may or may not pose a problem for a biographer." What I came to find over the next four years was that Bill was right: his life was not really all that much different from most of our lives. But I also discovered that he was able to make it far more interesting because of his imagination and tenacity, the two tools that served him so well for more than forty years as a writer.

Returning to his house after breakfast, we sat down at his kitchen table, where we began the first of many interviews. As Bill played multiple games of online Scrabble simultaneously, muttering under his breath to the players against whom he was competing, I opened my notebook and said, "So, I've got a few questions . . ."

1

Six Hundred Miles from Anywhere

By the middle of the 1930s, much of the world was mired in the grim realities of the Great Depression. Coupled with a dismal economy, events in Europe were rapidly moving towards a global war on a scale never before seen, holding in store a future that for many would seem, at best, as bleak as their present situation. While this time period served as the backdrop for literary works like John Steinbeck's *The Grapes of Wrath*, such novels were able to capture only a fragment of the financial realities facing families during this period. This backdrop led William Patrick (W.P.) Kinsella to rely on his own imagination throughout his life and shaped him into the writer he was to become.

W.P. Kinsella's father, John, was born to Patrick and Ellen Kinsella on May 15, 1896, in the now defunct town of Ashgrove, North Dakota, where Patrick was a postmaster, the post office being conveniently located in the family's farmhouse. With forefathers originally from Ireland, the Kinsellas, like many immigrants, moved westward, possibly spending time in London, Ontario, before settling in the rural North Dakota landscape. By the time he was four years old, just after the turn of the new century, Johnny and his family had moved to the small village of Rivière Qui Barre, Alberta. A mile from town his parents established a small farm where they raised their eight children.

After turning eighteen in 1914, John returned to the United States to enlist in the army, claiming his American citizenship, which he retained for the rest of his life. During this time, presumably as a stretcher bearer in France, he, like countless other soldiers in the Great War, was gassed, leaving him with tuberculosis and recurring bouts of pneumonia that plagued him for the rest of his life.[1]

While working with a doctor in the army who observed his aptitude for medicine, John was encouraged to pursue a medical profession in civilian life. Years later, having never followed that advice, John Kinsella lamented to his son, "My main regret in life is that I didn't have sense enough to do that," adding quietly, "Never let anyone keep you from doing what you want to do with your life." The advice stayed with Bill.

Following the war and his discharge from the military, John travelled extensively, visiting all forty-eight states and most of the Canadian provinces while working various jobs and playing semi-professional baseball along the way. By all accounts passed down in the family's oral history, John was an adequate third baseman, though his career never advanced beyond the level of commercial league teams. His stories of watching various major league teams play across the United States, including seeing the Chicago White Sox play during the infamous 1919 season, were the first exposure his son had to the game he would so often use in his writings. John returned to Canada in the mid-1920s and worked in the coal mines in Cardiff, a small town south of Edmonton. There, he fell in love with Mary Olive Elliot, whom he had met years earlier, though their relationship became romantic only after his return from his sojourn.

Mary Olive, called by different variations of the two names throughout her life, was born in Wingham, Ontario, on September 6, 1903, to Thomas Elliot, a mining engineer, and his wife, Rose. While Mary was still an infant, she and her parents and her sister Alba (older by eight years), moved to a homestead near Athabasca, Alberta, approximately seventy-five miles north of Edmonton, where Thomas returned to working in the coal mines. Three years later, the family's third and final child, Margaret, was born, and the girls spent the rest of their formative years in Athabasca.

By the time John Kinsella returned to Alberta to work in the Cardiff mines, Mary Olive's family was living in the area and would stay there until the last of the mines died out, leaving nothing but a few dilapidated buildings behind. It was during this time that John became interested in pursuing a relationship with Mary Olive, though they had known each other for some time before that. After completing grade eight, Mary Olive worked as a telephone operator in Westlock until the Elliot family relocated to Edmonton sometime around 1928. She and John married on April 15, 1929.

With his new bride now employed at Ramsey's Department Store on 101st Street in Edmonton, John began looking for a steady job as a plasterer, which he had worked as in Florida and California. Soon after their wedding, however, he suffered another bout of tuberculosis, and the doctors grimly predicted he had only six months to live. Compounding the young couple's problems was the lack of plastering work available as the economic depression strangling North America tightened its grip that fall, following the stock market crash in October. Not wanting to accept any government relief, John sold the Edmonton house his wife had inherited on 86th Street and used the money to first briefly rent a farm and later, in 1932–33, to purchase 160 acres of rocky and relatively worthless land situated between Lake Isle and Darwell, Alberta, some sixty miles northwest of Edmonton. As an adult, Bill would regularly comment that, because of the farm's remote location, the distance "might as well have been six hundred [miles]. Our only transportation was a horse and buggy in the summer, and horse-drawn sleigh in winter."[2] With few options for such rocky terrain, the Kinsellas raised and kept a few cattle, pigs and chickens, and planted a large garden that enabled them to can various vegetables for the winter.

The Kinsella cabin was large in comparison with other houses in the area, solidly crafted from logs, and identified by the stout brick chimney John constructed soon after he purchased the farm. The large kitchen on the house's north side faced a stone path leading off into the Alberta landscape. Nearly all of the family's indoor time was spent in the kitchen, where Mary Olive built a couch frame from pieces of lumber, filling it with hay and upholstering it with gunnysacks. The room was heated by a large, black, wood-burning cook stove, which the family kept going regularly to heat water brought from a well nearly 100 yards north of the house.

The front living room, which Mrs. Kinsella referred to as "the parlour," was a dark space, its only window shaded by the trees outside. And although the room had an old sofa bed and a wood-burning space heater, it was only used during Christmas, when the family would place a tree in the corner and decorate it with brightly coloured bulbs, thin strings of tinsel and small Santa Claus figurines. The kitchen, by default, became the family's key space and would, decades later, reappear in Jamie O'Day's narrative in the semi-autobiographical descriptions Kinsella wrote in *Box Socials* and *The Winter Helen Dropped By*.

On May 25, 1935, Babe Ruth hit the last three home runs of his career, against the Pittsburgh Pirates in Forbes Field. Meanwhile, 2,100 miles northwest, thirty-nine-year-old John and thirty-two-year-old Mary Olive welcomed their first and only child, William Patrick, whom they affectionately called "Billy." And while John had convinced his wife to move to the remote farm, she made it clear that, were they to have children, she would give birth in the hospital in Edmonton, a commitment she kept as they welcomed their newborn son that spring.

Raised in isolation, miles from the nearest town and with only horses for transportation, the boy would spend nearly the first full decade of his life with virtually no company other than his parents and his mother's sister Margaret, who moved to the farm and stayed with the family until she took a job in Edmonton when Billy was five years old. With no other children nearby, surrounded by vast open space, young Billy had few options other than his imagination for entertainment, something to which he later attributed his beginnings as a writer. A self-proclaimed daydreamer, he regularly created his own worlds, often with his favourite stuffed animals serving as the siblings and playmates he lacked. He gave the animals names like Puppy, Jabby, Helen, Scotty-Pat, Kitty, Jerry and Pinky, and they later became the inspiration for his first full-length short story, "The Blue Rabbits." They were also described in "A Tribute to Toys," one of his earliest paid publications, printed in the freelance writers' space, "Third Column," in the *Edmonton Journal*. More importantly to the young boy, however, they were his first friends on the Darwell farm.

One Christmas Eve, when Billy was no more than four years old, with the decorated tree lighting the otherwise darkened parlour, he alternated between bouncing on the kitchen couch and looking out the window, pressing his face to the glass to block out the glow from the lamplight behind him. His mother stood working at the stove in the kitchen telling him to watch out the window in the event he might catch a glimpse of Santa Claus as he made his way to the homes of good girls and boys. His father, meanwhile, was out in the barn finishing up the evening chores before joining the family inside the comfort of the cabin.

With growing anticipation, Billy pressed his nose against the cold windowpane. Suddenly, the frame was filled with Santa's face gazing back at him. With white hair and pink skin, Santa looked exactly as the boy always imagined he should. Though in the window for no more than a few seconds, the image left Billy in a near state of shock, yelling to his mother, "I saw him! I saw him!" His mother later recalled coming in to see her wide-eyed son, pale and shaking from a mixture of fear and excitement. The next morning, Billy awoke and went outside to explore the area on the cabin's east side. Noting the footprints on the ground beneath the living room window, he ran back inside to announce, "Santa Claus wears boots just like Daddy!"

Years later, while digging in the barn behind the feed box near where the cows were kept, Billy discovered a weathered papier mâché Santa Claus mask covered in grass and showing evidence of being chewed by mice. Though long past the age when he still believed in Santa, Kinsella recalled years later that the discovery made him very sad. In 1972, he used the memory as part of a four-part autobiographical piece entitled "Christmas Eve," which he submitted as an assignment for a creative writing class at the University of Victoria; Bill later recalled the story (never published) as "very badly written, sentimental, [and] melodramatic." The discovery, however, served to solidify his lifelong disbelief in anything fantastic or supernatural, though those elements were at the root of some of his most popular stories.

Bill Kinsella would later become a writer and university professor, though neither of his parents had attended school beyond grade eight. In spite of their limited education, Bill recalled that both John and Mary Olive wrote in clear, unadorned, standard English and spoke clearly, with proper grammar. And all three of his parents—Bill often referred to Aunt Margaret as his third parent—were regular readers and took turns reading aloud to him in the evening around the oilcloth-covered table in the cabin's kitchen, cultivating his imagination and his love of reading.

Lacking interaction with other children in the Darwell area, Billy often recruited the three adults in the cabin to be part of his games and imaginary worlds. His father, a hockey fan whose American background meant he cheered against all the Canadian teams, commandeered the only radio on Saturday nights when games were broadcast; Billy and Aunt Margaret, both uninterested in the sport, were forced to bundle up in heavy sweaters to play games of their own in the living room, away from the stove. Using Jell-O boxes as fences, the two created farms with small wooden and lead animals. Occasionally, the young boy would collect the boxes and tins from the few store-bought items in the house and set up a market where he would sell his products, cheaply to Margaret but at significantly higher mark-ups to his parents. As an adult Bill later joked that he "didn't know there were other children, and that [he] considered [himself] a small adult" until the family moved to Edmonton when he was ten years old.[3]

The relative isolation that kept the Kinsellas from experiencing the excitement and entertainment found in larger cities made what simple forms of entertainment they did have that much more valuable to them. With a small battery-powered radio their only continuous connection to the outside world, the family would gather around to listen to the news, and, on a limited basis, various music and popular shows that fuelled Billy's creative interests. They received primarily smaller Canadian stations and, from time to time, CKUA out of Edmonton, though on clear evenings after dark they would occasionally pick up reception from as far away as Salt Lake City. Although there were children's programs broadcast in the afternoons, including a serialized production of "Little Orphan Annie," Billy was never drawn to them. In fact, after listening to one such episode, he became afraid of what was going to happen next, so he purposely avoided the show when it came on, even going to bed sometimes at 5:30, when the show was broadcast.

Such fears, he concluded some four decades later in his personal notes, led to his dislike of the horror and suspense genre in books, shows and movies. Due to his "extremely active imagination," Kinsella concluded that as a child he "identified too closely with fictional characters [and] used to confide [his] worries to [his] mom" who provided reassurance to her young son. In a recurring pattern that continued into his adult life, Billy would focus on something else to feel anxious and apprehensive about. In spite of his later literary success and personal achievements, he recognized that from an early age he was "just a pessimist" and would "anticipate the worst, no matter the situation." Fortunately for the young boy, comedic broadcasts became a regular part of the family's life, huddling over the radio in the kitchen to hear the shows over the crackling static. Billy's personal favourite, *Fibber McGee and Molly*, provided much-needed relief from what were often extreme conditions in isolated circumstances. Most important to his emerging author's ear were the dramatic broadcasts and literary dramas. Though he did not always understand what he heard on these shows, he later realized that they helped him develop a taste for both literature and theatre, two lifelong passions.

With radio access often limited by the battery's power, the Kinsellas derived much of their entertainment from their shelf of books, which included Jack London's *The Call of the Wild*, Gene Stratton-Porter's *A Girl of the Limberlost*, Louisa May Alcott's *Little Women*, as well as *The Valley of Silent Men* by James Oliver Curwood, *The Desert of Wheat* by Zane Grey and one of the Tarzan books by Edgar Rice Burroughs, plus a number of children's books, including *Aesop's Fables* and a book about a family of cats, which Billy committed to memory at a young age. Thinking of himself as a small adult, he began referring to his parents as "Johnny and Olive."

Much as the early years on the farm shaped Billy's imagination and love of literature, they also had an impact on his musical tastes and his love for storytelling in songs, especially early country music. Because of the radio's limited power supply, Billy was allowed to use the gramophone, learning how to change the needles as a young boy. While the family had a rather extensive record collection, his interest never gravitated to instrumental or romantic selections, being drawn instead towards songs like "The Big Rock Candy Mountain," "The Wreck of the Old 97," "Mississippi Flood" and the music of Jimmie Rodgers, "The Blue Yodeler," whose popular tune "Moonlight and Skies" firmly solidified the boy's musical taste in traditional country music. Years later he would see Hank Williams perform, shortly before the musician's death on New Year's Day 1953.

Occasionally, a few extended family and friends would visit; however, even with limited interaction with other people living in the area, Billy came to know various members of the community, often seeing how they pulled together in times of need despite the distance separating them. One such neighbour, Max Furst, was a bachelor who lived in a drafty two-storey frame house in the Lake Isle community. When his home burned to the ground, Furst bought a new stove and bed, and relocated to the granary, where members of the community contributed various household goods, bedding and clothing to help him. The man was later the inspiration for the story "Hopfstadt's Cabin," for which Kinsella won first prize in the 1966 Literary Awards Competition sponsored by the *Edmonton Journal*.

During the Depression Billy's family and those in the surrounding area worked hard every day to simply eke out a living from the rocky ground in unforgivable conditions. During such times, the community often gathered for fundraisers to assist neighbours who were even less fortunate than themselves and who lacked resources due to whatever situation had befallen them. In one such case, Billy attended a box social, an event designed to provide entertainment, fellowship and a meal for those who attended. The women from the community contributed homemade meals in custom decorated boxes. Men would then bid on the anonymously boxed meals as they were auctioned off, spending as much as their limited funds would allow. Reflecting on the event years later, Kinsella recalled that, because everyone in the area either farmed or tried to raise cattle on the nearly unusable land, there were no rich people. Despite their own financial struggles, locals came together on this night to help raise funds for a family that had been burned out of their home.

Held at the Lake Isle Community Hall, a large log building, the event began with a card tournament with a one-dollar buy-in—the winners received a small prize with the rest of the proceeds going to help the family in need. Though John was out of town working in the city on a plastering job, Olive and her young son made the five-mile round trip to Lake Isle for a rare opportunity to socialize. A local man named Carl Voight bought Olive's meal and the three sat on the edge of the stage eating and visiting together. Olive had given Billy fifty cents to spend on some smaller baskets that had been brought by school girls and were intended to be bought by the boys from the school; however, since Kinsella was homeschooled and knew none of the girls there, his characteristic shyness prevented him from bidding.

Years later, Kinsella's first novel set in Canada, *Box Socials*, would explore the large immigrant community of the rural Six Towns area, a remote part of Alberta not unlike the place where he grew up. Kinsella's narrator, Jamie O'Day, describes the majority of people in the area as "hardworking farmers who made a marginal living in good times, but [who] were presently mired in poverty because of the Depression."[4] And while most of his baseball novels are set in Iowa, Kinsella often presents readers with rural communities of people in need of each other's generosity. Most notably, in *Magic Time*, the entire town of Grand Mound, Iowa, comes together and contributes time, money and merchandise to help bring the family of a local baseball player from Mexico to Iowa and set them up in a home, presented at a dance held in their honour. The dance, much like the box social from Kinsella's boyhood, demonstrates the community interaction and philanthropy Billy witnessed as a boy. Because these events were so few in number and happened so infrequently, their place in his memory indicates the depth of the impression they made.

Other than such benefit dances, card games held at the community hall, and occasional Sunday afternoon visits with neighbours, social events were sporadic at best. Even church services, which often fill a need for social interaction in rural communities, were non-existent. The sparsely settled area had such a diverse collection of ethnicities that no church was within a reasonable driving distance. The nearest place anyone considered a church was a type of mission nearly twenty miles away in Lac Ste. Anne. The tiny yellow structure along Highway 16, referred to as "the Church in the Wildwood," later served as the inspiration for the church described by Marylyle Baron, first in the story "Something to Think About" and later in Kinsella's second novel, *The Iowa Baseball Confederacy*.

In May of 1941, Billy turned six years old and was set to begin school that fall at the one-room Lake Isle School, two and a half miles away from the family farm. However, there were no other children Billy could travel to school with, so John and Olive made the decision to hold him back for a year. By the following summer, John bought a pony for Billy to ride to and from school. The young boy's greatest fear was not of attending school for the first time, nor of being surrounded by so many new people; Billy's trepidation came from the pony itself. The animal sensed his fear and often refused to follow commands. Even when the pony followed directions, Billy still had the challenge of learning to saddle him and trying to master tying him to a hitching post, a task he was never able to perform well, possibly because mild dyslexia prevented him from doing so. (Though never officially diagnosed, Kinsella stated that he often confused his left and right, and thought this may have contributed to the problems with tying up the horse.)

On the first day of school, John rode with his son, putting the pony in the school's makeshift stable and arranging for an older boy to saddle the animal for Billy after school let out. Billy made the trip home safely and without any trouble, and Billy and John made the trip the following morning. By the third day, Billy was on his own, though by his own admission he was "timid, not strong, and [...] dealing with a horse that was smarter than I was, and who had no desire to make a 2.5 mile walk on a brisk autumn morning."[5] After going not even half-way, just past the neighbour's house, the horse abruptly turned around to bring him home, and did the same the following day when the rider tried to return to school.

Knowing their son was expected to attend school, but faced with the problem of a horse that seemingly did not want to go to school any more than Billy wanted to make him go, John and Olive were left wondering what they should do. Billy professed his innocence, blaming the animal: "The pony just turns around when he feels like it. He's too strong for me." While that may have been the case, he later admitted that, had he made some effort to assert himself with the animal, he would have been able to make the trip. In the back of his mind, though, was how difficult the journey would be when the harsh Alberta winter settled in and he would be dealing with riding in sleet and heavy snowstorms. Recognizing the situation was going to present more problems for the family as the school year went on, Billy's parents decided he would continue his schooling via correspondence courses offered by the Alberta government.

Because of his lack of social interaction with children his own age, Kinsella's few clear memories of the days spent in the Lake Isle School indicate that it may have been more frustrating for him to be there rather than being homeschooled. The school comprised about twenty-five students from first through eighth grades, most of whom Kinsella knew at least casually, having lived in the area his entire life, though none of them ever became close friends. The only student who made any type of lasting impression was a young girl named Bertha, also in grade one that term. She came from an itinerant family that lived along the lakefront somewhere and disappeared permanently from the district later that fall. Her reddish-blonde hair and freckles, he later admitted, probably began his lifelong passion for red-headed women. It was also the first time he experienced being an outsider drawn to another outsider, something he would regularly experience in his adult life.

In general, Billy was appalled by the students around his age, many of whom did not know how to print their own name or even know the alphabet. Describing himself years later as "one of these people who woke up at about age five knowing how to read and write,"[6] he had already been writing one-page stories for his mother. Kinsella would likely have only been frustrated and grown resentful had he been made to continue attending the school.

John, whom Billy always suspected knew he was not actually putting forth much effort to get to the schoolhouse and who knew the weather would prevent his son from making the trip for much of the winter, contacted the proper authorities in the school district and arrangements were made for the lessons to be mailed to him. Although his mother had only completed eighth grade, she had served for a few months as a teacher years earlier, in her hometown of Cardiff. During the next three years, Billy was homeschooled with the curriculum that was sent to his family each week, and he completed four grades of school in that time.

One of the first assignments was to construct a modern frieze, unfamiliar at the time to both Billy and his parents. After referring to the large orange-covered *Webster's Dictionary* on the bookshelf, he was soon put to work retrieving old copies of *The Saturday Evening Post* and *National Geographic*, periodicals from the late 1920s and early 1930s, and back issues of the *Star Weekly* from the attic, so that his mother could cut out the pictures he chose, not yet trusting her son to stay within the lines. She also helped him glue the pictures in place, knowing her son would likely make a mess in the cabin. They completed what he later proudly called "a university-level frieze and scrapbook from a seven-year-old."

At some point during that school year, the district sent a representative whose job it was to visit correspondence students once a year to ensure they were progressing as planned. The Kinsellas, in preparation for this important visit, scoured the home until it was spotless. Then their energies turned to preparing Billy, who was bathed and dressed in freshly laundered clothes while being coached on every possible question the inspector might be inclined to ask. The boy soon gathered that if he failed in presenting himself well, it would reflect negatively on his parents, increasing the pressure on him to meet their expectations. The school inspector, upon his arrival, quickly recognized that the boy, reading at nearly a grade-five level, was already far beyond other students his age; his assurance put Billy and the family at ease, making all the preparations worthwhile.

Although no record of the district representative's comments about Billy's aptitude or Olive's teaching is known to still exist, there is one surviving note from the teacher at the local one-room school. In the note, dated exactly one month after Billy's eighth birthday, Mrs. Satermo, a Kinsella family friend, described Billy as "fully competent to take up to [grade two] work" and his mathematical skills were nearly what was expected for a grade three student. His reading skills were described as "excellent," and he had "good knowledge of the words" he read, even at that young age. Having offered minor suggestions to help him learn more advanced math problems and handwriting skills, Mrs. Satermo closed the letter by telling Olive, "You are to be congratulated on the fine work you have done teaching Billy at home."[7] The praise for both Olive's teaching and Billy's work validated the family's decision to homeschool him and demonstrated the boy's ability to achieve success in his work in an isolated environment, a trait that continued into adulthood.

Having been afforded the opportunity of progressing through the material more rapidly than if he had had to endure the one-room schoolhouse experience, Billy demonstrated such proficiency that he skipped most of grade two, remembering very little other than that he had to take an exam or two at the local school at the end of the academic year in order to demonstrate his competency in each subject, something he was able to do remarkably well considering the family's limited resources and the fact that his mother had no professional training as a teacher.

Even in elementary school, Billy had already demonstrated the strong will and defiance that came to characterize him as an adult. The one area in which he and his mother constantly disagreed was on the concept of whether it was better to do quality work or to produce a large quantity of work. Though his mother operated under the belief "if something is worth doing, it is worth doing well," her son always, even as an adult, felt "it is better to do more, even if quality suffers."[8] His approach would later keep him with any number of projects in the works, allowing him to shift between working on a novel and developing ideas for various short stories simultaneously.

While staying at home year-round certainly contributed to his inability to relate to people his own age, it also undoubtedly cultivated his imagination and love of fantasy. On long summer days, when the weather was clear and while the mosquitoes and blackflies were at a minimum, Billy often sat in the sun along the walls of the root cellar or on the rails around the pig pen to think. His ideas would simmer for weeks or months, sometimes even years, before he felt they were ready to be put down on paper. As an adult, he continued to spend lengthy parts of his day "dreaming about [. . .] work, about other projects [. . .]; I dream of revenging past wrongs, relive those scenes, visualize possible and impossible sexual fantasies." As a boy, however, his daily fantasies were more whimsical, such as when he strolled the north field, about a quarter mile behind the house, imagining the various flowers as a colony of six-foot-tall men who were his servants, to do exactly what he commanded, whether it be entertaining him or waging war against one another. Looking back on these daydreams, an adult Kinsella explained, "That is essentially what fictional characters are: they are real people in your imagination, whose lives, you as author, control completely. An author has the power of life and death in his characters." Living so far from potential playmates, Billy was left with his imagination and the rural landscape to feed his creativity, something that provided an escape from the challenges of growing up in the midst of economic hardships and the reality of the growing global crisis. He often created his own companions and entertained his family with tales of their exciting exploits. Two such creations, Rags and Sigs, are the earliest known Kinsella characters, regularly accompanying him around the farm, acting as his friends, playmates and confidants.

With no one else to play with, he sometimes bounced a rubber ball off a wall or roof and caught it on the fly or off the bounce. The games he created by himself often involved exotic teams competing against each other in sports that most often bore some vague similarity to hockey, the only sport of which he had any real knowledge, as he listened to the games on the radio with his father.

Throughout his life, almost without exception, those who did become his friends were the ones who sought him out, and Kinsella readily admitted he was "not one to make overtures" in initiating friendships. Though little is known of his father's early life, Bill remembered John Kinsella as a loner as well, though he was not unfriendly. John had three or four buddies from his army days with whom he stayed in contact, but beyond that the majority of his relationships seem to have been acquaintances from the plastering trade, most of whom his son remembers as hard and heavy drinkers. While John may have had a beer or two after work in the summer months, he was not one who regularly drank, and Bill never recalled a time when his father was drunk. One of the most common traits in Kinsella's baseball novels is strong father-son relationships. Even when a character's father is absent, due either to geographical distance or death, the son, often the novel's narrator, is left reminiscing over touching moments with him.

However, John and Bill were never extremely close, though Bill found it difficult to explain why. Remembering his father as a "kind and amiable man" who "was always good to [him]," Bill recalled, nearly thirty years after John's death, that there remained a distance between them. "I suppose the distance was placed there, unintentionally, by my mother and my aunt. There was always a feeling in the air that my father was tolerated, like a large and often disobedient pet, but a pet no one would dream of getting rid of." And while he described his father as being an enjoyable presence during his early years, Bill admitted that they became more distant as he got older, though he felt they would have grown closer together had John lived longer.

Though his parents were not necessarily unhappy, Bill later determined it may have been a situation in which his mother was a much more astute financial manager than her husband, but, as many women during the time did, she allowed her husband to mishandle the family money, deeply resenting it in the process. Bill picked up this resentment from his mother as he spent far more time with her than he spent with his father. In fact, Bill could only recall one time, perhaps at five or six years of age, when he was alone with John. With both Kinsella women gone to the city, leaving the boy and his father home alone for the day, the younger Kinsella looked forward to not having to wash. Both Aunt Margaret and Mary Olive scrubbed the boy clean several times a day, and he made John promise he would not have to wash that day if he chose not to.

Like many children born during the Great Depression, some of Kinsella's earliest memories were set against the backdrop of World War II. "As the Kennedy assassination has been the most telling historical event of my lifetime," he later reflected, "so the Japanese attack of Pearl Harbor was the most memorable day for previous generations, and, just as my anguish at the death of President Kennedy embedded itself in my children's minds, so December 7, 1941 is etched in mine. I really did not know what was going on but sensed a grave situation when I encountered one." On that early December morning, one he described as "an average winter day," it was warm enough that John hitched up their two horses, Barney and Babe, to the sleigh, covered his family with blankets and buffalo robes and made the four-and-a-half-mile trip to the shores of Lake Isle to see the Satermo family, whom the Kinsellas occasionally visited. It was from the Satermos' radio that the Billy and his family learned of the Japanese attack and President Roosevelt's declaration of war the next day. Billy noticed how subdued everyone was. His father and Ancher Satermo, a Norwegian immigrant, were Americans and the United States would soon be at war. While not fully grasping the magnitude of the situation, the boy sensed that the world and his life would be forever changed as a result.

Though too young to fully understand the reasons for and implications of the war, as a Canadian, he "knew the Americans were right and everybody else was wrong." Very carefully, using his mother's scissors, he would cut out Japanese and American soldiers from the comics page and pictures of real soldiers from the photo section of the *Star Weekly*. When spring weather permitted him to play outdoors, he lined up the paper cutouts in battle formations along the path on the home's south side, where ice could still be found in the mornings and where snow banks were still formed against the logs. Backing up from the figures, Billy threw jagged bits of ice, rocks and marbles at them until the cutouts were either wounded or killed. The Japanese, regardless of how much they might have outnumbered the Americans in his battles, always lost in these encounters.

World War II remained a presence in Billy's life until the war in the Pacific ended in August 1945. John Kinsella, watching the war unfold for four years from his farm, spoke of his own unpleasant experiences from the Great War and often told his son how thankful he was that Billy was too young to be involved in World War II. With the exception of the constant stream of war-related news reports, however, the war had little effect on the family. Already living on limited income and only the barest of essentials they could not grow or produce on their farm, the notion of the "war effort" occasionally struck them as absurd. Killing their own beef, fish and chicken, and making their own butter, the Kinsellas had little use for the ration booklets, sending them to Aunt Margaret or letting Billy use them as playthings.

John Kinsella, though frustrated at his lot in life, worked hard to provide for his family, too proud to accept any type of government aid. Unfortunately, his lungs weakened from being gassed during the war, he was frequently sick with chest colds and bouts of tuberculosis. During the winter of 1943–44, a mysterious fever incapacitated him for several weeks, leaving Olive the only person to work on the farm. One day, John's illness became so dire that his wife and son walked to a neighbour's home to use their phone to call the doctor. The spring thaw had begun, and the roads were ankle deep in mud, making their trip that much more unbearable and making it difficult for the doctor to get to the farm.

As the war drew to a close, and with the economic, social and educational possibilities on the farm as dismal as they had ever been, the family began to explore the notion of moving into Edmonton. Having only made occasional trips into the city, Billy found the idea of living anywhere close to it unfathomable.

Kinsella's first real memory of leaving the farm to visit Edmonton was when he was eight or nine years old and a family friend drove him and his mother the ten miles to the Jasper Highway, where they met the bus at Fallis Corner. The bullet-shaped bus was dirty on both the inside and the outside and had to navigate the soupy gravel highway as it pulled to a stop at the station. For a boy who had minimal experience beyond the farm, the bus ride was itself a thrilling experience.

Stepping off the bus, about an hour later, at the depot on 102nd Avenue across from the Eaton's department store, the young boy suddenly found himself overwhelmed by the crush of people on the sidewalks, the traffic lights and the tall buildings, some as high as seven or eight storeys.

Billy and his mother stayed with Aunt Margaret, who had moved into the city in the early 1940s. Heartbroken at the thought of losing his aunt, someone he considered a second mother, he'd begged her to take him with her in her suitcase. Her moving may have, however, led to Kinsella's early development as a writer, as he started writing her letters, each one beginning, "Dear Aunt Margaret: How are you? I am fine."[9]

The trip briefly reunited Billy with his favourite aunt, with whom he had been so close in his early years. He also saw his first colour movie at this time. And now, with a wave of optimism resulting from the war's end, and the hope that a move to the city would improve John's health, the family's finances, and provide Billy opportunities for a childhood in a school with people his own age, the Kinsellas prepared for what would prove to be a turning point in their lives.

2

Edmonton

Late August 1945 brought significant changes for the Kinsella family. The war in Europe had been over for only three months and the Japanese surrender had taken place mere days earlier. As the war had drawn to a close, John and Olive discussed their son's education, specifically Olive's feelings of incompetence in continuing to teach Billy through the grade-five correspondence courses. The family sold the farm to George Lund, the farmer living adjacent to their property, and moved into Edmonton, where Billy could attend public school for the first time in his life and where John would be more likely to find work.

The city was still filled with American troops who had been stationed there during the war, making it difficult for families to find adequate housing. To complicate matters, the war effort had resulted in few new homes being constructed, meaning nearly every available space in town was already rented. John Kinsella spent that summer working in the city. When Olive and Billy moved to town to join him, Olive found the second floor of an older frame house at 11236 87th Street in the Parkdale district, only a block from where she and John had lived before moving to the farm years earlier.

The family's new space was much smaller than the cabin in Darwell, forcing them to bring only the most necessary personal effects and clothes, and leave most of their furniture back on the farm. The quarters, though cramped, were warm and clean, and while having to share a bathroom downstairs with the couple who owned the house may have been difficult for some, for the Kinsellas it was a luxury after years of having only outdoor toilets. Settled into a new city and a new home, Bill saw his life "changed completely and irrevocably forever."[1] The next month, for the first time other than the few days he spent in the schoolhouse at Lake Isle, Billy attended a regular school full-time, at Parkdale School. Despite the lack of classroom education for his first four years of schooling, he was immediately recognized as one of the brightest students in the class of thirty-five. His comfort with the workload and material, however, far exceeded his comfort with the other students. As he continually recalled to audiences as an adult, having spent his first ten years on the farm with his parents and Aunt Margaret, before moving to Edmonton he had played with other children his age only a few times in his life.

For many children, playing sports is one of the easiest ways to immerse themselves into the world of their peers, and Billy's first contact with baseball occurred during the initial week in the new school. Having never played the game, he stood to the side at recess watching the other children, when suddenly somebody handed him a bat and said, "Yer up!" Though normally right-handed, he stepped to the plate as a left-handed batter before making contact, driving the ball into left field. Not knowing what to do, he stood watching the ball while his classmates yelled at him to start running. Someone grabbed him by the arm and pulled him towards first base. Unfortunately, the joy of making contact was soon replaced by the embarrassment of the ball being thrown back and him being called out.

Years later, still stinging from the incident, he recalled, "The worst thing was I had shown my stupidity in front of everyone. Children are especially cruel to anyone who is different, and I had all my weaknesses pointed out to me in no uncertain terms." Compounding his embarrassment was the fact that he wore bib overalls to school and sported a haircut given to him by his mother, making him self-conscious of the stark contrast between himself and his classmates, nearly all of whom had grown up in the city. Because he was so unused to contact with other children, Billy was never certain whether someone was teasing him or being serious.

As he continued adjusting to life in Edmonton, especially at school, Billy discovered that unlike other children his age, he had no ability to skate, swim or ride a bicycle. Even as an adult who had made a name for himself as a writer, he continued to maintain, "Those things are totally irrelevant to an adult and still, [I] always will bitterly resent the children who made fun of me because of those lacks." In fact, he took immense pleasure when he saw some of these childhood acquaintances in dead-end, blue collar jobs, taking great joy thinking of them "in their stupidity and mediocrity" and wondering, "How much good did being able to skate and swim and ride a bicycle do [them]?" Already demonstrating the hyper-competitive attitude that would motivate him as an adult, young Billy soon began looking for opportunities that would afford him a chance to stand out from the crowd.

In Edmonton, for the first time in his ten years, Billy was able to observe on a regular basis other family dynamics and gauge how much his own life at home differed from that of his friends, particularly those who had siblings. One day his friend Arden Barrett invited him home for dinner with his parents and two sisters. Watching another family's dinner routine and interactions with each another, Billy saw what it was like to be part of family with multiple children. He had never particularly wanted any brothers and sisters of his own, and this feeling was further confirmed as he watched the contentiousness between his friends and their siblings. His attitude was summed up years later in the short story "Nursie," when he wrote, "Nursie really knows how to hate. She has brothers and sisters."[2] Unable to understand how siblings could be so quick to forgive each other after fighting, he later commented, "If someone crosses me, it is forever. I *never* forget and I seldom forgive."[3] Indeed, his grudges against those whom he felt had slighted him personally or professionally in later years became legendary among friends, family and peers.

The move to Edmonton ultimately resulted in Billy making more friends than he had ever had while living in the country; but one of the main reasons for the family's move to the city, his schooling, eventually drove a greater wedge between him and his father. In the early months of his first year in public school, Kinsella brought home a math test on which he had scored 77%, placing him second in the class and well ahead of many students who had failed. Rather than praising his son or offering any other encouraging words, John said, "Seventy-seven percent is only two points above seventy-five. That's only three-quarters." Fearing he would burst into tears while trying to speak, Billy said nothing and never again showed his father any paper or exam. Recalling the scene decades later, Kinsella was still "incoherent with anger" and admitted that he "was never particularly close to [his] father after that." And while he claimed he never wrote autobiography, examples of strained father-son relationships or fathers who are altogether absent often appear in both his short stories and novels.

During the Easter break of 1946, in a preview of what would be many bouts with illness in his life, Kinsella caught a cold and developed a terribly sore throat, causing his mother to confine him to bed. When Billy did not improve, the family doctor was called, but since he was busy attending to other patients, an associate was sent who diagnosed the illness as tonsillitis and prescribed medication. Rather than getting better, the condition worsened. With Billy's health continuing to decline, John called the doctor to demand a visit from the physician himself. By the time the doctor arrived, Billy was drifting in and out of consciousness, feeling lightheaded, as though he was floating above the bed. Immediately after arriving, the doctor realized the seriousness of the situation and called for an ambulance to rush the boy to the Royal Alexandra Hospital.

Kinsella was soon injected with penicillin, a drug still considered a miracle as its use was in its infancy. Without the medicine, the strep throat that was closing up his airway might very well have been fatal. Fortunately, his condition improved after a few days, though he'd lost a significant amount of weight and remained weak for several more days. Staying in the hospital nearly three weeks, he was unable to return to school until the last days of classes for the year. Though none of his new friends came to see him, the class did take up a collection and sent him a fruit basket. After Kinsella missed nearly all of the last three and a half months of the school year, his grades were never again outstanding. His teachers constantly remarked that he had the ability to do much better work, but his motivation to excel academically had simply disappeared.

At age eleven, Billy Kinsella's world consisted of his farm experiences in Darwell, times he rarely looked back on with any fondness, and his new life in Edmonton. There were a number of soldiers still in the area following the end of World War II, and Billy had his first opportunity to interact with Americans who had come to the city as part of the war effort. Behind his home was a row of low buildings that included a garage, a machine shop, a hen house and the home of an American soldier and his wife. Known to everyone in the area as the "Little American," the soldier was short but looked heroic in the tan gabardine uniform that Billy considered far more dashing than "the shit-colored, wooly uniforms with the wooly berets or trough caps" worn by the Canadians. The Little American had married a Canadian girl of Ukrainian heritage and made her famous in the neighbourhood when he bought her a squirrel fur coat. Though from South Carolina and presumably not very wealthy, the soldier soon won Billy's admiration. After a lifetime of not being near any real stores, Billy went window shopping one day, and the soldier saw him eyeing a bin of chocolate-covered graham crackers. The two chatted for a few minutes, and the American filled a small bag with the treats and bought them for him.

Another day, the soldier spotted Billy alone, as he often was so soon after moving to Edmonton, and took a red bandana and showed him how to tie the corners and fold it like a parachute, weigh it down with a small rock and toss it into the air. Though he pretended to understand how to execute the folds himself, Billy never was able to master it, despite having hours of fun with the American's creation.

In late spring, the soldier and his wife were reassigned elsewhere, and no one in the neighbourhood ever heard from them again. Years later, Kinsella fondly recalled the man's kindness. The man, and his efforts to reach out to a young boy who often saw himself as an outcast in his new home, appeared in *Box Socials*, in Jamie O'Day's friendship with a character known only as the "Little American Soldier."

In July, after nearly a year in the cramped quarters on 87th Street, the Kinsellas moved to 11315 79th Street, where they lived on the third floor of a large yellow stucco house. More spacious than the single room in which the three had been living, these accommodations included a living room, a bedroom looking out to the street, and a kitchen at the back of the house where Billy slept on a couch. Around the same time as the move, John Kinsella made the decision to go into business for himself as a plasterer. The most noticeable and immediate result was that the family, for the first time ever, had their own telephone. With telephones being nearly impossible to come by following the war, it was easier to obtain one for a business, which is what John did.

The move also resulted in Billy attending a new school that September. Cromdale was located less than a block from his new home, and Kinsella started grade six much like he had begun grade five—knowing no one. Unfortunately for the introverted boy, the students at Cromdale were not nearly as friendly as those at Parkdale, many of them having known each other for years. Kinsella's only close friend that year was a bully named Jack who lived next door and was a year behind in his schooling because he, like Billy himself, had been sick for much of the past year and was still in the process of recovering.

That fall, Bill attended his first semi-professional baseball game at Renfrew Park, located in the flats below downtown, a park later made famous when "Truckbox" Al McClintock got to play on an all-star team and bat against Bob Feller in Kinsella's novel *Box Socials*. Kinsella's friend Grant Argue asked him if he wanted to see a game after school, so the two boys took the bus to watch two teams from the four-team league face off, an experience Kinsella later recalled as the event that got him "hooked for life." Billy and Grant returned several more times, and Kinsella was even able to talk his father into going with him to a game or two on Sunday afternoons. Since the league was not allowed to charge admission on Sundays, they took up a silver collection, meaning Billy got in for a nickel instead of the usual quarter. When he was unable to attend the games in person, he would listen to them on CKUA, a 500-watt radio station from the University of Alberta, cheering for the Calgary Purity 99s for the few seasons the league existed. Having fallen in love with the sport, he closely followed the 1946 World Series between the St. Louis Cardinals and the Boston Red Sox, the first he clearly remembered. Rooting for the Cardinals, largely because he liked the brilliant scarlet uniforms, he soon became enthralled with names like Harry "The Cat" Brecheen, Howie Pollet, Enos "Country" Slaughter, Harry "The Hat" Walker, Red Schoendienst, Terry Moore and Joe Garagiola. Cheering hard against Boston slugger Ted Williams, Billy was thrilled when the Cards won the series and was equally disappointed when the team faded the following season.

With few close friends, Kinsella once more retreated into worlds of his own creation, playing by himself with games he made up, many of which were played on paper, though he also created a baseball game with dice, keeping statistics for the entire league. The teams' names were taken from the standings he read in the *St. Louis Sporting News* and included places about which he knew little but that sounded exotic to him, such as Mobile, Burlington, York, Tyler, Chattanooga and Ogden. Years later, many such small cities would resurface in short stories about minor league and independent league teams. Though he had yet to begin his writing career, the ability to create fictional narratives from the world of baseball had already started to manifest itself. The names of the towns and their representative teams provided him a small window into a world unknown to him at the time.

Despite the potential his teachers saw in him throughout his academic career, Kinsella often struggled to maintain his grades. The three months he missed at the end of his grade-five year, for instance, caused him to miss work on decimals and fractions. The result was that math, a subject he had found easy before the illness, now became difficult, and remained so for him into his adult years. Never interested in subjects that did not come to him easily, he neglected to do the work and focused on what came naturally for him—specifically

English or any class that offered writing assignments. In social studies, for example, students were periodically assigned a report addressing material from the textbook, with the best paper being read aloud to the class. Deciding to write the best paper one week, Billy put forth the type of effort his teachers longed for from him in each of his subjects. Much to his fellow classmates' surprise, his paper, not one by the same two or three students whose work always earned the best marks, was read to the class. It was a feat he never again achieved, his rationale being, "I knew I could do the best work if necessary, but the material was uninteresting so why bother?"

Though he often seemed complacent or indifferent towards his schoolwork, and though he detested playing most sports, Kinsella "always had a great desire to win, to be best at something." This proved somewhat challenging when, by his own admission, "I was very picky and couldn't see competing at things I wasn't interested in." Academically, his only real interest was when he was asked to write about a topic of his own choosing for his English class. Unfortunately for him, these types of assignments were only given twice a year.

For Halloween in 1946, the school hosted a costume contest, with prizes to be awarded. A family friend had a yellow clown suit that had belonged to one of her children. Olive then painted Billy's face to complete the look, and he went to the party. Despite having no real initial interest in dressing up, Billy was named as one of the five finalists for the costume prizes, giving him a small level of recognition he craved among his classmates. The winning outfit was determined by audience applause. Only two costumes other than his own stuck out in his mind. One was worn by a large boy, who had possibly failed a grade or two, who arrived wearing a velvet weskit and a real sword sheathed in a long scabbard. The other was worn by a Trevor Henderson, who came from one of the poorer families, the children often arriving at school appearing pale and undernourished, wearing ragged and ill-fitting clothing.

Trevor had constructed his costume by taking two large sheets of cardboard and creating a sandwich board on which he had glued various magazine covers, making himself look like a magazine stand.

Impressed by Trevor's originality and inventiveness, Kinsella was frustrated when the student who "had done nothing but drag a weskit and sword out of mothballs" won. As he would later discover during his time as a university student and again when he began writing regularly, "people with imagination and originality get short shrift from the plodding masses." Decades after the fact, Kinsella mused, "Trevor Henderson, if you're still around—you had the best costume. I wonder if you ever think about how you should have won the contest?"

Unfortunately, Billy's health issues resurfaced that winter, with a prolonged bout of pneumonia that kept him out of school once more for several weeks. Compounding this setback was the fact that John Kinsella's health also deteriorated during that winter, keeping him confined for several weeks as well. Both Billy and his father went to see an older doctor who recommended deep-breathing exercises for both of them, a regimen that lasted exactly three days before they were abandoned. The younger Kinsella was left with a nagging cough he was unable to lose. Late in the school year, before classes let out in 1947, he had his tonsils removed, once again forcing him to miss several days of school and preventing him from doing his schoolwork.

The next school year, while largely unmemorable for him, was the first time Kinsella made a deliberate effort to ignore what he came to see as "bureaucratic stupidity." Mr. Loeb, the grade-seven math teacher, issued a requirement that students should keep all their notes while solving problems and then write down the correct answer to each problem beside them. Failing to see the value or purpose in the mandate, Kinsella simply chose to ignore it, living in fear for the entire year that he would be called on to produce the work, would fail to do so and would receive a whipping with the strap reserved for such punishment. While he was never caught, he proudly recalled the event as one of the first stances he took against arbitrary and meaningless requests from people in power. This attitude became more dominant in his personality as he became older.

By grade seven, in improved health, Kinsella had begun regularly spending time and playing games with a circle of several friends. This year was also when he began attending the professional wrestling matches that were held at the Stock Sales Pavilion. Regularly used for cattle shows and smelling of livestock and manure, the pavilion was transformed each week into a showcase of wrestlers. The first night he went, Bill won the lucky program number prize, two free tickets to another week of wrestling, and the next week he took his father. While John was not terribly impressed with the staged antics the wrestlers put on, Billy found it to be enjoyable and soon began attending with his friends and following the results in the local newspaper.

In junior high school, at the end of each year, the students who had not met expectations during the year were required to write final exams for those classes. At the end of grade seven, for the first time ever, Billy had to write these exams. In addition to failing health class, a half-course offered in conjunction with physical education, he was required to write for science and math. Never one to take notes, he maintained the philosophy that if he could not recall it on his own or it was not written in the textbook, then it probably was not worth him making an effort to remember. As there was no textbook for health class, Billy borrowed notes from one of his classmates, allowing him to memorize the bones of the body and the organs well enough to pass the exam. Under the threat of being held back a grade if he did not pass all seven required subjects, he met each standard and made it into grade eight.

Kinsella made his first attempt at writing fiction during his grade-eight year. His first short story, "Diamond Doom," was about baseball, specifically about a murder at a ballpark. Just two pages long, the story was passed on to his friend Walter Shore who, upon finishing it, drew a seal with crossed ribbons and the letters S.S.A., or "Shore Seal of Approval." And though it would be many years before he made a name for himself as a writer, Billy enjoyed the process of creating a story that entertained, which would be the primary measure he had for his work in the coming years.

During the spring term, Kinsella participated in the Boys' and Girls' Fair. The event was affiliated with the local YMCA and several rooms in the building held displays ranging from penmanship samples to baked goods. After attending the event the previous year, he explored the dozens of categories listed in the information booklet, and chose to enter in the writing category. While his first story earned only Walter Shore's seal of approval, his entries in the Boys' and Girls' Fair earned him ribbons from the sponsoring organization, though he later suspected this may have been due to a lack of entries in the category. Pleased that he had a venue at which to present his work, he admitted that comparing the winning story to his own pieces would be similar to "comparing a story by F. Scott Fitzgerald to a plumber's grocery list." For several years after, Kinsella remained involved with the fair, attending meetings and supervising events such as the badminton tournament, the dog show and the chess tournament, but never became active in the organizing or administrative sides of the group. The recognition, however small it may have been, gave him more of the attention he desired and provided the creative outlet he lacked at school.

While he had made several friends by grade eight, Bill had never had a girlfriend, though his interest in girls was growing. He and his friends would gather and rate the girls in their class based on what they, as thirteen-year-old boys, thought sex appeal to be. Though his friends gravitated towards those girls who were more athletic, Bill simply could not conceive being physically close to a girl who was stronger than he was. This same group of boys all came from similar backgrounds; none swore, smoked or ever talked about sex as a physical act. And while Billy felt a connection to these boys, his introverted personality left him feeling incapable of developing a romantic relationship with any girl—though he had made at least one attempt to show his affection for a girl the previous school year, an effort that for many years he kept a secret.

In the spring 1949, a girl named Florence had begun attending Cromdale, sitting at the opposite side of the room from Bill. Still inexperienced in dating and making connections with female classmates, he began admiring her from a distance, fantasizing about being with her—not sexually, but simply as a close companion. Girls at Cromdale School were forbidden from wearing blue jeans, and Florence often wore a yellow and green plaid wraparound skirt with a large safety pin to hold it in place. One day while catching the bus in downtown Edmonton, Billy saw Florence wearing a pair of tight, faded jeans. Even as an adolescent, he was attracted to women wearing blue jeans, especially those who realized how attractive they were in denim.

Later that spring, Kinsella purchased a pair of kitten-shaped pink barrettes set in a tiny blue box with cotton batting. He took the purchase home and kept it hidden in the kitchen, where he slept on the couch. By Monday morning, he could hardly contain his excitement as he left for school early, quickly walking the block from his house to the school and going inside as soon as the doors were opened to students. Before any of his classmates had arrived, he quietly entered the classroom, opened the lid to Florence's desk and placed the small box inside, where it would be the first thing she saw that morning.

Still feeling the excitement of his secret mission, Bill went outside and walked back home, where he played in the yard until it was time to go to school. Arriving in time for the first bell, he made sure he was with several people as he walked into school. By the time he entered the classroom, Florence had already discovered the gift and the mystery had become the talk of the class. Kinsella coolly asked someone what had happened, acting as disinterested as possible when given the details.

All the girls in the class gathered around Florence during recess, guessing at who may have given the gift. Much of the speculation centred on a boy who sat in the back of class and had already announced he would not be moving on when their grade was promoted, choosing instead to become a carpenter. Amid the boy's strong denials, a few other names were mentioned, but not one person ever suggested that Bill Kinsella might have had anything to do with the mysterious gift. The event was a point of discussion for the next several days, but it remained a mystery. Bill never disclosed to Florence that he was the one who had given her the secret gift, preferring not to spoil the surprise and imagining her wondering "who in hell it was."[4]

Having never worked a job beyond a few chores on the farm, by the summer following grade eight Kinsella began to grasp how hard his father worked to provide for his family. Bill had been made to feel guilty because he had never shown an interest in his father's work as a plastering contractor. In fact, Jack Warring, a next-door neighbour and classmate of Bill's, showed far more interest in John's work, even tagging along with him a few times, something that gave Bill enough of a reason to dislike him.

In an effort to keep peace with his dad, Bill reluctantly agreed to help out and woke up early one day that summer to leave by seven o'clock with John and Jack. The job involved putting the stone coat on a new house, and that day they mixed cement in a mortar box, then carried it up the scaffolding in buckets to the plasterers, who spread it on the wall, so John could then use a coal scuttle and small shovel to toss white stone chips into the wet cement.

Though the job was tedious, Bill was sure to not complain to his father, doing everything asked of him. At the day's end, John seemed happy that his son had worked with him, so much so that he paid both Bill and Jack for the day's labour. While he appreciated the income, Bill loathed the idea of having to work such a physically demanding job, an attitude he held for the remainder of his life.

In the fall of 1948, for the second time since coming to Edmonton from Darwell three years prior, the Kinsellas moved, this time to a home John and Olive purchased at 11445 83rd Street. It was a small two-bedroom, yellow and reddish hued stucco house. The original structure had been remodelled and added to and, as a result, had parts that were dark and unheated, but for the first time since living on the farm in Darwell, Bill had a bedroom all to himself. While the house was something to call their own, its inadequate heating and the damp walls in Bill's bedroom did nothing for the family's health. As with every other winter, John battled illness throughout the coldest months. Bill's health, however, had improved significantly after having his tonsils removed two years prior. By the spring of 1949, though he had avoided any major illnesses, Bill began having pains in his side.

The family doctor determined his appendix needed to be removed, but that it could be postponed until the summer months.

In an attempt to improve their new house, John prepared to have new insulation installed and to re-stucco the outside of the structure. In anticipation of the stucco, Bill and Jack had agreed to scrape the house for fifteen dollars each. Jack completed his half of the house very quickly, but the pains in Bill's side increased, causing him to stop working until after his appendix was removed in June. After a few days in the hospital he began a slow recovery at home, and the remainder of his summer was spent dealing with surgical pain that was often worse than the original symptoms.

As the summer wore on, Bill felt guilty and tried to repay to his father the money he had not earned by completing the job, but John refused, and Bill eventually set up the scaffold and finished the job. Hating every moment of the work, he later recalled that the experience "helped forge a life-long aversion to manual labor." Saying he "would rather go hungry than do work like [the scraping],"[5] Kinsella made it his mission to avoid the type of job his father did on a daily basis, further emphasizing the disconnect that had grown between father and son.

With the new house came a new pet and a realization that would shape Kinsella's religious worldview for years to come. Having failed at earlier attempts at keeping a pet while on 79th Street, including some goldfish and a turtle, the family got a black kitten soon after moving into the house on 83rd Street. Less than a month after getting the cat, however, it was run over, and the family got another they named Patty—they had gotten it on St. Patrick's Day. Two months later, Patty drank antifreeze that John had left out on the back porch. After a visit to the vet failed to save the cat, Bill, for the first time in his life, prayed. Even as a young teenager, though, he "felt religion was sappy" and he "couldn't bring [himself] to believe any of it." Seeing it as the last hope for saving Patty, he prayed anyway, feeling that anything, no matter how absurd it seemed, was worth doing to save his cat. Years later, thinking back on the prayer, he admitted, "the very concept of kowtowing to the supernatural is so totally silly I still cannot fathom how anyone with an IQ over 90 can help but laugh at the ludicrousness of it." Though it would take several more years for him to fully embrace his atheism, the incident demonstrated a confrontational mindset towards authority figures, whether real or imagined.

Despite the updated insulation and stucco, the dampness that filled the inside of the house remained, and John and Olive decided to sell the house and move yet again, this time choosing to purchase a partially built home at 12726 71st Street in north Edmonton, a move that appalled their teenage son. In a rundown neighbourhood, the unfinished house was appealing to his parents because of its low price. The owner, a Ukrainian man, was dying of cancer and had to sell two houses he was in the process of building at the time.

The Kinsellas had to move from 83rd Street in early October, but the new home was not yet habitable, so the family was forced to find a temporary living space. With quality housing still in short supply following the war, the only available place was downtown in a building called McDougall Court. Bill fell in love with it. With no yard to mow and close proximity to stores, restaurants and a theatre, living at McDougall Court gave Bill a taste of what was possible in a larger city, something he would enjoy years later when he was able to afford a place in a downtown area. Though his parents spent nearly all their time working on making the new house livable, Bill was thrilled with each delay that set back their move-in date.

That fall, Kinsella returned to Parkdale School, where he was entering grade nine. This year, he felt much more at ease. Mr. Nichols, Bill's homeroom and math teacher, a man in his early forties with gold-rimmed glasses and curly, greying hair, impressed him as both a pleasant man and a good teacher. Years later he would use the teacher's physical description for that of Silas's mentor in what became known as his "Indian stories."

Bill had scored well on an IQ test, and his teachers regularly commented that he could do much better if only he would apply himself, but he continued to feel unmotivated to excel in areas that held no interest. With very few athletic abilities, he saw no possibility of getting recognized on sports teams. And since his one passion, writing, offered no possible outlets at that time that would gain him recognition, he "was left to wait and hope something would come along."

That fall, needing a new jacket as the weather began turning cooler, Bill made a choice that went against the grain of the largely conservative styles of his schoolmates and gave him a level of recognition he had never known before. Another boy in his class owned a blue satin jacket with snap buttons and virtually no collar, something quite unlike the windbreakers most of the students were wearing. After finding out the jacket was not at all expensive and also came in maroon, Kinsella purchased one. Recognizing that "a person who dresses bright but tastefully stands out" gets noticed, he made the decision "that until some other means came along that was how [he] would attract the attention and acclaim [he] deserved."

In grade nine Kinsella got his first experience in dating. His first girlfriend was May Sorlie, a black-haired, blue-eyed, freckled girl who lived with her grandparents near Kinsella's house. The tentative relationship primarily involved taking long walks and holding hands after school, and a few kisses, and died out as it became too cold to go walking after school.

Kinsella never told his parents anything about his school or his friends that he absolutely did not have to. Somehow, however, they heard about his having a girlfriend, and embarrassed him by asking his friend Dave Page about it when he came by the house to visit. This began what turned into a lifelong habit of Olive and Aunt Margaret talking about Bill in the third person while he was in the same room with them. On the up side, John was so pleased about his son's interest in girls that Bill's allowance was raised. The experience, however, made Bill vow to never tell anyone anything about his personal life, and he fiercely guarded his privacy into adulthood.

Although Bill and his father were never very close, even when the family was living on the farm in Darwell, they were usually able to maintain a relatively civil relationship with one another. In fact, Bill's last real confrontation with John, over a fairly trivial matter, took place during Bill's ninth grade year. He had spent the day playing with his friend Glen Boyce, and the boys walked through Borden Park around nine o'clock that evening, hoping to catch couples searching for some privacy. Finding nothing worth watching in the park, the boys parted ways and Bill set off on his thirty-minute walk home.

As soon as Bill walked into the house, John went into a rage, partially because of the late hour and partially because a washer from a garden hose in the basement had fallen into a drain, something John blamed on Bill. Though it seemed insignificant to his son, John was furious with him, lambasting Bill for an hour, reminding him of the sacrifices the family was making so their son could get a good education.

There were moments, however, when Bill impressed his parents with his ability to deal with stressful, unexpected circumstances. When he was fourteen, Bill was at home with his father's oldest brother, Patrick, who had a heart murmur and, for a brief time, lived with the family. When John took a job working on a hotel being built in Barrhead, a town seventy-five miles to the northwest of Edmonton, Olive went with him to spend the night. Sitting at the kitchen table with Patrick, who was known by the family as "Uncle Bud," Bill watched him tip back in his chair, exhale a sigh and die. Bill was able to compose himself and call the funeral home to make the arrangements to claim the body.

In spite of the sometimes tumultuous relationship with his father, Bill harboured an abiding respect for him and the pride he took in his work. After the family settled into the house at 12726 71st Street, John installed a mirror and imbedded it into the wall, surrounding it with a plaster border that was later enamelled to give it the shine of a snow sculpture. Years later, in 1982, Bill took his then wife, Ann Knight, to the house and knocked on the door. When a woman answered, he told her the house had once been his childhood home and asked if he could show Ann his father's handiwork. Though the rest of the house had long since deteriorated, the fireplace and mirror were as beautiful then as they had been when his father first crafted them.

Rarely if ever comfortable in social situations, Bill suffered in the spring of 1950 what he would recall years later as the most embarrassing moment of his young life. Though he later admitted he had far worse things happen to him, none of them occurred at an age when he was so easily humiliated. One weekend evening, as Bill and Dave Page were out walking, they decided to call on a girl named Maureen Rowan. Though both boys were uninvited and the visit was planned on the spur of the moment, Maureen was happy to see them. At her mother's suggestion, she made fudge and they all three sat around the kitchen table talking awkwardly. During the conversation, Bill asked for a drink of water, which Maureen was happy to get for him. Just as he was taking a long drink, Dave made a humorous remark, causing Bill to choke on the water, spitting it across the immaculate blue and white tile floor. Remembering how their hostess got a cloth to wipe up the mess, Kinsella later said he wished he would either die or disappear: "I don't think I have ever been so embarrassed." The event only reinforced his dislike for circumstances over which he had little or no control, preferring to remain isolated instead.

Searching for extra income, in between grades nine and ten Kinsella took his first paying job other than working with his father from time to time. Beginning in late June, he delivered the *Edmonton Bulletin*, a daily magazine for the area. Bill picked up his allotment of eighty papers, then walked them six blocks back to where his route began. Traditional routes paid five cents for each paper delivered per week, but because Bill's route was scattered across a broad territory he was paid seven cents for each paper.

The $5.60 he made each week was enough to keep him with spending money in his pocket, new clothes on occasion and a few gifts for others. When Olive returned from a few days away, Bill gave her a china bulldog named Winston. It cost Bill five dollars and remained with Olive for many years after her son moved out. Bill also allowed himself personal purchases. One of the first things he bought with his new wealth was a record player, a small portable model that cost nineteen dollars and played only 78 rpm records. As often as possible, Kinsella added to his music collection—radio was still largely filled with talk and music that he found uninteresting.

In grade ten, Bill began attending Eastwood School near 120th Avenue. With a full load of classes, including English, social studies, Latin, science, algebra, physical education and a half year of vocational guidance and bookkeeping, he soon discovered that high school was much more difficult than what he had experienced at Parkdale, particularly the math and science courses. It was during this year that he also became more public in his stances against those he viewed as mindless authority figures.

Each morning the principal, a World War I veteran whom the students called "Pappy" due to his resemblance to Pappy Yokum in the *Li'l Abner* comic strip, would assemble the students in the study area. Standing on a chair he would read a Bible verse while the students saluted the Canadian flag. Kinsella made a point of leaning against the wall, keeping quiet, but trying to show as much contempt as he could for the entire ritual.

It was a tradition at that time for the grade-ten students to participate in Frosh Week, during which they were supposed to wear beanies and act subservient towards the upperclassmen. This infuriated Bill, and he took the hat off almost immediately after it was issued to him and threw it in the nearest trashcan, refusing to participate in a tradition that fed what he would later call "the sheep mentality."

But this was also the year Bill fell in love. Sitting across the aisle and a row in front of him was Irene Kerr, a girl with short, dark hair and beautiful brown eyes. Simply looking at this girl made "his insides [rearrange] themselves, and [his] breathing became unstable in that wonderful, frightening way love has of disengaging a person from their senses." Unfortunately, Bill's anxiety once again got the best of him and he was rarely able to bring himself to say more than an occasional hello to her. Even if he could have brought himself to ask her out, there were few places for teenagers to go. The main one was Club Stardust at the Highlands Community Hall, but the only event hosted there, unfortunately, was a dance every month or so. By then Kinsella knew he was not a dancer.

Later in the fall, following the elections for student council, a dance was held after school. Despite his inability to dance, he went anyway. In the gymnasium decorated to fit the "Shine on Harvest Moon" theme, Bill listened to the music, desperately trying to work up the courage to ask Irene for a dance. Though he never mustered up the nerve, later he admitted that he had "fantasized about it so much [he] might as well have," creating a fiction in his mind that far surpassed the evening's reality.

As fall continued, Bill quit the paper route, having discovered that he had to work much harder to make average grades in high school than he had had to just a year earlier. Much of his free time was spent by himself, often walking alone over two miles to Clarke Stadium for Friday night football games. Though he regularly spent time alone, Bill did make some friends. One friend, Len Leigh, looked years younger than his classmates and often seemed out of place. Len had teeth chipped from a swimming pool accident and no athletic ability whatsoever, and other boys in the class called him Little Beaver, after the character from the Red Ryder comic books. Together, he and Kinsella were called Mutt and Jeff, from the popular comic strip of the time: Bill was the tallest boy in class and Len was, by far, the shortest.

In an effort to relate with people his own age, something Bill found difficult, he agreed to attend a party with Barbara Klatt, an outgoing girl from his class, who had invited him. The party was hosted by another schoolmate, Barbara Mercer, and included ten or eleven people from their class. Having no idea what teenagers did at parties or what was expected of him once he got there, Kinsella worried intensely for a week after accepting the invitation, nearly calling and claiming to be ill.

Shortly after arriving, he realized he knew no one else, had nothing to say to those who were there and had no idea how to conduct himself in that type of setting. The anxiety drove him into what felt like a semi-catatonic state. Though the rest of the teenagers at the party, especially Barbara Klatt, were nice to him, he simply sat there "like a lump," realizing that many of the boys from Eastwood would have given anything to be on a date with Barbara. Telling everyone he was feeling ill, Kinsella glumly watched his "chances of being 'somebody' in high school melt away." The long walk along the railroad tracks to North Edmonton was, he later recalled, "the most depressing of my life." Unfortunately, the anxiety-induced nausea he first felt that night was a feeling that plagued him for years in any important social situation.

By December, the embarrassment had abated long enough for Bill to summon the courage to go on his first real date. Though he still longed for a date with Irene Kerr, he chose not to ask her out. Instead, after dialling all but the last digit of her telephone number several times, he asked Patsy McDowell, a slim, pleasant girl from his class, to attend a Christmas dance, and she agreed to go. Kinsella called on her at home and the two rode the bus to the dance. Dancing only the slow numbers and sitting out the fast songs, they kissed at least one time when someone held a sprig of mistletoe over them. Bill later took comfort in the fact that "the evening was not a disaster, as I nearly expected it would be—it is hard to figure out why a person keeps thrusting themselves into potentially disastrous situations—but I guess hoping that situations that were bad previously will turn out better next time, is what life is about."

He managed to control the waves of nausea that kept creeping to the surface, despite a couple of close calls, and his date was "very considerate of [his] nonexistent dancing ability." After the bus ride back to Patsy's house, the couple shared another kiss at her back door. "We didn't need any mistletoe for that," Patsy told him before they said goodnight. Walking home in the clear winter night, Kinsella decided that his "first date had gone surprisingly well." His shyness, however, resurfaced and he never again asked Patsy out, unable to imagine what they would do on other dates. Though he longed for companionship, he later realized he was too immature at the time for a relationship.

In Bill's grade-ten year he was presented with an outlet to showcase his creative skills. Having studied J.M. Barrie's *The Admirable Crichton*, the class was given an assignment to write a new third act, leaving it up to each student whether the play would end happily or sadly. Both Len and Bill threw themselves into the project and, while most of their classmates wrote two or three pages, Bill submitted a finished copy that was at least ten pages, complete with dialogue and stage directions. He was rewarded with a grade of 95%. The best part for Bill, however, was not the grade but the thrill of seeing "the story pouring off my pen and [feeling] the ideas forming in my mind." Sadly, it would be twenty years before he found another such outlet in an academic setting.

Just as his inability to dance no longer prevented him from attending functions, neither did his lack of athleticism prevent him from trying new sports. In the spring of 1951, at Len's insistence, Bill began playing tennis, a sport he would continue playing as an adult. While he did not care much for the game, he was drawn to the fact that Irene Kerr lived right across the street from the Eastwood tennis courts. Bill also began playing golf during this time, a game he grew to enjoy so much that he soon had his own set of clubs and would play regularly, often by himself.

Sometime after Easter that year, Bill began working Saturdays in the fruit and vegetable section at Eaton's, a large combination department and grocery store. Though he did not necessarily enjoy the work—mostly trimming lettuce and cabbage leaves, stocking shelves and sorting produce—he did enjoy the perk of being able to eat all the fruit he wanted, especially when the weather turned cold. At fifty cents an hour, the four dollars he brought home each week enabled him, from grade ten on, to buy nearly all his own clothes, books and sports equipment, while still saving a few dollars in the bank account his parents had set up for him at the Bank of Montreal when he was twelve. The job included a 20% employee discount on clothing, something that allowed him to add to his growing collection of brightly patterned shirts, which he had grown to love. Working full-time during the holiday season and whenever the store needed additional help during special sales or promotions, Bill would continue to work at Eaton's off and on until he finished grade twelve.

As the school year drew to a close, Bill's grades once again meant he would have to take the written exam, though this time it was for just one class: Latin. Failing to grasp the most basic aspects of the subject, he had known by Christmas that passing it was a lost cause. He passed the rest of his classes, however, with average grades. Had it not been for an elaborate system of signals, signs, toe taps and head scratches he and Len Leigh had devised to be used during algebra exams, he may have also had to take the written exam for that class.

After failing his Latin exam, Bill turned his focus towards finding a summer job, and he landed one the following week at a lumberyard that had gotten a contract for hundreds of Quonset huts. Given the mundane task of hammering nails into floorboards in specific spots so that the flooring would be solid, he made between $1.10 and $1.20 an hour, working eight hours each day. Though he felt a great sense of pride in finding the job and being hired on his own, he also quickly realized how much he hated the work. Seeing it as nothing more than "hard, stupid work, where you could only hope for thundershowers to save you from eight hours of idiot's work," he knew after the first day on the job he did not want to work there for the entire summer. Fortunately, after his first day off, he went back to work only to be told the fifty people who were originally hired had been trimmed to fifteen and he would no longer be employed there. Collecting his paycheque and relishing his newfound freedom, Kinsella went back to Eaton's to get on the part-time list and promised himself he would never again do any kind of manual labour.

Starting grade eleven, Kinsella decided to commit himself to his schoolwork in an effort to live up to the potential his teachers since grade five had been telling him he had. He began doing work that placed him in the top 10% of his class. He found the work to be fairly easy, though it meant he had to apply himself more rigorously than ever before in subjects for which he cared very little. By the time the first report cards were issued in mid-October, Kinsella found himself on the honour roll for the only time in high school.

His plan for continuing with his academic success was curtailed when he became terribly sick in mid-November, this time with chicken pox. He had to miss over three weeks of school, and didn't open a book during that time. By the time he was well enough to return to classes he felt lucky to not have failed any subjects, after missing vital parts of chemistry, French and geometry. His grades would never recover.

That winter, despite his trepidation towards social situations, Bill decided to attend a basketball game, not because he had any interest in the sport, but because he was hopeful of making contact with a girl at the dance that was scheduled to follow the game. After nearly two years of wishful thinking, he saw Irene Kerr, who was then attending Victoria High. Dancing several times with her that evening, Kinsella later claimed it was "a wonder I didn't glow like fluorescent watch hands in the semi-darkness of the Eastwood gym." When the evening came to a close and the gym began to empty, Bill gathered the nerve to ask Irene if he could walk her home. Though she declined his offer, she did so with such graciousness that he didn't feel hurt. He had no way of knowing that it would be the last time he would dance with her.

With the end of his high school career quickly approaching, Kinsella met with Mr. McCoy, the school's counsellor, to discuss his plans for the future. Soon after sitting down, Bill emphatically stated that his primary goal was to be a writer. Rather than encouragement or help implementing a plan to make that goal become a reality, Mr. McCoy dismissed his comments with a ten-minute lecture on how unadvisable that career path would be. Instead, the counsellor suggested rather strongly that Bill opt for a more traditional career path in engineering, accounting or law and then begin writing as a hobby once he had established himself in some such field. Decades later, after he had won multiple awards and had become one of the best-known Canadian writers, Kinsella stated, "I think there is a special place in hell for [McCoy]," who had a position that significantly influenced the sixteen-year-olds who came to him for long-term guidance, only to be steered away from their passions towards safer, more traditional options.

During this same time, Kinsella took a preference test designed to clarify a student's aptitude towards certain career paths. It comprised a series of questions that were answered by punching pins into rows of papers for hours on end. He soon realized the exams could have little accuracy as they were so easily manipulated, even by teenagers like himself. When presented with a question such as

"Which of the following would you rather be? A) nuclear physicist; B) cowboy; C) dishwasher," Kinsella assumed the examiners thought most people would choose the first answer, thereby assigning them some form of scientific score on the results. Instead, he chose the last answer honestly, as he was realistic enough to know that a physicist would have to study immense amounts of mathematics, and his reality was that, after graduation, he "was never going to have anything to do with math, science, or [physical education] as long as [he] lived." Since he did not like the outdoors, he could not imagine being a cowboy, so he chose to answer as honestly as he could: of the three, he would rather be a dishwasher. When the results came back, he had scored a 99% in writing, a 2% in scientific aptitude and a 0% in mechanical aptitude. To him, the exams "showed that I didn't have an aptitude for anything acceptable," so law was suggested as an option for his future career path. Having already failed Latin and seeing nothing that would persuade him to ever study it again, he quickly dismissed this suggestion, still fostering the aspiration of becoming a writer after he graduated.

The Kinsella family was never very religious, but during the winter of 1951–52, Bill overcame his aversions and decided to explore religion on his own, joining a young people's group at a Presbyterian church next to Parkdale School. Though not close friends with anyone who attended, he did have acquaintances from his Parkdale days, including a girl he had vaguely known in elementary school, and Bob Fanning, who, when they were in grade five, had briefly persuaded Bill to attend Cub Scout meetings with him.

The ten or twelve teenagers were led by an enthusiastic young pastor, but Kinsella found the group uninteresting and was unable to recall years later any type of religious discussion they had. Instead, the group held several social events that included playing games and dancing. After going to a few of the group meetings and events and going so far as to attend a church service, Kinsella found it all a bore and soon abandoned his exploration.

After two years of being required to take at least one written exam at the end of the school year, Bill ended his junior year by passing all his classes, allowing him to look for summer work once more. Not wanting to get anything remotely resembling the construction job he had hated the previous year, he applied to the City of Edmonton for an open position as an assistant playground director, scheduled to run from mid-June until Labour Day weekend. Though the pay was fairly low for that time, around twenty-five dollars a week, the job was not demanding, and suited the seventeen-year-old boy nicely.

Once hired, Bill was assigned to Kitchener Park, located in one of Edmonton's older neighbourhoods. Working from 11 a.m. until as late as 9 p.m., he was left in charge of the older children, playing volleyball and softball, coaching boys' and girls' teams to play against teams from other playgrounds. Aside from a few potential youths at risk, whom he felt were there to make the staff's lives miserable, he came to enjoy the work. One of the job's greatest benefits was that it allowed him to play an early eighteen holes of golf before walking the few blocks to the park for work. In fact, Kinsella golfed more that summer than any other before, and wished there were lessons available to him. Though he was largely self-taught and played with a cheap set of eight left-handed clubs, he was still able to shoot close to par on the local municipal courses, cultivating an interest in a game he continued playing years later.

Across from the park lived Freddy Bell, a man in his forties with Down's syndrome whose parents seemed very old at the time to the teenaged Kinsella. Always wearing a felt hat, Freddy was good-natured with red hair and freckles and a pot belly, someone who was always kind-hearted and gentle with the smaller children who came to the park. Over thirty years later, when working on his second novel, *The Iowa Baseball Confederacy*, Kinsella developed the character Missy, John and Marylyle Baron's forty-something daughter with Down's syndrome, based on Freddy, even keeping the red hair and freckles.

Kinsella started his grade-twelve year in September of 1952, deciding not to work part-time that year as he anticipated the schoolwork would be more rigorous than in years past. Additionally, since he had failed Latin in grade ten, he would not be able to earn his senior matriculation, which required at least a hundred credits, with certain mandatory subjects. As a result, he would have to take at least part of what was then referred to as second-year-twelve to make up any necessary requirements for graduation.

Despite his best intentions entering the school year, Bill found his schoolwork to be nearly impossible as his only interest was in English. While most students feared Miss Ethel Anderson, who taught English that year, Kinsella was one of the few who genuinely looked forward to her class each day as it was the one class that afforded him an opportunity to show his intelligence and aptitude. While grammar and sentence structure came naturally to him, his favourite part of the class was the literature portion, which consisted of reading a book of poetry and a book of essays, though Miss Anderson also had the class read one Shakespeare play and *The Importance of Being Earnest*, neither of which appealed to the aspiring writer.

What he most looked forward to were the essays they had to write, which allowed him to demonstrate his impressive vocabulary. Rather than turning in whatever he had written on his first attempt, he began revising his work, going as far as to rewrite some essays three times. In one such paper, Kinsella decided to use several complex words, including "infinitesimal" and he was terribly disappointed when he saw the terse note Miss Anderson had attached to it, saying pointedly, "Use simpler words." Though furious at the time, Kinsella knew that she was correct. He later admitted that her comments on that essay became his credo in fiction writing, "for storytellers don't need a big vocabulary; they need to use everyday words in an interesting manner." As a result, one of the characteristics of Kinsella's fiction, something many critics would come to praise, was his eloquent use of a fairly basic vocabulary. When Bill's first novel, *Shoeless Joe*, was published in 1982, he included Anderson in the dedication, making her the only non-family member mentioned.

Besides English, Bill found his social studies course to be fairly interesting as it was taught by a former major in the British army, who focused primarily on World War I. French, a class for grade elevens, appealed to Kinsella only because he found it easy. The teacher seemed to be unqualified to teach French and had the students sing songs in French until one bright female student pointed out that one song translated as "It's so good to sleep with my blonde girlfriend," thereby ending the daily singing.

The rest of Bill's courses were what he could only describe as "pure hell," a combination of algebra, trigonometry, physics and chemistry. Because he never learned to use a logarithm book, he was unable to score more than 25% on any of the tests in trigonometry. He fared not much better in physics, only surviving the class by memorizing the formulas, hoping to at least be able to apply some part of them on the final exam.

Despite the challenges of his course load, Bill still chose to write for the *Gazette*, the school's student newspaper. He wanted to be the paper's editor, but he was not elected, losing the position to a boy named Stephen Stiles. Recognizing that the new editor was not as hard a worker as he was, Kinsella took on the responsibility of advertising manager in addition to writing several columns. With a small staff and an editor who was unable to fulfill his responsibilities, Kinsella and a classmate, Harriet Stuckburg, did the majority of the work on the first edition, which barely made it out by Christmas.

After the holiday break, Stiles stopped attending meetings, so Bill assumed leadership of the staff and wrote most of the remaining columns himself. With help from Harriet and a few others who proofread the material, they managed to publish one more edition by June, though by Bill's own admission, "it wasn't very good. But I [was] proud to put my name in it as Editor-in-Chief." The last edition was nearly dead before it was assembled when after the new year, Kinsella, as a student council representative, heard a rumour that the yearbook staff had made the decision that there was not enough advertising revenue to justify both the *Gazette* and the yearbook. Since they knew the *Gazette's* leadership was weak, they had decided to appropriate the $300 set aside for the final edition and cancel the *Gazette's* remaining issue.

Hearing the news around noon on a Friday, Bill recruited a handful of friends who spent that afternoon and the following day selling a full complement of advertisements for the final issue. With both the budget money and the newfound advertising, the paper was committed to publishing, thereby preventing the takeover of their funding. Though it would still be several more years until Bill got into sales full-time, he learned a universal business truth that weekend: "Get them before they get you."

Kinsella's grade-twelve year was, by far, his busiest. Having started his high school career as a shy introvert, he had developed into someone who had a growing circle of friends, was involved in various capacities with the Boys' and Girls' Fair and served on the student council and the social committee. And while he had never found much success in most school-related athletic endeavours, Bill played in a number of badminton tournaments, often making it as far as the quarterfinals before being eliminated.

Kinsella's life took a dramatic and unexpected turn in March of 1953. His father had felt unwell for a while that winter and thought he might have an ulcer, so he made an appointment to visit his doctor. Taking one look at the x-ray, the doctor quickly rushed John to the hospital for exploratory surgery, during which they discovered he had developed stomach cancer. Realizing there was little they could do as it was at an advanced stage, the doctors closed the incision, giving him approximately three months to live.

Not knowing how to react to the news, Bill felt bad for his father but never really communicated his feelings about the situation with either his family or his friends. John gained his son's admiration when he demanded full disclosure from medical staff, not wanting bad news to be kept from him, despite the severe diagnosis. While Bill's parents had made preparations for John's surgery, transferring all bank accounts, the house, and the family's car into Olive's name, Bill had carried on with his life. Having seen other people abandon their normal day-to-day lives when confronted with a crisis, Kinsella promised himself he would not give in to the pressure of the situation. In fact, with the exception of his friend Dave Page, once the diagnosis was made, Kinsella did not even let his friends know how gravely ill his father was.

As his school year began to wind down, Bill's life was filled with activities that gave him something else to do other than watching his father's health deteriorate. Sometime in mid-April, he participated in the High School Badminton Championship, playing in the mixed-doubles event with Verna Bourcier. He was also occupied with the annual graduation dance that was approaching, an event that necessitated asking someone out well in advance to give her time to get a dress. He mustered the nerve to call Verna for a date, something he had wanted to do for a long time, but she told Bill she was already going with someone else, an answer that was not altogether unexpected. To his dismay, he didn't see Verna at the dance, leaving him to assume she had declined his invitation in the hope that someone else would ask her instead.

Trying to work up the confidence to ask out Irene Kerr, he debated too long, realizing he was too late when one of his friends, Gordon Arbuckle, announced he would be taking Irene to the dance. While not jealous of Gordon, Bill was "angry at [his] own complete stupidity for not asking her." Though there were other girls he thought might agree to accompany him to the dance, he ultimately decided, with all the trauma going on with his father's situation, he would attend the event alone, if he attended it at all. About a month before the dance, however, Beth Reid from his chemistry class asked if he wanted to go with her and he accepted, giving him one more thing to deal with. He did take some relief in knowing he did not have to worry about impressing her, so he had none of the pressure he would have felt had Irene or Verna accepted the earlier invitations.

The dance was to be held on the evening of May 15, 1953, the day after the commencement exercises for the high school's graduation class. Bill's enthusiasm was dampened by the realization that he would likely fail some of his required coursework, meaning he would have to return to school the next month to write the exams, or the following fall to complete his classes. Even more troubling, though, was realizing how critical his father's condition was.

Following the exploratory surgery, John Kinsella had tried to work but found himself unable to do so. His fatigue became more debilitating as the cancer continued eating away at his stomach. He was in serious pain for a few days leading up to Bill's graduation, and pills were unable to curb it, so Kinsella's cousin Margaret, a nurse, came to the house to administer shots of morphine. Nearly bedridden by his son's graduation day, John was forced to stay home and Olive attended the exercises alone.

With the graduation dance temporarily distracting him from the deathwatch at home, Bill formulated a plan that he desperately hoped would once and for all win him Irene Kerr's affections. In the 1950s, school dances still incorporated the tradition of dance cards. While Beth and her friends had taken care of nearly all the details, leaving Bill with the sole task of buying the corsage, he asked just one thing from her—that she exchange one dance with Gordon Arbuckle and his partner for the event, Irene Kerr.

That spring, Bill had come upon Dale Carnegie's writings. Though he recognized much of what the renowned motivator wrote was "bullshit," he was drawn to Carnegie's positive attitude and his notion that people can accomplish anything they want provided they set their minds to it. Long ago, Bill had decided he wanted Irene and he saw the last dance of his high school life as the opportunity to finally accomplish his goal. Beth arranged to exchange dances during the sixth dance, just after the scheduled intermission, and Bill promised himself that in the ten minutes he had with her on the dance floor, he "would manage to win Irene over, and would arrange to call her the next week, and [they] would start dating and in a year or two get married and live happily ever after." Unfortunately for Bill, the fantasy he had created in his mind failed to come close to matching the reality that unfolded.

Managing to not make a fool of himself during the first five dances of the evening, Bill excused himself at the intermission and went to the restroom to comb his hair and check for food in his teeth. Stepping into the indoor garden at the hotel, he rehearsed his lines before going back into the ballroom to sit with Beth for the rest of the intermission. Time seemed to drag on more slowly than it ever had before that evening, due in no small part to the band taking a longer than expected break. Upon returning to the stage, they announced that, because the break had run so long, the decision had been made to cut the sixth dance from the program. The rest of the evening went by in a blur for the heartbroken Kinsella, and, arriving home at dawn after the party he attended following the dance, he later recalled, "I was probably as depressed that morning as I have ever been."

The next month, Kinsella's problems only worsened. Knowing he had little to no chance of passing the approaching exams, seeing his father's health rapidly fade, and faced with having to make plans for earning a living, he was more uncertain that spring than he had ever been before. Even if he somehow managed to pass the exams, he had no interest in attending college as he knew he would still be required, as an English major—the only field of study he would seriously consider—to take the obligatory math, science and physical education courses.

Perhaps most troubling for Kinsella during this time, and something that had an impact on him for the rest of his life, was that his father, knowing his death was imminent, had turned to religion, something his son was growing to despise. For nearly all of his adult life, John Kinsella had been a staunch opponent to religion, the Catholic Church specifically, and his son was infuriated when his father "went crawling back to them." The parish priest at Rivière Qui Barre, a Father McIntyre, was someone whom Bill would describe decades later as "a fat old slob with an alcoholic face," and he was a person John himself had often ridiculed. However, as his health continued to deteriorate, John called on this very priest, who visited the Kinsella home numerous times during the last weeks before John's death. Bill, appalled at his father's decision, avoided being home when he knew the priest was going to be there. On the one day when he was home as Father McIntyre appeared at the front door, Bill left out the back.

Years later, decades after his father's death, Bill still expressed anger at his father's actions: "Even after all these years I cannot forgive my father for what he did. Not having the guts to stand by your principles is unforgiveable. I mean I would have stuck by him if he'd killed or robbed, but to be such an incredible coward . . . not to have the fortitude to stick by the principles by which he'd lived his life, and to crawl back to hypocritical simpletons he had scorned. . ."

John apologized to Bill for what he did, saying only, "You can't understand how they indoctrinate you." Not offering much of a response at the time, Bill later thought, "I wanted in the worst way to denounce him as a coward, to chase that smelly old slob of a priest out of the house, and tell my pious relatives to get out of the house and take their goddamned religious medals with them." Never one to embrace any type of confrontation, Bill instead chose to go to the municipal golf course, where he often spent his evenings and weekends playing alone and escaping from the mounting pressures. Despite knowing John was nearing death, Bill and his mother never discussed the diagnosis or its finality. "We knew dad was going to die. What was there to say?"

Near the end of June, around the same time as the school's grade twelve departmental exams, family members converged on the Kinsella house. Bill's uncle Tom and aunt Lizzie McNamara, John's oldest sister, offered sympathy, and his cousin Margaret continued to provide morphine shots to temporarily alleviate the pain.

After drifting in and out of consciousness for several days, on June 22 John Kinsella slipped out of it for the last time. The family knew it would only be a matter of hours until his end. He had wasted away from 165 pounds to perhaps 120 pounds, and his breath had become shallow and laboured. Around 5 a.m. on June 23, 1953, Uncle Tom came into the basement to wake his nephew, saying, "You'd better get up, son. I think your dad's near the end."

Kinsella walked upstairs and took a place in the hallway by the bedroom door. The priest had already come to administer last rites a few days before, and now the family gathered together while John's breathing briefly became erratic. Suddenly, the breathing stopped, the room grew silent and cousin Margaret said simply, "He's gone." Olive, who had been standing just inside the bedroom doorway, went out to where Bill stood, put her arm around him and said, "There are just the two of us now." Bill had no reply, and that brief interaction was the only discussion they ever had about John's death. Neither of them cried.

Feeling a great sense of relief that his father's illness and the deathwatch, which had been lingering over the house for three months, was over, Bill soon turned his thoughts to the trigonometry exam scheduled for nine o'clock that morning. Though he could have told the principal what had transpired and obtained a deferral for the test, he instead chose to tell no one about his dad's death, thinking that postponing the exam he had no hope of passing would only give him cause to worry until the supplemental exams in August.

That afternoon, when the undertaker had been contacted, Bill accompanied Uncle Tom downtown to help pick out a casket. The only conversation he had with his mother about the funeral was when she asked him to not go golfing for the next day or two, something to which he agreed, despite his desire to avoid the house, where "all the self-righteous, pussyfooting relatives" had converged.

The tension between Kinsella and his relatives over their religious beliefs continued growing. The service was to be held at a chapel not far from the family home. Most important to many of his father's relatives, however, was the decision to have John interred in the Edmonton Catholic Cemetery, where he would be forever separated from his wife and son, neither of whom would ever profess a belief in the Catholic tradition. While Olive's response was simply, "It doesn't matter to me," her son saw it as a major victory for "those religious hypocrites who always regarded my mother and I as second class citizens because we didn't share their fantasies of the supernatural." Had it been left to Bill, John would have been buried in a neutral cemetery, if for no other reason than to spite those relatives. When some remarked to Bill following the service and burial how brave he had been to not cry, his only thought was how pitiful they all were for relying on a religion he viewed now more than ever as worthless.

Following the funeral, while waiting for his exam scores, Bill decided to look for a full-time job rather than the summer employment he'd had in previous years. He was hired almost immediately by the Alberta government to perform various tasks for the Publicity

Bureau of the Department of Economic Affairs. In early August, Kinsella's examination results arrived, and none of the scores surprised him. As expected, in English he scored in the 90% range and social studies in the low 70s, in the 60s in French, in the 40s in both physics and chemistry, the 30s in algebra, and in the low 20s in trigonometry. By the middle of the month, having taken a brief vacation and with less than two months on the job, he decided he did not want to pursue a career working for Economic Affairs, choosing instead to go back to school in September and complete his grade-twelve requirements. Attending school in the mornings to take French III and Math 12, a replacement course he found significantly easier to manage than the more difficult courses he had failed in the spring, he was granted permission to take Physics II and Chemistry II via correspondence, allowing him to work the rest of the day. By this time Eastwood High School had been made into an elementary school, so Bill attended classes at the brand new Eastglen Composite High School.

At the start of the school year, Olive had taken a job with the government in the Correspondence School Branch, a job she would keep until her retirement years later. Around the same time, Aunt Margaret moved in with them, taking over Bill's room, and Bill claimed his own space in the basement. The women would live together for nearly four decades, both providing encouragement to Bill as he made his way in a world very much uncertain for them all.

Bill needed to find a new job, and a friend who had worked as a page at the Edmonton Public Library recommended him as his replacement. Though he found the work mundane—one of the worst jobs he ever held—he was able to maintain full-time status, working from two o'clock in the afternoon until ten o'clock in the evening and nine to five on Saturdays. While attending school in the mornings during the week, he had little time for anything other than work and school, and found it nearly impossible to keep up with his correspondence courses. He soon discovered, however, that he was only required to complete half the lessons in order to be eligible to take the final exam, so he devised a strategy to memorize the necessary formulas, do the minimum amount of work required and "hope for the best" on the exams. Rather than focusing on producing quality work, Bill was more concerned with simply doing enough to complete his graduation requirements, to offer him more opportunities for employment.

While he had dated occasionally during high school, it was only when he returned to complete his graduation requirements that he developed his first serious love interest. Ruth Foth invited Bill to the annual Sadie Hawkins Day dance and though he did not realize it at the time, her looks—plump with red hair and freckles—would become the type he found himself attracted to as an adult. After that largely unmemorable first date, Bill and Ruth continued dating during the winter of 1953–54, mostly in secret. Bill met her parents and thought he had done everything he could to make a good impression, but Mr. Foth, a German who worked for Canada Packers, immediately seemed to dislike him, and told his daughter to not see Bill anymore.

Often meeting downtown, where they could watch a movie and spend time together, the young couple grew increasingly fond of one another. Knowing he was eligible to attend the graduation dance once more in 1954, Bill hoped it would go better than it had the previous year.

It was during this time that Bill became good friends with Ian Spence, who also worked at the library. During one slow evening at work, the two began making up poems about Mr. Hyde and Mr. McCoy, the principal and vice-principal at the high school. Insulting and irreverent, the poems avoided anything profane or obscene. When they had written them out, Ian proposed making duplicate copies to distribute at school. Kinsella would later refer to the incident as "my first published poem." Once Ian typed the pieces, making sure they could not be traced back to either of them, they stayed after work to make nearly a hundred copies. Carefully destroying the original stencil and any extra incriminating copies, Kinsella carried the pages home and put them in a binder so no one would discover their work at school the following day.

The next day, around noon, Bill took a portion of the poems to the restroom at one end of the building. Ian, knowing he would be a prime suspect because he was the only student known to have a mimeograph machine at home, even though the copies were made at the library, recruited two classmates to distribute copies in one other boys' restroom and one girls' restroom. Unfortunately, Mr. McCoy, the vice-principal, stepped into the restroom just minutes after the copies were left there. Despite the administrator's best efforts to confiscate all remaining copies before they were dispersed among the students, about twenty copies did get carried off and were passed around for the rest of the day.

Having left for work at the library immediately after the poems began making their rounds in school, Kinsella was contacted later that evening by Ian, who had, as predicted, been accused. Denying any involvement and conveniently presenting from his binder a sample print made from his personal mimeograph machine at home, he was let go due to a lack of evidence. Because Kinsella was never one to cause a scene or be disruptive himself, no one suspected him, though this did not prevent him from destroying as a precautionary measure the single copy of the poems he had saved and hidden. Though only a handful of friends even knew who was involved, the escapade became legendary. In fact, when he later encountered graduates from Eastglen in business situations, Kinsella learned that they had also heard of the poem and its mysterious circulation. It was the first time he had achieved recognition, albeit anonymously, as a writer.

In June of 1954, Bill once more sat down to write the exams required to pass grade twelve and, again, applied for a job within the provincial government. Having quit the library job in May, deciding it was impossible to continue once the weather turned nice again, he had nearly a month off while taking the exams and waiting for the results. In early July, he accepted a position with the Alberta government, working for the Department of Lands and Forests, Homestead Branch. With the official title of "correspondence clerk," Bill was mainly responsible for overseeing a group of several hundred homestead leases, primarily located in the Peace River area. As people leased land from the government and began working the land or building homes on it, over a period of years they would earn the title to the land. Corresponding with the inspectors in the field who evaluated the land to be sure the specific improvements were being made, the office then determined if the people had earned the title. Kinsella soon recognized the lack of urgency involved with the position—some correspondence would go months without being answered. He devised a more efficient system of form letters and filing, and found he was able to quickly catch up on his work, leaving him more free time during the day to work on his real interest: writing fiction.

Liberated for the first time in years from the burden of having to study subjects like math and science, he was able to go right back to writing stories as soon as the exams were over. In August, the long-awaited test results arrived and while he easily passed French and just barely survived math, he once again failed both physics and chemistry, earning a 46% in each class. He appealed the grades and, perhaps because the school was considering consolidating the classes the following year, and perhaps because they felt sorry for him, each score was raised to 50%, meaning that he was finally finished with high school. He earned his senior matriculation, making him eligible to attend college, though he would not enroll for another sixteen years.

During his time with Lands and Forests, Kinsella came to know Stan Cherkas, a young man his age who was waiting until he turned twenty-one to be eligible to join the Royal Canadian Mounted Police. An amateur boxer, Stan and another friend entered a local boxing tournament, which Bill followed with interest. Though Stan was quickly knocked out, the boxers from the Cardston Club had fighters with names like Eddie First Rider, Frank Wolfchild, and Elias Tailfeathers, among others, that Kinsella would later make famous in his "Indian stories."

After years of being plagued with debilitating awkwardness in social situations, Kinsella finally sought relief from a doctor. In a visit to Dr. Hay-Roe, the father of two of Kinsella's fellow Eastwood students, Bill explained the chronic upset stomach that nearly caused him to vomit in these situations. The kindly older doctor assured the young man that the problem was in no way uncommon and that it would pass with age. Dr. Hay-Roe then performed a number of manipulations and adjustments to Kinsella's spine and lower back, claiming they would help him relax. Reflecting on the experience, Kinsella later concluded the root issue was purely psychosomatic but that the assurances from the doctor that day helped more than did the actual treatment. That summer was the last time in Kinsella's life when he suffered from these problems, though he still preferred avoiding uncomfortable social situations.

Because he only wanted to take classes he was interested in, Kinsella had decided not to go to university. But nearly fifteen years after writing his first one-page story for his mother while living in the cabin back in Darwell, he began writing seriously in the fall of 1954, and enrolled in a night school creative writing course at Victoria Composite High School. The creative writing class was taught by Margaret Coleman Johnson, who had published fictional pieces in a number of magazines, and was someone Bill saw as "a gentle, encouraging teacher." And while most of the students, Kinsella admitted, "were very bad . . . she somehow managed to find something positive in even the most horrific piece of drivel." The encouragement helped motivate him to continue writing stories.

His earliest pieces as an adult were largely, by his own accounts, poorly written. The first piece, titled "The Hangman," is "a dreadful cliché of a story that, if it ever finds a publisher, will be in *Worst Canadian Stories.*" This early wave of stories included some science fiction, a genre of growing interest to Bill, and a story he called "Candide," which was read by University of Alberta professor Dr. W.G. Hardy, a longtime supporter of the Canadian Authors Association. Hardy's response was harsh but helpful to the aspiring writer. He told Kinsella he was "'as full of clichés as a bagful of crap,' but that if [he] put his mind to it [he] could probably make a living as a writer." Irish-born John Patrick Gillese was, at that time, the only Alberta writer able to make a living at the craft, but much of his work consisted of small articles for relatively insignificant publications and Kinsella wanted no part of such a life.

Around this time, and in spite of his admittedly rough beginning, Kinsella was able to call himself a published writer as his first pieces appeared in the *Edmonton Journal*. The newspaper regularly set aside the third column on its editorial page for submissions from freelance writers. The first of the three pieces he had published in the paper was "A Tribute to Toys."[6] In the June 18, 1955, issue, his piece "Dictation" was printed, and later that summer "Summer Glory" was included. All three pieces were published under the pseudonym Felicien Belzile. In October, his first short story, "These Changing Times," was published in the *Alberta Civil Science Bulletin*. Just three months later, in January of 1956, they published what Kinsella felt was a "not-bad fantasy story" titled "I Walk Through the Valley."[7]

And while he relished these early publications, these were the last ones he would see for a number of years. Though he still had the desire to write, the reality of life after high school and making a living severely limited his ability to commit the time necessary for writing. At a time in his life when many people feel unlimited possibility on their horizon, Bill entered into nearly two decades of frustratingly tedious jobs, tumultuous romantic relationships and a series of events that, except for the birth of his two daughters, left him feeling lost.

3

The Lost Years

E dmonton in the 1950s became known as the oil capital of Canada, with a population that grew as quickly as the economy did. For Bill Kinsella, it was a time of personal growth and maturation as he worked to find his place in the world. Bill and Ruth continued seeing each other, and soon after finishing secretarial school, Ruth took a job with the Department of Lands and Forests, working one floor below Bill. By early 1955 the couple was engaged, though they kept the news from her parents, while making plans for Ruth to move out of their house. Looking back, Bill noted they were products of "the repressive 50s" when "young people didn't leave home when they became self-supporting."[1] Eventually, much to Bill and Ruth's dismay, her parents found out about the relationship—though when confronted, both Bill and Ruth denied it.

Because of her parents' attitude towards him, Bill had to take advantage of whatever opportunities he could find to be with Ruth. Though most of their dates involved meeting downtown, there were times when they were alone at her house. Every Sunday evening, Mr. and Mrs. Foth went out visiting relatives in the area. On one such evening, however, her parents returned at least an hour earlier than they usually did, pulling into the backyard to park while Ruth and Bill were trying to be intimate. Although there was a front door, it was never used, so Bill's only chance of escape was through the clothesline door. Many homes in Canada once had these doors, which enabled one to access an outdoor clothesline from the comfort of the indoors. Bill exited via the clothesline door into waist-deep snow, still scrambling to get fully dressed. The story was later reworked, with Ruth's name changed to "Sonja," into a first-person narrative titled "The Clothesline Door," included in the anthology *The First Time: True Stories, Volume 2*, a collection of stories by Canadian writers about their first sexual encounters. That fall, despite having tried multiple times to weather the obvious opposition from Ruth's family, the couple broke up for good.

Kinsella dated various girls after this, though none seriously. One was Norma Brummet, the file clerk who regularly delivered homestead files to his desk at work. She lived with her sister in an upstairs suite across from the office building and was engaged to a milkman. She wasn't particularly excited about the engagement and confided in Bill her desire to break it off, but her father, the head of a large Germanic family, would not entertain any change in his daughter's plans. Norma began making excuses to her boyfriend, choosing instead to spend time with Bill, often driving around Edmonton with him at night.

They also spent their lunch hours at her apartment, as it was so close to the office. One afternoon, Norma's fiancé walked in, catching them both in the suite, leaving Bill certain his "time was up." And while the boyfriend was upset at the situation, Kinsella realized the man "knew he had her father on his side and was content to hang in until the wedding in July." Despite the interruption, Bill and Norma continued spending time together, Kinsella later admitting his fondness for her had grown to love. Though they had vague discussions about going away together to Vancouver, "things like that just weren't done" and the relationship, such as it was, soon ended.

In early July, Bill received a note from Norma inviting him to the wedding. Having already made plans to attend the Calgary Stampede the same weekend, he opted not to attend the ceremony, something he still regretted years later, wondering "what might have been, or what should have been. The possible connections we miss by such small margins; if times had just been a little different." Even after, or perhaps in spite of, his marriages and other romantic relationships, the idea of missed connections and lost opportunities would feature in his fiction.

Early in 1956, growing restless with his government job, Kinsella began actively searching for other employment, something that would allow him to advance towards a successful career in another, more rewarding field. Equipped with both a strong work ethic and an equally strong desire to be recognized, he was hopeful when a company by the name of Personal Finance showed interest in him; however, because they could not hire anyone under twenty-one, he made arrangements to start with them the week following his twenty-first birthday. Taking his remaining holidays from the government job, he cleaned out his desk one evening before leaving, and mailed his letter of resignation from Vancouver while he was on vacation.

Upon returning to Edmonton following that getaway to Vancouver and Seattle, Bill officially started with Personal Finance in June. The new job required him to collect delinquent accounts and verify the addresses provided by loan applicants, all the while being expected to study the finance business with the hope of an early promotion to assistant manager and, perhaps, manager soon thereafter. Part of this preparation included a lengthy correspondence course he was required to complete as part of the job. Within a week of starting, due in no small part to the course being "boring and stupid," he had decided he would not stay there long. While he could tolerate the work itself, it became clear that people in management positions had the title but not a commensurate salary to go with it.

About this time, Kinsella was at his friend Jim Warne's house when he met Myrna Salls. Her older sister Florence had been a boarder at the Warne home until she got married, giving her room to another sister, Doreen, whom Myrna had come to visit in Edmonton while she sought a job for the summer. Bill and Myrna immediately made a connection, and he helped her to get a job as an assistant play-ground director with the recreation department, the same position he had held in between grades eleven and twelve. Within two weeks of Bill meeting Myrna, her father died after suffering a stroke. The middle of nine children, Myrna lived on a farm about ten miles west of St. Paul and 120 miles from Edmonton. Upon first visiting her house, Kinsella was struck by it. Though clean inside, "the house itself was [a] slant-roofed shack, right out of *Tobacco Road*." Like Myrna, Bill had grown up with limited resources on a farm and had lost his father at a young age. Bill may have felt an even closer connection to Myrna because of these similarities.

By August, not finding any excitement in the position with Personal Finance and dreading the thought of having to continue with the correspondence course, Kinsella once again explored the job market. Fortunately, his friend Gordon Arbuckle worked for Retail Credit Co., a company that worked primarily with credit and insur-ance investigations, and Bill discovered they were looking to hire a credit reporter—a position he was quickly hired for, to begin working in that fall.

By summer's end, Bill and Myrna had fallen in love, though she soon had to return to high school back home in St. Paul. He visited her nearly every weekend until her oldest brother, Delmar, bought a house in Edmonton and moved his mother and the rest of the family into it in early 1957. Soon after the move, Myrna quit school and began working as a clerk with the Toronto-Dominion Bank.

Within the first three months, Kinsella began feeling comfort-able with the work at his new job, doing credit reports for mortgage and finance companies and following the strict set of rules he was given. What he quickly learned was that in order to meet the quotas set by the company, the reporters simply could not carry out the types of investigations they were supposed to. As a result, he "wrote a lot of fiction over the years at RCC," providing what information was required without having actually followed protocol to obtain it.

Myrna and Bill began seeing each other nearly every night, often merely driving around town listening to the radio, which at that time was playing artists like Elvis Presley, Fats Domino, the Everly Brothers, Chuck Berry and Marty Robbins. During this same period, Kinsella began taking a course in radio announcing from the Canadian Broadcasting Academy, which was operated by two employees of CHED Radio. Though he felt confident in his voice over the airwaves, he also admitted later that "at that time [I] would have panicked at having to adlib a line." Upon completing the course, he was offered a job with CFCW, the local country music station in Camrose, Alberta, at a starting salary of $190 per month as the nighttime disc jockey. Kinsella was intrigued by the job offer, but was already making $240 a month at RCC, and was barely able to exist on that. He had made a similar decision while still with the government when he turned down a position as a cub reporter with the *Edmonton Journal* because the pay cut would have been far too drastic for him to live on.

In December of 1957, after dating for nearly a year and a half, Kinsella and Myrna were married in a ceremony attended mostly by family members, though Bill's friend Dave Page served as the best man. Following a small reception at the Sallses' house, the newlyweds spent their first night together at the Mayfair Hotel in downtown Edmonton. Calling it "a disaster from the first," Kinsella said later that their sexual inexperience left them each "more than a little inept" and that their first sexual encounter "was a tremendous disappointment," adding that "it was about seven years before I found out sex could be sensational."

The newlyweds rented a basement apartment at 10714 76th Avenue, just a few blocks from Bill's office at RCC. The weather that winter was bitterly cold and their new home was only marginally warmer inside than out. Fortunately, they had placed their names on a waiting list for an apartment on 83rd Avenue just behind where Bill worked, and they got a call the following spring that an opening had come up for them. Soon thereafter they moved into a more comfortable one-bedroom apartment on the main floor. During this transition, Kinsella bought a 1957 Royal typewriter, the one he used well into the 1980s, to allow him to complete most of his typing at home. Along with the new marriage and the new home, Bill was promoted to insurance investigator, giving him the freedom to travel around Edmonton. He paid visits to neighbours of auto and life insurance applicants and made inquiries into the applicants' health, finances, drinking habits and other such information, which he compiled for the company.

Bill soon came to the conclusion that Myrna was unable to understand her husband's career ambition and his drive for success and recognition. He later acknowledged that she may have very well "been happier with a man who worked half the year and drew unemployment and stayed home the rest of the time." Envisioning himself in the role of rescuer, he expected Myrna, since she had come from an impoverished family, to be more grateful that he had provided her a home, a car and new furniture. Instead, she seemed not only uninterested in the material possessions he provided, but unwilling to pay the price necessary for success.

By the time the couple moved into their new apartment, Myrna had become pregnant. Their first daughter, Shannon Leah, was born that fall on November 12, 1958. They had not planned on having a baby so soon after marrying, and Bill was not terribly excited about becoming a father at that point in his life. He was, however, glad the baby was a girl as he never particularly cared for boys. Like many first-time fathers, Bill was struck by how tiny and fragile his new daughter was, though he was equally mesmerized by her beauty from the day she was born.

A month after Shannon's birth, what Kinsella called "one of the beautiful experiences of my life" took place. While in downtown Edmonton in Woodward's department store, he happened to walk through the toy department. The seemingly mundane event caused him to feel "such a rush of love for [his] daughter," like nothing he had ever felt before. He bought her a small, yellow, scented frog she ended up keeping through her childhood. And while his love for his daughter offered a reprieve from the frustrations he felt towards his work and the tension in his marriage, the rest of his life continued pressing down on him.

With a new baby in the mix, Bill and Myrna had very little social life. Other than an occasional party or a night of bowling each week, they would spend one day each weekend at her mother's house and one day with his mother. His resentment at work was compounded by the correspondence courses he was required to take. Bill believed "they were artificially complicated to give the illusion that . . . the job was difficult rather than quite straightforward, something anyone with good verbal and written skills could do." He did the minimum work required for him to keep his position, and even this was done haphazardly.

In 1959 the company split up its insurance and credit reporting operations in Canada. As a result, the head credit reporter, who was set to be promoted to manager, resigned just a week before the new arrangement was announced. Kinsella had experience in credit reporting, was next in the line of seniority, and in the fall of that year, at age twenty-four, became the manager of the newly formed Retailers Commercial Agency. Though it sounded more impressive than what he had been doing before, it came with only a small increase in salary, coming out only twenty dollars per month ahead of what he had been making. For most of the next two years, while Kinsella was branch manager, the Edmonton office was among the top earners out of some sixty-five branches in the company.

Though his work and ambition served the company well, Kinsella felt unappreciated by RCA. In 1960, after a successful year, rather than offering a cash bonus, the company mailed Kinsella a framed certificate of excellence, something he kept for years as a reminder of how unappreciative large corporations often are of those who work for them.

Similarly, Bill felt Myrna was never suitably impressed with the success he had garnered. Adding to the tension in their marriage was the fact that she was not a reader, nor did she ever encourage her husband's ambition to be a writer. He later considered this one of the greatest disappointments in their marriage. At one point, when he was still trying to write while working for RCA, he had composed a piece for the *Edmonton Journal* and gave it to her to read. Barely glancing at the manuscript, she simply responded, "This is kind of dull, isn't it?" The lack of support only served to exacerbate the growing rift between them.

By late 1959, the Kinsellas' marriage was on shaky ground, but they continued to try to make their way as a family. That spring they had relocated once again, this time to a house at 9284 77th Street on Edmonton's south side. The two-bedroom house had a separate suite in the basement, so Bill and Myrna rented the entire house and sublet the basement. After they had settled into the new home, the owner offered to sell it to them for a reasonable rate. Although Olive Kinsella offered to front her son the $2,000 down payment, there were second and third mortgages in addition to other loans already taken on the house, making it impossible for the family to purchase.

But Bill and Myrna kept searching and by August had bought a two-storey house at 6054 107A Street. The purchase strained their already meagre finances, and in an effort to ease some of the financial difficulty, Bill proposed taking in a boarder or two as the house had extra bedrooms they weren't using. Myrna was unable or unwilling to share his enthusiasm, ultimately deciding no boarders would live with them. With no other obvious alternatives, Kinsella began driving taxi, working Sundays to earn extra money for the family's grocery bills.

That fall, Myrna began having an affair. She confided to their friend Kay Harper about the relationship, and Kay, who had been Bill's friend first, reported back to him.

Bill was not ready to give up on the marriage, feeling obligated to stay together for their daughter's sake and thinking that being separated would only create more complications for them. In an effort to salvage the relationship, he began seeing a counsellor affiliated with a free service offered by the City of Edmonton. When he came home after the first visit, Myrna suggested that he move out of the house. Holding his ground and telling her he was not going anywhere, he responded that she was free to leave, but if she did, Shannon would stay with him. Realizing how serious he was, she agreed to see the counsellor with him.

During their sessions, Myrna complained to the counsellor that Bill was spending entirely too much of his time working. His complaints focused on their sex life, which he found utterly unsatisfying, perhaps due to both of their mutual inexperience, though her poor housekeeping and cooking bothered him as well. Myrna responded that their sex life was fine except not frequent enough for her tastes. Ultimately, despite their difficulties, they elected to stay together. The counsellor did not discourage them from thinking of having another child, often bringing it up in their sessions, and by the late spring of 1960, Myrna was pregnant once more.

On February 28, 1961, she gave birth to another daughter, Erin Irene, who later picked up the nickname "Boo" from her sister, after Yogi Bear's cartoon sidekick, Boo Boo. And while another baby did little to improve their relationship, Bill's plan was "to simply stick it out until the girls were grown. We didn't fight much and so the kids didn't suffer. I planned to just plug along."

In the winter of 1960, though they could not justify the additional expense in the family's budget, Kinsella spent over $300 to attend the popular Dale Carnegie course on public speaking. After a shaky first public speech, Bill improved and even won several prizes, and was given the opportunity to speak at the graduation banquet. Decades later, he still referred to it as "probably the best $300 I have spent in my whole life," as it enabled him to anticipate rather than dread book readings, lectures, and question and answer sessions once he was an established writer. He became known for his relaxed, efficient delivery and comfortable style at book events. He denied any fear of any public appearances or television and radio interviews; in fact, his enjoyment of speaking grew in correlation to the size of the crowd.

Bill grew continually more dissatisfied with his job at Retailers Commercial Agency. Despite operating one of the company's most cost-efficient branches, his annual salary was still below $6,000, and the prospects of a raise did not look good. Hearing from an acquaintance in the insurance business that there was good money to be made there, Kinsella began looking into the possibility of yet another career change. While he was successful in his position at RCA, there were few corporations looking for a similar skill set. So he considered going into sales, where he would have an opportunity to advance based on his performance and to make much better money to support his family.

Multiple companies showed interest in him, and Bill began the process of choosing one. After telling RCA how unhappy he was about his bleak possibility for advancement in the company, they offered him a sales job, though it may have meant relocating to the United States and would not likely come open for a year or more. Bill chose to move into the insurance business with Standard Life, primarily because of a guaranteed salary and paid 90% of commission upfront, where other companies paid just 50% in the first year.

Soon after taking the new job, Bill found out that "insurance companies, next to banks, are the most repressive and biggest thieves in the world." He was a successful salesman, but quickly realized his loathing would prevent him from being able to produce. His feelings about insurance companies would emerge in his stories later on, and he unapologetically stated, "I mean every word of it. They are blood-suckers of the worst ilk." After only six months on the job, he quit to take up a brief stint in publicity and advertising before realizing that company was in a precarious financial situation.

He left just a week before the company filed for bankruptcy, losing most of his commissions as a result, and began selling advertising for the Yellow Pages in the fall of 1962. Unlike the other sales jobs he had before, the new position provided the opportunity to work overtime, and the sales staff worked on compiling the book during the month after the sales window closed. As a result of this system, he was able to earn significantly more, and for the first time in his life, felt optimistic about his financial future. In just his first year, he worked his way into the top sales position. Myrna went back to work as a bank teller in 1963 and between them the family's financial problems finally seemed to be nearly solved.

But the marriage finally unravelled completely in the fall of 1963. During this time, Jerry and Florine Beauchamp, Myrna's sister and her husband, had separated, and Jerry visited the Kinsellas' home a few times, bringing his friend, an unemployed, itinerant land surveyor, with him. Myrna and the friend began having an affair. Following some agonizing weeks of consideration, Bill made it clear he would no longer tolerate the situation as it was, letting Myrna know she was free to leave but that, if she chose to do so, Shannon and Erin were going to stay with him. In early November, Myrna moved out, and Bill, who was into the months when he was able to work overtime, had to pay for a full-time babysitter to watch the girls five days a week.

With the sudden unexpected childcare expenses coupled with the cost of hiring a lawyer to handle the divorce, Kinsella was forced to take out a second mortgage on his house. While the situation seemed to improve after Myrna and her lover moved to Calgary, Bill had trouble keeping a babysitter hired. Until late February the following year, when the overtime period ended, he went through a succession of sitters who were often both incompetent and unreliable. However, that month when the divorce was entered into court records he was awarded custody of Shannon and Erin. Years later, after he had been divorced from Myrna for more than twenty-five years and had been married twice more, Kinsella would admit that he did not know the whole story of what happened to lead to the dissolution of his first marriage, concluding that only Myrna knew for sure the real reasons.

In the spring of 1964 Bill ran an advertisement in the local newspaper, offering free rent to a single-parent family in return for babysitting. Mrs. Evan Barclay, a war bride who was left with three children when her husband died, answered the ad. Having solved the childcare issue, Kinsella spent that summer attending auctions to buy tricycles and bicycles, which he would spraypaint and affix new handle grips with tassels to before reselling them for between five and ten dollars more than he paid for them, thereby bringing in a little more money.

In early 1965, for the first time in years, he started writing again while taking a night school course at Victoria Composite High School. And while he later acknowledged that he "didn't turn out any even passable fiction," the course was beneficial in that it once again got him into the habit of writing. Though his fiction output was not what he would have hoped, that spring he began writing an article for the *Edmonton Journal* on its weekly editorial page, "The Journal for Dissent." The piece, entitled "Let's get rid of the dogs in this city," was what Kinsella described as "a tongue-in-cheek tirade" in which he had obviously "overestimated [the] intelligence of the reading public by about 90%" as "literally thousands of people believed what I wrote and I had to take the phone off the hook for days." Established as a controversial writer following this first article, he continued submitting pieces for the next two and a half years, though none of them were able to generate even a fraction of the controversy the first one did.

In June, while Bill was dating off and on following his divorce, his friend Kay Harper introduced him to Mickey Heming, who, like Kinsella, had endured a failed marriage. Mickey was living with her family in Paradise Valley, about 125 miles east of Edmonton. Kinsella corresponded with her for a few weeks, then met her for the first time that July when she had to bring one of her four children to Edmonton for an eye examination.

Mickey "was a plump little redhead" with whom he immediately felt a connection. He took her to a Klondike Days event the first day they met and followed up by taking her and her daughter Lyndsey and his two girls to the park for the day. The new couple spent that night together, and Kinsella experienced what amounted to a sexual awakening. Describing his sex life with his ex-wife as "not very pleasant work," he'd reached a point where he believed sex "was not what it was cracked up to be." He later remarked, "While I regret not getting started seriously writing until I was 35, I regret not discovering the joys of sex until I was 30 or more. I often think of the fun I could have had for the previous 15 years." Bill and Mickey's obvious chemistry laid the groundwork for a stronger connection than the marriage he had just ended and gave Bill reason to be optimistic about their relationship.

Mickey's divorce was not finalized until September, but she and Bill decided they would marry when they were able. In the meantime she and her children moved into Bill's house as quickly as possible, as Mrs. Barclay and her children had vacated it. As an early honeymoon, Mic and Bill took a brief vacation to Calgary just before the move. Immediately after the Labour Day holiday, Bill began working overtime four or five nights a week to offset the family's increased costs. The marriage took place on September 10, 1965, just two months after they had first met, and Kinsella found himself with a new wife and four additional children to provide for.

Even with the changes in his personal life and the overwhelming amount of overtime he was working, Bill continued to make time to write. He submitted pieces to the "The Journal for Dissent" in the *Edmonton Journal* and to another section of the paper called "Writer's Corner." His approach in many of these was a self-described "Erma Bombeck style" of humorous caricatures of his neighbours, including an older man three doors down who spread grass seed and fertilizer in the snow during early springtime and "the organization queen who looked like Attila the Hun in drag." The Kinsellas had a large, pie-shaped yard, which Bill hated but the neighbourhood association maintained must be kept cut. Though he found it much easier to let the grass grow, "the fucking neighbors always complained to the weed inspectors." In addition to furthering his lifelong disdain for seemingly arbitrary and senseless bureaucracies, these people and their attitudes towards the rules kept Kinsella well-armed for his newspaper pieces.

Following the move, Bill and Mickey's children had to adapt, some of them to a different environment and all of them to new family members. Bill later reflected that Mickey's children were often threatened with punishment, but that she would often not follow through. Additionally, when they returned from visiting their father the children would often attempt to abide by different rules. In the midst of this, Mickey became ill in late 1966, becoming so depressed that she required hospitalization for nearly a month. Years later, Kinsella would recall that his new wife "had always had feelings of inadequacy, brought on . . . by a haphazard upbringing, [and] even though she was an excellent mother and wife, she felt she was not doing a good job, to the point where it got her down." Though she remained on medication for several years afterwards, and experienced later bouts with depression, none matched the seriousness of this first instance.

During the spring of 1966, Kinsella entered an annual contest held by the *Edmonton Journal*, submitting in both the fiction and non-fiction categories. He won his first award for writing with a first-person piece titled "Hopfstadt's Cabin," winning the non-fiction category despite the fact that "there wasn't a discernible fact" in the story.[2] The $100 cash award was a welcome bonus, but the real prize was having his picture in the newspaper. And while the win encouraged him to keep writing, Kinsella kept applying himself to his regular job in an effort to continue his financial recovery. That year was an important one for his career with the Yellow Pages as word came down that there would be a sales supervisor job available in 1967 and the top salesman in 1966 would have a significant advantage over other applicants. Looking back years later, he realized the announcement was "a cheap, nefarious scheme to get probably $100,000 worth of extra advertising revenue without having to pay for it."[3] He made his yearly quota by June, as did his primary competitor for the job, and for the rest of the year Bill worked with the sole focus of winning the promotion.

By year's end, Bill was only a few hundred dollars in sales ahead of the second-place salesman, but since he had prior experience in a supervisory position, he felt all but certain the job was his. To his disappointment, he was passed over, not because he was not qualified but because he "didn't have . . . the right attitude." As Bill put it, "What was required was that I believe what I was doing was important." Though he felt he was doing excellent work, he never once believed that selling advertisements for the Yellow Pages was important. Once he was denied the promotion, he began searching seriously for another job. Until one came along, he made the decision to do only enough work to meet his quota. As a result, his sales dropped significantly the following year. Knowing that he had sold between $50,000 and $60,000 in extra advertising for them, with no hope of getting the promotion, made him "eternally bitter at the miserable treatment [he] received."

Kinsella spent most of 1967 working just two days a week. Many days, he would come to work to clock in and head home shortly after that. Fortunately, this gave him the freedom to write more than he had been in recent years, and he even submitted some pieces for publication. And though *Playboy* magazine rejected his story "The Girl from Cemetery Hill," the fiction editor, Robie Macauley, sent him "a lovely rejection letter" telling him they would have taken it except there was a policy at the time that the magazine would not buy stories with "down" endings. Coincidentally, several years later, in 1981, Macauley was working at Houghton Mifflin when the publisher bought the rights to Kinsella's first novel.

That spring, while on vacation in Victoria, British Columbia, Kinsella fell in love with the landscape and climate. Mickey had lived there when she was younger, and her parents had recently moved back to the area. Looking around, the couple decided that rather than waiting until their retirement—as did many people wanting to leave the harsh Alberta climate and live in Victoria—they would move while still young enough to enjoy life there. With no job possibilities in front of him, Kinsella set out to look for work in Victoria. He quickly realized it was all but impossible as employment was scarce and he had no professional contacts in the city. Even with six years of exemplary sales results and experience, he was unable to secure a job in the field.

They decided to move anyway, confident that Bill would find something before they arrived in town. In what could be considered a bad omen, when Bill went back in midsummer for some job interviews, his suitcase was lost, and he had to rent a suit to wear to meet prospective employers. During one interview, with the *Victoria Colonist*, he was asked why he had no affiliations with service clubs or community activities. In truth he had always considered these types of organizations to be little more than an excuse for members to get out of their houses in the name of public service, reverting to "the grade-school-boys-tree-house-mentality," and had never considered joining, even for the sake of a job.

Though still without a job, when they moved to Victoria at the end of October, Kinsella was finally free of the bitterly cold winters he had lived through for over thirty years. The family moved into Mickey's parents' old house at 1440 Jamaica Road, a three-bedroom split level home with a sundeck that backed up to the tree line of nearby Mt. Douglas. They had just a few dollars left after the sale of their home in Edmonton, Mickey's share of the money from the home she had owned with her ex-husband, and Bill's pension fund, and Bill immediately began pursuing ways to provide for his family here.

He began entertaining the idea of starting his own business. While in sales back in Edmonton, he had sold advertising to a man who owned several pizza franchises in the area and who was willing to sit down with Bill to explain the financial side of it. Bill made an initial plan to work for at least a year before opening a restaurant and was pleased to discover a new shopping mall being built at McKenzie Avenue and Shelbourne Street, just south of where the family now lived. It was slated to open in the fall of 1968, and Bill went ahead and leased the space for a pizza restaurant there.

There were only two pizza places in Victoria at the time, one downtown and another in a shopping centre. While Bill was looking for something to generate income until he was able to open the restaurant, he discovered that the pizzeria downtown, Mario's Italian Restaurant, had closed. Digging into its history, Kinsella found out that a young man named Mario had moved to town and opened the place at 1819 Douglas Street, remodelling the existing building. He added a lowered ceiling, installed by an older Italian carpenter. When the carpenter came to collect payment, Mario, whom others described as immature and abrasive, laughed and claimed that since he was only eighteen, he was not responsible for his debts. The carpenter went back home and got a gun, returned, and "ventilated Mario in several places." Mario's reputation outside his family was such that, as Bill gathered from those from the area, the killer had "decidedly improved society by his act."

After Mario's murder, his brother, Elio, attempted to supervise the Victoria business from Vancouver. Perhaps not surprisingly, with the boss away most of the time, the employees mismanaged and stole from the operation. Kinsella contacted Elio in Vancouver in the hope of purchasing the business from him. Because Elio was desperate to sell, Bill managed to talk him down to $6,000, approximately what it was worth. It did, however, come with an established clientele, keeping him from having to endure the lean times most new restaurants are forced to suffer through until a customer base is in place.

On December 1, 1967, Caesar's Pizza officially opened for business, despite the fact that Bill had never before made a pizza until that day. He and his staff did have "a lot of nerve" and a competitive spirit that made them confident of their ability to succeed. In spite of their lack of restaurant experience, the endeavour was successful from the day it opened. Projecting a minimum volume needed to simply pay living expenses and keep the doors open, the business exceeded all those expectations from the beginning. Holding fast to sound business principles such as never hiring out what could be done in-house, always buying used equipment, only buying what was absolutely required to do business, and being very judicious with advertising, the restaurant was soon thriving. As welcome as the financial success was to him, Kinsella was even more gratified that he was finally able to demonstrate that he was a competent manager, which he felt he had never before been given the opportunity to prove.

Word about the restaurant soon got out and its popularity grew. Despite the awkward layout and informal location, it attracted clientele from all walks of life, including navy sailors and young people, who would fill the jukebox with money, especially on Saturday nights when people would bring in their own wine or beer. The restaurant also became a popular place for a local motorcycle gang that, according to Kinsella, was "extremely well behaved because there weren't many places where they were allowed to hang out." In addition to spending a large amount of money, the bikers "also kept the navy types in line" as "the sailors tended to come in drunk and were occasionally offensive [and] also liked to act tough." Kinsella recalled, "The bikers *were* tough, so they didn't have to flaunt it. If a sailor got rowdy, he was suddenly hustled up the back steps and out to [the] alley."

The next three years, though exciting for him as the business grew, were also among the busiest years Kinsella had ever known. For the first time, he answered only to himself at work; however, this also meant that he alone was responsible for the success or failure the business would have. He took immense pride in the fact that Caesar's Pizza was not only surviving, but thriving. Unfortunately, it left Bill no time to write. From the fall of 1967, when Bill was getting the restaurant ready to open, until September of 1970, he stopped writing altogether. Still, the restaurant's success made it all worthwhile for him. Years later, Kinsella explained the success as "a way of saying 'I told you so' to the idiots who didn't recognize your ability or worse, were afraid of it . . . There is nothing a bureaucrat fears more than an employee who is smarter than he is. I suffered that for years."

In the spring of 1970, Kinsella had the opportunity to move the business to the corner of the block. Sometime during the previous summer, the French deli located there had sold out to a Montreal businessman who transformed it into a traditional restaurant. Realizing the location wouldn't work for a non-specialty restaurant, Kinsella simply bided his time and watched it happen. Then he approached the landlord, offering to take over the lease to the space. He also purchased the tables and chairs and the large cooler in the kitchen area. Fortunately for Kinsella, the previous owner had spent a sizeable amount remodelling, allowing Kinsella to move "up in class by about 70%." Now, rather than being just "a pizza joint," they were "an Italian restaurant," offering pizza, spaghetti, ravioli and other dishes. They opened in time for the tourist season, and exceeded expectations once more, allowing Kinsella to hire a manager and several new staff. That year he and Mickey took the four children still living with them on an extended vacation to Disneyland.

The time away from the business gave Bill the freedom to reflect and begin thinking about what he wanted to do next. He was finally in the financial position to be able to step back from work and he was certain of one thing: he wanted to write again.

4

Back to School

Finding himself in a position where he was no longer living paycheque to paycheque, Kinsella entertained the idea of taking classes at the University of Victoria. Though he was unsure after so many years removed from high school if he would even be capable of doing work at a university level, he enrolled for the fall term beginning in August of 1970. His university career got off to an inauspicious beginning as he and Mickey were in Hawaii for two weeks, causing him to miss the first day of classes. The creative writing course met at eight o'clock in the morning, which was difficult for Bill as he was often working at the restaurant until past midnight. Designed for beginning students in the field, the class was taught by the poet Derk Wynand, a recent graduate from the University of British Columbia. In the first semester Wynand required students to write a variety of forms, including a one-act play, poetry and short stories, and whatever the students themselves found most interesting during the second semester. After years of working in jobs he loathed, Bill was ecstatic at the idea of finally having a dedicated outlet for his storytelling.

Most of the twenty or so students enrolled in the course fretted over the number of pages they were required to produce; however,

Kinsella bombarded Wynand with manuscripts, writing a story, play or a collection of poetry each week, later causing the professor to joke that "he had one folder for the work of 19 students and one folder of equal or larger size for [Kinsella]."[1]

For his first university assignment, a one-act play, Bill went to his earlier efforts for the *Edmonton Journal* in which he had made fun of the people living in his neighbourhood. Taking the title from a poster he had seen in a store, he called the piece "Yea Though I Walk Through the Valley of the Shadow of Death, I Will Fear No Evil, for I'm the Meanest Son of a Bitch in the Valley." Many of Kinsella's early efforts are housed in his private collection or at Library and Archives Canada, but this manuscript did not survive. His next play, "On the Turf," about street life, and a short piece from the following year "about a mouthy kid writing to Ann Landers," met the same fate, though a copy of nearly everything else he wrote in school survives. Soon, he began saving copies of his drafts.

Kinsella thoroughly enjoyed his introduction to higher level creative writing classes, though he observed that "after seeing the quality of work submitted by many of my classmates, [I] never had any doubt about my ability to do work at the university level. Then, as now, 50% of the class were close to functionally illiterate." The greatest benefit for Kinsella was having Wynand's helpful feedback and encouragement, despite the professor openly admitting that he did not know enough about fiction to be of any real help. Having the poet read his work was enough to make Kinsella want to continue. Additionally, Wynand provided the class with a list of some fifty books he felt would be beneficial for aspiring writers. Bill was shocked when he saw the list and realized he had only read one of the books. He had always been a voracious reader, though not of quality fiction before then. Astounded by his ignorance, he went to the library and the bookstore, and by the end of the semester, he had read all fifty books and more. Kinsella recognized the value reading had for a budding writer and would teach it to his own students years later: "Reading will teach a prospective writer more about craft than any course. I harp on reading constantly when I teach writing and students who have the stamina to serve their apprenticeship eventually agree with me."

Balancing his daily duties as a restaurant owner with his coursework, Bill continued to write and read steadily as he progressed towards his degree. In January of 1971, while sitting at home contemplating ideas for another short story, he remembered an Indigenous girl he knew only casually who was married to a white man. Initially drawn to the idea of writing about the problems her husband might have had in bringing his wife home to meet his conservative parents, Kinsella decided that concept was too reminiscent of *Guess Who's Coming to Dinner*. Deciding instead to reverse the usual racial stereotypes, he began writing a story that would answer the question "what would happen . . . about the Indian girl bringing the straight white man home to the reserve?"[2] The end result was "Illiana Comes Home," the first of several dozen of what he would call "Indian stories" written over about thirty years.

The story would lead to his reputation as a humour writer and set the stage for his first published collection of short stories, introducing readers to the voice of Silas Ermineskin. And while he was adamant that his work was far better when he wrote stories that were completely fiction, he recognized that his choice of the name Ermineskin was based on "subliminal knowledge." He had passed the Ermineskin Reserve many times over the years, but it was only when he next returned to the area four years after the story was written that he noticed a sign with the name on it. Once he had selected Silas for the narrator's name, the majority of the remaining tribal names were borrowed from the Blood and Sarcee Reserves (now the Kainai and Tsuu T'ina Nations' reserves) in southern Alberta, as Kinsella felt the family names on the Ermineskin Reserve were not colourful enough for his purpose in the story.

Although Silas narrates all of Kinsella's Hobbema stories, the humour in the stories emerges mainly from Silas's best friend and regular companion, Frank Fencepost. Obnoxious, belligerent, irreverent and having no formal education, Frank suggests a unique perspective into how humour is used on reserves to counteract the oppression often felt at the hands of settler society. Frank began as Kinsella's interpretation of the trickster character common to many Indigenous stories, though "Illiana Comes Home" was not written to be humorous; Kinsella "intended it as a bittersweet comment on race relations." Only after reading the story aloud during his creative writing class and hearing his classmates' uproarious laughter did he recognize the humour in Silas's narrative. The original version lacked details later suggested by playwright Lawrence Russell, who taught another creative writing class to which Bill brought the story, in 1974. By the time he presented it to a third class, taught by W.D. Valgardson in 1975, the story was nearly in its finished form and Kinsella was encouraged to submit it for publication.

In February 1971, Bill developed a stomach ulcer that restricted him to a bland diet for six weeks. Working from five o'clock until closing, then going home to write until the early morning hours, often drinking only coffee and soft drinks, certainly did nothing to help his ulcer, but after the issue cleared up he began considering taking a heavier course load during the following school year. That fall, he decided to enroll in three courses: an advanced writing course taught by Leon Rooke, an advanced composition course taught by Velma Gooch and an introductory English course taught by Mel Faber.

In the meantime, Bill decided to enroll in a summer course, "Studies in Literature," which introduced him to academic literary criticism, something he later grew to loathe. Kinsella was drawn to the reading list of about a dozen novels and collections covered in the six-week course, including works by Samuel Beckett, Ernest Hemingway, D.H. Lawrence, Thomas Pynchon and T.S. Eliot.

Though the readings themselves proved interesting, Kinsella later described himself as "incredulous," as he could not fathom how a writer could "have all these layers of meaning in mind" when composing their work. He felt that the writer most likely had no such symbolic meanings in mind when writing. Ultimately, he dismissed the field, saying, "The interpretations were made up by academics— here was a whole growth industry relying on someone being able to see things that weren't really there." And while he disagreed with most, if not all, of the critical methods introduced in the class, he discovered "that in order to get a degree in English it was unnecessary to learn a single fact, but only to read and put interpretation on what you had read—the more outlandish the better. I was perfectly suited for this pursuit. I was a storyteller—a born liar."[3]

Kinsella despised the "lit crit game," in which "the students with the best imaginations received the best marks." Even in his introduction to the discipline, he was "terribly cynical about the whole process." Maintaining that students should always be required to read a high quality and high quantity of books, his own teaching approach included questioning them to ensure the readings had been completed. Requiring the students to create their own interpretations, however, was to his mind "a non-learning process, and completely useless." To his thinking, interpretations could be considered and discussed in class, but should never be created by anyone other than the writer of the work in question.

As he had in high school, Kinsella grew increasingly frustrated with bureaucracy and the attitudes of people in positions of power at the university. Older now, he became more intent on finding ways to fight the system and expose the fallibility of such people and rules, if only to himself. During his time at the University of Victoria, he would write papers on books he had never read, and once recorded a professor's lectures in class and then transcribed them for a fifteen-page paper in another course. Perhaps his most blatant disdain for the system, however, was demonstrated when he submitted an intentionally plagiarized paper for a Shakespeare course. The professor who assigned the paper announced to the class, "I've read everything ever written on the plays we'll study, so if you plagiarize, you'll get caught." Viewing this more as a challenge than as a warning, Kinsella got to work. Finding an obscure book on the playwright, he verified that the university library had only the one copy before promptly checking it out to keep until after the paper was graded. He then copied the chapter word-for-word, submitted it and received several enthusiastic comments from the professor and a grade of 85%. Kinsella "sat and smirked for the rest of the course."

Not all of his academic experience, though, was negative. In Alastair Watt's class, for instance, he chose to avoid "writing deadly dull research papers" his classmates were submitting, choosing instead to write "a conversational story-like essay [in which] two men have been locked in a basement, assigned to turn E.M. Forster's novel *A Passage to India* into a screenplay. Both men loathe the book and consider it about as exciting as watching water find its own level." Although the effort earned him an A, the grade came with a stern warning from Watt "that the mark could just have easily been an F" and an instruction to write a traditional essay for his next paper. Some fifteen years later, when Kinsella was appearing at a book signing in Toronto, his former teacher appeared and recounted the story of the unorthodox paper.

The restaurant continued to flourish and the Kinsellas were more financially sound than ever, allowing Bill to keep taking classes during the day while working at night, maintaining a steady schedule and turning out a new story every week or two. By the winter of 1971–72, the effort began bearing fruit as he was published in a literary magazine. Put out sporadically by the university, the magazine was published as a supplement to UVic's newspaper, the *Martlet*, and though not widely circulated it was a beginning for Kinsella.

Although the business was doing well and he was making steady progress towards getting a degree from the university, Kinsella's family life was not without its share of challenges. During that fall term, his daughter Shannon ran away from home. She usually waited tables at the restaurant on Saturday nights, a job that provided a steady income for the twelve-year-old. However, as she drew closer to turning thirteen, her father noticed a change in her attitude. She became, according to Bill, "sullen and snippy," and decided she no longer wanted to work. The day after her birthday party at the restaurant, Bill was woken up by a phone call from his ex-wife, Myrna, letting him know that Shannon was with her in Edmonton.

He soon found out that she had made a call for a taxi the evening before and then snuck from the house to take the cab to the airport, where she caught an early morning flight by herself to Edmonton. Upon arriving there, she hailed another cab to her mother's place, where Myrna was living with her new husband and their two young daughters. Shannon was determined to live with her mother in Edmonton, so her parents transferred her school records there with the understanding that she could return to Victoria any time.

During the summer of 1972, Bill made a commitment to attend school full-time, working towards a degree in creative writing. The decision meant selling the restaurant, but he found a buyer relatively quickly. Being a full-time student for the first time since he was in high school nearly two decades earlier was a big adjustment. He later recalled that during this period of his life events ran together more than at any other time and even the courses he took blurred together in his memory. Though he had primarily written short stories up until this point, a poetry workshop with Robin Skelton, "probably the best all-round instructor" Kinsella ever had, soon changed that. Though he had never written anything more than "rhyming doggerel" before the course, by Christmas break Kinsella was not only writing but publishing poetry. For the first time, he realized that he "had considerable talent but it was unfocused." Still, when in his third year he had to choose between writing poetry or fiction, he opted for fiction for two reasons: first, his own tastes were more aligned with reading fiction—poetry failed to provide the same enjoyment; and secondly, he still felt being a fiction writer offered him a more realistic possibility to make a living as a writer, as "poets *always* have to teach to supplement their meagre income from book sales," something Kinsella had no interest in doing.

While working towards his degree, Kinsella was able to keep from using the savings he and Mickey had accumulated after selling the business, though he did have to look for some part-time work to help meet the family's expenses. He took on a job two days a week for B.C. Forest Products, where he shovelled sawdust off the mill's roof and completed other menial tasks. The job reminded him that he loathed manual labour, and before long he decided to drive a taxi, even though it brought in less money.

Bill began driving occasional shifts that fall for Victoria Taxi and ended up working steadily on the weekends for them for nearly four years. He also drove full-time during the summer months and during the Christmas holiday season. Between working twelve weeks for them and then drawing unemployment for several months, he was able to devote most of his time towards writing and completing his degree.

Seeing how much Bill was enjoying his time as a student, Mickey decided to take courses at the university as well, discovering, as he had, that the work came easily to her. Having produced some promising pieces as a playwright and poet, she decided to begin working towards a degree in creative writing. Their decision was largely based on the rumour that the Creative Writing major, unlike English, did not require learning a foreign language.

After the business sold, the Kinsellas made the decision to sell their house on Jamaica Road and rent a small cottage a few blocks away on Torquay Drive. That summer, Erin went to Edmonton to visit her mother and Shannon. Erin soon decided she also wanted to move to Edmonton and Bill agreed to the arrangement, since on his frequent visits he'd found Shannon seemed happy there. He later described this as "the one decision in my life that I regret."

During the fall 1973 term, Bill was introduced to someone who would forever change not only his writing, but also his life. That fall, acclaimed writer W.D. Valgardson began teaching at the University of Victoria. Kinsella had been given a copy of the writer's collection *Bloodflowers* and had been impressed, describing the book as a "collection of Hemingway-like stories set in Manitoba, about real people. They were tough and tender, full of hidden symbols and layers of meaning." Kinsella went on to review the book for the *Martlet*, "and raved on about the book, probably too loud and long." Though he had yet to meet Valgardson, Bill was struck by the power of the writer's storytelling and the structure of his prose.

At the registration day for that semester's classes, Robin Skelton called Bill over to him, and introduced him to Valgardson. Years later, Kinsella would often discuss what he referred to as the Implied Author

Syndrome, in which readers craft a version of the writer in their minds based on the writer's style. Since Valgardson's fiction was often "about rough, tough fishermen and loggers," Kinsella had assumed the author was "a 6'4" Viking who would wear a mackinaw and carry an ax." Instead, he was introduced to a short, slightly built man with receding blond, curly hair, not at all like the man he had pictured.

Kinsella enrolled in Valgardson's fiction writing course that year, something that would have a huge impact on his work. Towards the end of the school year, just as Bill was getting ready to graduate, Valgardson gave him the most valuable piece of advice of his career. Taking a couple of Bill's stories as examples, Valgardson said, "Look, you are warming up for two pages before you start your story. And you are winding down for a couple pages after the story ends." He then tore off the first two pages and the last page or two. Bill was thrilled to finally meet a teacher who understood his craft and how his style could be improved—someone who could not only see what he was trying to accomplish in his writing, but was able to help him do it. And while other professors such as Rooke, Wynand, Skelton and Russell had each made a special effort to help Bill, it was Valgardson who provided the advice that helped him take his writing the next step towards being publishable.

In May 1974, Kinsella officially graduated, though he decided not to attend his convocation, held on his thirty-ninth birthday, as he was averse to the pageantry of such events. He enrolled in a summer school session in the education program. The province was in need of high school teachers, and there was a special internship program that enabled Kinsella to receive a scholarship. The program involved six weeks of intensive coursework, after which the students could teach at a reduced salary for a year. The following summer, they would take summer school again, and obtain a teaching certificate. At the outset of the program Kinsella was hired by the North Vancouver School District, and he and Mickey made plans to move there by late summer.

In June, Bill travelled to Vancouver to spend a day at the school and meet the staff he would be teaching with. That one day was enough to change his mind about his career path. Though he respected the effort the other teachers obviously put into their work, he saw them as "too competent and particularly too dedicated," whereas he was looking at teaching solely as a way of supporting his writing. Additionally, much of the work in the school involved team teaching and, as had been the case since his childhood, he preferred working alone. Upon returning home, he dropped out of the education program. He planned to write for at least a year while continuing to drive a taxi on the weekends to pay for the family's necessities.

Bill began applying Valgardson's advice to his writing, which immediately resulted in him producing better quality work. Though he had already graduated, he took Valgardson's course again, this time auditing it. He showed Valgardson a few of the Silas Ermineskin stories he had written, including "Dance Me Outside," "Panache," "Horse Collars" and "Penance," and was thrilled with the professor's response. He offered editorial advice and suggested that Bill get them out in the mail to various publications. The stories, all of which were later included in his first published collection, reflect a developing sense of language and a voice that readers and critics alike came to identify with the Hobbema stories. And while he was writing at a steady pace, producing far more pages of work than anyone else he knew, he also knew he had yet to develop "a sense of discipline—the business of setting a definite quota for [himself] and sticking to it."

Written that spring, "Dance Me Outside" was inspired by Cathy Ford's brief poem "Another Same Old Story," which Bill had read years earlier in a Vancouver magazine. He was struck by the feminist poet's ability to tell in just twenty lines the story of two brothers and their friend murdering an Indigenous girl and getting away with the crime. The punishment was meted out when the girl's friends "danced him outside and castrated the bastard with the lid from a tin of brown beans."[4] Bill had filed the poem away until revisiting it with the idea of turning it into a short story. Remembering how much his classmates had enjoyed the voice of Silas Ermineskin in "Illiana Comes Home," he explored the idea of using the same characters on the reserve and continuing with Silas as the narrator. Though "Dance Me Outside" is much darker in both subject matter and tone than his first Hobbema story, both helped Bill address the issues of marginalization and power struggles found on Canadian reserves.

"Panache" was inspired by a column in the *Globe and Mail* dealing with the word, which Bill had never heard before. He copied down the definition and began thinking of ways it could be incorporated into a story. Feeling as though he "sort of had the hang of Silas' lingo," Kinsella had begun consciously searching for ideas to be used in stories narrated by him. He set "Panache" in a real-life coal mine near Jasper, Alberta, and incorporated people from his own life into the plot, including Gran and her husband who were based on his in-laws at the time. As was usually the case when he finished writing a story, there was little he found that he would have wanted to change. Editing while he worked on the stories left Kinsella with final drafts that required little if any revision related to the plot or characters before sending them to the publishers. Months after he completed "Panache," he took a tour of the actual mine when he was in the area, but even then he didn't find anything that compelled him to revise the story.

The other two stories Valgardson suggested be edited for submission, "Horse Collars" and "Penance," took their inspiration from existing works, one fairly obvious and one more obscure. Some months after reading the Sonja Croucher story "Toffee Apples," Bill took the idea of a young Jewish girl living in London whose father is away in jail and transformed it into another story set on the Hobbema Reserve. He doubted Croucher herself would be able to recognize "Toffee Apples" in "Horse Collars," which explores a dysfunctional family and power struggles through the story of a father who pimps out his own daughter for financial gain.

"Penance" was what Kinsella later called "the most technically perfect story in *Dance Me Outside*." Using what he thought was "perfectly obvious symbolism" borrowed from the story of Christ's birth and the Magi's journey to see the child, Kinsella was amazed years later when none of his students recognized the references or symbols. He changed the wise men into three somewhat comical Indigenous men on motorbikes, guided by a searchlight rather than a star in the heavens, suggesting "that perhaps a new virgin Mary was born there in that manger, but had to be sacrificed because even the small world where she was born wasn't ready for an event of that magnitude." Kinsella wrote the first paragraph based on an actual pilgrimage to Lac Ste. Anne, then left the story untouched until Valgardson suggested that he have Annie, an Indigenous character who already has eight children and is married to a drunkard, be pregnant. The rest of the story quickly formed in Kinsella's mind and was completed soon thereafter. This is the first example of Kinsella—who was agnostic at the time, a few years away from becoming an atheist—borrowing from biblical references to incorporate religious symbols and iconography into his work. While many of the references in the Silas stories make fun of organized religion and criticize the perceived hypocrisy of Christians, this story is one of the few in which he uses Christianity in a marginally positive manner.

During the summer of 1975, Bill and Mickey returned to Hawaii, spending two weeks on vacation in Honolulu. Within the first ten days, a time he later described as "one of the most productive periods of my life," Bill wrote four more stories that would be included in his first published collection less than two years later. Two of the pieces, "Caraway" and "Butterflies," were inspired by stories Mickey had been writing. Reading her rough outline of a story about a young girl struggling with drug addiction, Bill was struck by the butterfly symbolism, and when Mickey's story failed to develop, she gave him permission to transfer the idea to his fictional Hobbema Reserve and write it in Silas's narrative voice. Throughout his career, Bill incorporated attributes of people he knew into his fictional representations. Winnie's physical description in "Butterflies," is based on his youngest daughter, Erin. Taking full advantage of the butterfly imagery, something he would use more elaborately years later in *Butterfly Winter*, Kinsella consciously employed symbolism connecting Winnie and butterflies that were caught and pinned to a board.

The idea for "Caraway" was taken from a teleplay Mickey had been working on. The script was about a woman whose daughter dies under suspicious circumstances, resulting in the Catholic Church's refusal to bury her in their cemetery. Bill repeatedly asked Mickey,

"What does she do with the body?" Mickey took his suggestion to have the body burned in the front yard, but it was never used in the final version of the unproduced teleplay. Never one to waste material that has already been written, Bill set out to write a story that centred on a coffin-burning scene. The three paragraphs in "Caraway" describing the coffin and Ruth Buffalo's body being burned are, in Kinsella's own estimation, "the 'best' I have ever written."

Perhaps the most memorable aspects of "Caraway," however, are the story's opening epigraph and the ways in which Joe Buffalo, the older Indigenous man who loses his daughter, is able to circumvent the Catholic Church's authority. Starting the story with a fictional epigraph about the caraway plant's white blooms being used "to condemn the spirit [of a dying or recently deceased person] to eternal fire," an entry attributed to the fictional *Tales of the Great Spirit*, Kinsella gives the story's events an air of authenticity—backing up his frequent claim, "Where I need facts, I invent them."[5] Kinsella's epigraph explains Joe Buffalo's actions later in the story when he places caraway blossoms on Russell Bevans's eyes as he dies. Following the northern tribes' beliefs in the plant's supernatural powers as detailed in the epigraph gives Joe's actions purpose and clear explanation.

Because her death is a suicide, Joe's daughter cannot be buried in the Catholic cemetery. And so Joe burns the body so that he can take the ashes and bury them there late at night, undercutting the church authority's power over his daughter's soul. Though "Caraway" is subtler than some of his later stories in which he is critical of religion of any kind, Kinsella demonstrates in it his disdain for those religious bodies that abuse their authority over well-intentioned people. This anger towards the Catholic Church mirrored Bill's own anger following his father's decision to return to Catholicism shortly before his death.

After years of writing in relative obscurity when he was able to write at all, by 1975 Bill saw success in placing his work with more well-known, reputable publications. In the same week "Illiana Comes Home" was accepted for publication by *Canadian Fiction Magazine*, he received word that four other stories had been accepted elsewhere. To celebrate, Bill and Mickey took Valgardson and his wife, Maryanne, out for Chinese food. During this time, Valgardson suggested Bill attend graduate school, recommending his own alma mater, the University of Iowa Writers' Workshop. With a glowing letter of recommendation promised from Valgardson, Kinsella sent the program samples of his work in January of 1976. Meanwhile, Valgardson sent samples of Kinsella's work—two Silas Ermineskin stories, two fantasy stories and two more traditional pieces—to Michael Macklem of Oberon Press in Ottawa, his own publisher, for consideration.

While waiting to hear back from Iowa, Kinsella began teaching for the first time, offering a night school writing class at James Bay Community School and an afternoon course at the Silver Threads Centre in downtown Victoria. Volunteering his services would gain him some work experience for his curriculum vitae in the hope of earning a coveted teaching assistantship in Iowa, should he be accepted into the program. And though he enjoyed teaching these classes, his also recognized that it took skills he did not yet have. But he realized the students enjoyed listening to him read stories, and he would continue doing this in every creative writing course he ever taught. Finally able to see real progress towards his goal of making a living as a writer, Bill was excited about the future. However, his personal life had once again become unstable.

After ten years of marriage to Mickey, their relationship was, as he would later describe it, "running dry." She was often jealous, not only of women, but of men with whom her husband was friendly, too. Bill remembered that she was "particularly unreasonable about [his] friendship with Lee Harwood," one of his closest friends, a "big, blustery, ex-biker with a heart of gold" who hailed from Ontario. At the time, Lee was managing a number of Victoria-area bands. One evening he took Bill and Mickey along with him to tour the clubs and lounges where the bands played. At one point while they were travelling together in the same car, Mickey got angry with both men, and began driving wildly down the road. Bill suggested that she "smarten up," at which point she stopped the car and told them to get out. It was already past midnight, and Lee and Bill called a cab to take them back to Lee's car, and then went back to Lee's place for the rest of the night. Mickey was furious.[6]

In addition to his marital problems, Bill was having trouble with his daughter Erin. Although Shannon was doing well living in Edmonton, Erin was not. She ran away from home numerous times and had experimented with drugs, then returned to live in Victoria after too much arguing with her mother. Unfortunately, Bill was unable to do much better with Erin. She was, he said, "simply determined not to succumb to any authority," a trait she shared with Bill himself. Unable to get help from counsellors and social workers, by 1976 she had moved back to Edmonton to live on her own.

Amid the turmoil in his family life, Bill received his much anticipated acceptance letter from the Iowa Writers' Workshop and was scheduled to begin classes in August of 1976. That March, feeling as though "Mickey was simply hassling [him] too much," he moved out of the house on Torquay Drive. Taking his 1967 Rambler, his typewriter and other writing materials, a few books and some clothes, he moved in with Bev Morrison in the home she rented at 16 Government Street. Bill had first come to know Bev when she enrolled in the writing course he had volunteered to teach. Originally mistaking her for a high school student, he found out that in fact she was divorced and had school-age children.

Kinsella remembers Bev being a "very vulnerable young woman." She had endured what can only be described as a traumatic upbringing, raised by alcoholic parents and experiencing sexual abuse and rape. Bev, Bill later recalled, was the sort of person he told his writing classes about, "the one in ten whose life is so bizarre no one would [believe] it if it was written down." The living situation on Government Street presented its own unique circumstances. Morrison's two children lived with her, her ex-husband lived in the basement suite and her married sister in an upstairs suite. Though it could have been uncomfortable, Kinsella recalled that the few times he met Bev's ex-husband, Jack, he "was polite and . . . long-suffering," and perhaps "still in love with Bev." Kinsella admitted years later that he would also "always be a little bit in love with her," but believed they "never could have had a long term relationship." He thought "it was obvious that Bev was exacting a certain revenge from all men, by captivating as many as she could, and then casting them loose after they were in love with her." Bill, on the cusp of a second failed marriage himself, certainly had his own personal issues, to complicate the situation even more.

A few weeks after Bill moved out of his house with Mickey and in with Bev, Lee came to town and went to dinner with the new couple. That night, Bill developed an illness that that would linger for nearly six weeks. It was never diagnosed, but was possibly related to the stress in his personal life. He ran a fever for weeks, was constantly fatigued and developed a terrible cough. Unable to pinpoint what the exact problem was, doctors thought at one point that he might have leukemia. Bev was away for a good part of this period, having found her father after many years of estrangement. She and the children went to visit him in Ontario, leaving Bill to suffer on his own for a couple of weeks. And while being sick prevented him from doing much during that stretch, he did find the strength to write "Mr. Whitey," a story loosely based on one Bev had told him.

In early June, as he was making preparations for his move to Iowa, Bill travelled to Hamilton, Ontario, to help Lee and Maggie move back to Victoria. Covering the 2,500 miles in a week, Lee and Bill encountered "more problems than anyone should have to face in a lifetime," including flat tires, running out of gas and nearly running into a ditch on the Trans-Canada Highway while a hitchhiker was driving the car. Before leaving Hamilton, Lee introduced Bill to Barbara Kostynyk, a probation officer who was married but who, in Kinsella's opinion, showed an interest in Lee. Meanwhile, Bill found himself captivated by Barbara, wishing that "she would have looked at [him] once the way she looked at [Lee]." Though Bill was envious of Lee's confidence around women and his ability to attract attention, he believed Lee was equally envious of Bill's writing and intellectual pursuits. Bill's friendship with Lee would be one of the most long-lasting of his life, with neither man expecting anything other than friendship from the other.

Back in Victoria, waiting to leave for Iowa, Kinsella had ended his relationship with Bev and was living with Lee and Maggie and their son, Kenny. With Shannon in town and Erin visiting during the summer, Bill was able to reconnect with his own family before heading to graduate school. Meanwhile, Michael Macklem at Oberon Press had returned the stories Valgardson had sent him. Included with the stories was a letter saying that, though Kinsella was clearly a writer with talent, the collection was so diverse that it seemed to have been written by three different authors. As a result, Oberon was not inclined to publish it at that time. While he was disappointed, the decision came as no surprise to Bill as he had come to accept that rejection was a significant part of any writer's life. He did, however, have eighteen Hobbema stories, written mostly over the previous two years, and he soon packaged them together, sending a much more cohesive collection to Oberon in mid-July. They accepted it for publication the following spring and released it under the title *Dance Me Outside*.

As the summer wore on, Bill tried to reconnect with Bev, but the relationship never rekindled, despite his best efforts. He dated Mickey a few times in the waning days of his time in Canada, and they spent his last three nights in Victoria together, but it had become clear that the relationship was all but over at that point. With no strong romantic interest tying him to Canada, with his daughters able to take care of themselves, and with a clear path ahead of him towards the writing career he had always envisioned, Bill set his sights on Iowa City.

5

Iowa

Bill boarded a bus in Langley, BC, a city to the east of Vancouver, to start the three-day trip to Iowa, a journey that launched one of the most significant periods of his life. Though it often seemed to him the bus spent more time stopped than actually moving, he finally arrived in Iowa City and took a taxi to the International Student Center, where he picked up the boxes of books and personal items he had mailed to himself before leaving home. On the way to campus, the cab driver told Bill that the town had been the inspiration for the fictional River City in Meredith Willson's *The Music Man*. And though the story turned out to be incorrect, Kinsella used it a few years later when he described the town in *Shoeless Joe*—the first of many anecdotes from his time in Iowa that would find their way into his work.

As the only incoming Canadian student, Kinsella was grouped with the international students and given a booklet of instructions on "how to get along with Americans," despite the fact his own father had been American. He had arranged to be housed in a dormitory, but had to wait until a vacancy opened up for him. In the meantime, he was assigned living quarters in a lounge on the twelfth floor of Rienow Hall, along with seven others, including two Chinese students, a man from Sierra Leone, and a law student who had arrived after completing his Ivy League undergraduate education.

Once he had been assigned his own room on campus, Kinsella shifted his focus to registering at the Workshop. He enrolled in a fiction workshop taught by Rosalyn Drexler, a seminar on the novel led by Robert Anderson, an undergraduate poetry course outside the workshop and a freelance journalism workshop in the Journalism Department. In addition to his own course load, Bill was teaching a university course for the first time. The freshman literature course consisted of approximately twenty-five students and required him to teach a dozen books during the fifteen-week term. Among the required texts were *The Odyssey* and *The Adventures of Huckleberry Finn*, neither of which he'd enjoyed himself, though he found recorded versions of Homer's work to be particularly helpful, especially since, as he put it, "90% of my freshmen students were barely capable of writing a bad essay on How I Spent My Summer Holidays, and were quite incapable of analyzing anything."[1] In fact, a few students admitted to Kinsella that they had finished high school without ever having written an essay. Recognizing, however, that the difficulties they had with the course were compounded by the fact that he was a subpar teacher, Kinsella was able to make up for some of his pedagogical shortcomings by being "a fair storyteller, [having] a good sense of humor and [being] able to make fun of both the course and the university." He regularly referred to the university as "Big Brother," and would openly criticize the level of bureaucracy involved in earning a college degree.

Although the Iowa Writers' Workshop had a glowing reputation, and despite the fact that his former teacher and mentor had recommended him for the program, Kinsella found himself "tremendously disappointed in the workshop itself" as it had "no deadlines and no organization of any kind." Frustrated that a significant number of his fellow graduate students in the fiction workshop seemed to be writing at a poor undergraduate level, with little knowledge of proper sentence structure or grammar, he saw no point in even reading their work. Adding to his frustration was his observation that the instructor, Rosalyn Drexler, though a good writer of some renown, seemed to be afraid of the group and offered little substantive feedback on their work. The situation grew so unbearable in the course that multiple students (though not Kinsella) complained, resulting in each student submitting a critique of their work, giving Drexler something to read aloud to the class, though she never provided much substantive feedback of her own. The entire process, Kinsella recalled later, was "a 100% waste of time." Having expected higher quality work from the students and better quality instruction from his teacher, he became "totally and completely frustrated by the workshop" and began using the time to write.

Around the midpoint of the semester, Bill submitted a completed story to Drexler, an 8,000-word piece called "The Girl from Cemetery Hill," hoping she would offer some written feedback to him as he felt it was not working well in its current form. Drexler held on to the story until the semester's end, at which point she was obligated to return it. As she removed it from her desk Kinsella could see there was not a mark on it. Her only feedback, delivered in her thick New York accent, was: "I really liked your story. It had s'many good ideas in it." Kinsella felt both "[his] mother" and "any service station attendant in Iowa City could have given [him] better criticism." If nothing else, the experience inspired him to make sure to provide his own students with substantive feedback intended to help them improve their craft.

Around this time, and with his frustration with the workshop mounting, Bill was asked to critique a fellow student's work, a piece that he saw as being particularly lacking in quality. Pointing out all its flaws, he concluded that the work was at best at the level of an undergraduate freshman. And while he never felt what he said was wrong, he later regretted embarrassing the other student by voicing his opinions in the venue, and afterwards took the time to write her a note of apology.

Though Bill had shared his low opinion of the graduate program with Vance Bourjaily, one of the Workshop's faculty, none of the problems were ever resolved. However, he made the decision to take the fiction workshop with Bourjaily during the next semester, in hopes of a better experience. Fortunately, the problems were mostly limited to the one workshop course. He appreciated the instruction from Clarence Andrews and Dick Wheelwright, who co-taught the freelance journalism workshop that semester. And while he viewed Robert Anderson's class as little more than a "gossip session," he did appreciate that professor's storytelling abilities.

While many students took refuge in the social events offered by the program, during his time in Iowa City Bill only attended one such function. He thought the worst place for a writer to find material to write about was anywhere he would be spending time with other would-be writers. The event he attended was held at Bourjaily's home in a converted schoolhouse west of the city and did little to change his mind about time spent at such functions.

After being in Iowa City a little while, Bill attended an open reading in College Green Park where a group calling itself the Iowa City Creative Reading Series met during good weather. He also discovered the local chapter of Parents Without Partners and "set about to find a girlfriend." Though interested in women, Bill had no interest whatsoever in feeling obligated to attend the parties and dances frequented by university students. During the first PWP meeting, he met Ardis Jane "R.J." Moore, a teacher in Victor, Iowa, a town nearly forty miles from campus, who, like him, had children who lived elsewhere.

By this time, Kinsella had found a room where he could board in a house at 619 North Johnson Street, allowing him to leave the dorm room on campus. The house was owned by a young office worker at the university and her husband. Bill had no restrictions on who visited his room and as a result, R.J. was soon spending weekends with him. Still married to Mickey at the time, he warned R.J. that he was not yet certain what his future plans might be. She was not dissuaded.

In the freelance journalism workshop during the first semester, he chatted a few times with a red-headed woman whose hearty and appealing laugh he found inviting, though he assumed she was married. A week or two later, the woman mentioned to Bill that she was acting in a local production of *The Man Who Came to Dinner*, and offered him a free ticket to the show. Since the show was a mile or so outside town, and Bill was without a car, he let someone else have the ticket. And while he missed the show, he did make sure to give the woman, Ann Knight, his telephone number, offering to loan her a copy of Joyce Carol Oates's *The Wheel of Love*. The next week, she called to invite him to the symphony, which he reluctantly accepted— it would mean missing the meeting of the Iowa City Creative Reading Series, and his taste in music was more along the lines of the Statler Brothers and Willie Nelson.

Though he had no interest at all in the music, he was very interested in getting to know Ann. Meeting him outside the performance hall, Ann "wore jeans, a denim jacket and boots, the sexiest outfit [he] could imagine a date wearing." They began snuggling together during the show's second half, and afterwards she drove him back to her house on South Johnson Street, just a few blocks from where he was living, where she rented rooms to students from the university. While sitting in the living room in front of the fire, Kinsella learned that Ann had arrived in Iowa from California with a husband but had divorced.

During their first evening of lovemaking, Ann, an aspiring writer herself, showed Bill her diaries, various correspondence and a journal she had shared back and forth in the mail with a friend in Michigan, and he took the material home to read. Sitting at his kitchen table until three o'clock in the morning, immersed in reading her words, Kinsella became more smitten with her by the moment. They saw each other again in class the following day, and went out for lunch afterwards, a rare treat for her since her work schedule in the Health Center information office on campus usually meant she was afforded no such opportunity as she worked through lunch.

The next weekend, Ann stayed over with Bill at his place and he soon realized she "was exactly what [he] had been looking for," deciding within a few more weeks that he no longer wanted to date anyone else. Having to break off the relationship with R.J. proved difficult because they'd gotten along well, but she lacked the passion he had found in Ann. However, according to Kinsella, Ann "came from a very repressive background; her family were religious fanatics who were dominated, brainwashed and completely controlled by religion." And while he sensed that Ann did not completely buy into her parents' beliefs, he felt she "still wasted too much of her life on the useless ideas of the supernatural." By this point Bill had fully accepted his atheism. In any case, Ann's strong religious leanings were not enough to dissuade him from pursuing a relationship with her.

By the end of his first semester in Iowa, and in the first stage of what would grow into a long-term relationship with Ann, Bill was writing steadily, mostly Silas stories, and had completed fifty pages of what he hoped would develop into a novel. Once classes were finished, Bill flew back to Victoria and stayed with friends for what proved to be an emotionally trying Christmas break. By now it had become obvious to him that there was no hope for reconciliation with Mickey, as their relationship had only deteriorated during his time in Iowa. Though she reiterated her desire to stay with him, Bill had moved on. The day after Christmas, he left for Edmonton to spend the rest of the holiday season staying with his friends Kay and Roy Harper, and visiting family in the area, including his daughters.

Kinsella "was tremendously happy to get back to Iowa with Ann." Before the break, they had agreed that he would move into her house and pay her, since part of the basement in her house had been vacated. Although happy in his relationship with Ann, Bill was upset that Mickey had been so heartbroken when he had ended their relationship for good. She professed her love to him in numerous letters during their separation, stating that she wasn't interested in a divorce, though she ultimately agreed with him that the divorce was necessary for her to move on with her life after him.

Bill continued to write, completing five stories in January 1977, though the output slowed due to his course load and teaching schedule once the spring term began. To avoid thinking about his relationship troubles, he channelled the stress into his writing, resulting in his largest single output in such a short time, surpassing the four stories he had written during his vacation to Hawaii with Mickey nearly two and a half years earlier.

Of the five he completed that month, three were Hobbema stories narrated by Silas. With *Dance Me Outside* scheduled for release a few weeks later, Bill was already looking ahead to his next collection, which would include these pieces in addition to thirteen other tales told from Silas's viewpoint.

During this stressful time, Kinsella began to be plagued by stomach troubles. Believing his ulcers to be caused by emotional strain, Kinsella would ultimately visit a campus psychologist in East Hall. After numerous sessions with the therapist, in whose abilities Bill had almost no belief, he confided as little as he possibly could and eventually stopped going to the appointments. And though he was admittedly guarded, Bill did repeatedly speak of the guilt he felt over leaving Mickey, instigating their eventual divorce. In discussing Bill's emerging relationship with Ann, the therapist observed that Kinsella was "hovering in limbo between a desire to invest [himself] in what sounds like a comfortable relationship and the need to protect [himself] from a bout of guilt similar to [his] guilt over Mickey should [he] also break-up with Ann and hurt her in the process."[2] Fortunately, though he abandoned therapy, his health improved on its own.

When *Dance Me Outside* was published that spring, critics and readers were struck by the authenticity of Silas's voice. Jim Hill proclaimed that Kinsella's "imaginative triumph in this book is his narrative voice."[3] The stories were told in the voice of a young Cree man with little formal education living on a reserve, and although framed in a humorous style, readers recognized the serious subjects being addressed. Reid Powell commented that the book "brings to public attention a promising writer who interests himself in significant subject matter," and said that Kinsella's fiction "deserves wide distribution and careful reading."[4]

Because Bill was a white writer seen to be addressing issues of oppression and marginalization faced by the Indigenous people living on the reserves, his stories were considered for their social commentary. Patricia Morley recognized the power of his short stories: "Stories that show the Indian community from the inside are relatively rare in Canadian literature. Stories that treat pain and deprivation without tears are even rarer. Kinsella's fiction does both . . . The stories are controlled by a great sense of humor and strong feeling for form."[5]

Despite having little contact with the Indigenous population beyond limited interactions from his cab driving days, Bill was hailed by some as being one who "tells the life of the Canadian Indian better than anyone else has."[6]

Some later critics commented on the collection's content, understanding the seriousness of the issues confronting the real people living on the reserves. Brian Burtch, for instance, argued, "To some extent, the short stories centre on well-established themes of assimilation, pathos and racism facing Indians on the Hobbema Reserve near Edmonton and elsewhere," while recognizing "Themes of oppression do not, however, monopolize Kinsella's writing."[7] Many even saw *Dance Me Outside* as having value beyond the literary world, viewing it as a way of addressing the cultural disconnect between white and Indigenous people. Burtch also thought Bill's first collection "made a considerable contribution to our understanding of Native-White conflict," while Reg Silvester saw Kinsella as making "a significant contribution to Prairie literature that will surely gain wider recognition."[8]

What negative reviews there were usually addressed individual stories that, when compared with the others in the collection, were seen as unremarkable and lacking in substance. Generally, however, *Dance Me Outside* was a critical success and quickly became one of Oberon Press's most popular books. Kinsella was thrilled to have his first book published, but while he was grateful to have it in hand, by the time the book was released he considered those stories "ancient history" and had already nearly completed another collection.[9]

When his first year's work in Iowa was completed in June, Bill made the decision to take a break from the university and from his budding relationship with Ann to spend the summer with Lee and Maggie, who had moved back to Hamilton, Ontario. At Lee's home one day, while everyone else was attending a wedding Bill stayed behind to write and sort his friend's large record collection. When Barb Kostynyk called the house, Bill invited her over and they spent the afternoon making love. Captivated by her looks (dark-eyed and slim), he was equally taken with her intelligence and independence.

He soon decided she "was exactly what [he] had always deserved as a partner" and "set out to win her over, and did in a very short time."

However, he was unsure about what to do about Ann back in Iowa. While he considered her "very sweet and loving," he also could not comprehend a future with her outside of their mutual attachment to Iowa City, predicting their relationship would end upon his graduation from the program. Having made what he thought would be a final decision, within a week's time he had "all but moved in with Barb" in Hamilton. She had separated from her husband and Bill was fairly certain that his brief relationship with Ann was over.

Ann and Bill had already planned a trip for her to visit him in Canada that summer, but she surprised him by arriving a day and a half sooner than he was expecting her. Covering for Bill, Lee called Barb's house at 10:30 on the night Ann arrived to let him know she had arrived early, at which point Kinsella "had to get out of one bed and hurry to another." Having been saved from what could have been a disastrous situation, Bill fell into line and spent the next week with Ann, including a trip they made together to meet Michael and Anne Macklem from Oberon Press in person for the first time. Soon after that, Ann left to attend a conference at Purdue University and then return home to Iowa City, leaving Bill her car so he could travel to visit friends and family and do various promotional appearances for his book. During his travels, he spent a considerable amount of time keeping in touch with both Ann and Barb, delaying his decision.

By the time he arrived back in Hamilton, Bill had come to the conclusion that his future was with Barb, and they began making plans together. Bill was still in possession of Ann's car, though he felt it was unfair for him to have it when he had no intention of continuing their romantic involvement, so he drove back to Iowa City to return the car and end their relationship. After telling her he was involved with someone else, they decided it was best for him to move out of her house, so he rented another room starting in early August before catching a bus back to Hamilton to be with Barb.

Kinsella continued writing throughout the summer, working primarily on a borrowed typewriter on Barb's sun porch. The stories included "Black Wampum," "Goose Moon" and "Pretend Dinners," the last written specifically for Barb. As the summer dragged on, however, he started having doubts about his decision, wondering if he was doing the right thing in leaving Ann. In Barb, he finally had what he had long felt he deserved: "a beautiful, loving partner who encouraged [his] writing, [and] was quite willing to let [him] stay home and write full time." However, the nature of her job as a probation officer for the federal government left Barb used to being in the position of making decisions and being able to change people's lives.

Bill was, by his own admission, "absolutely resistant to change," and he had begun to notice how, often in small ways, Barb was attempting to remake him. For instance, she wanted him to start taking off his wristwatch at night and hanging up his clothes instead of leaving them on the floor. She began encouraging him to dress differently, buying him plaid shirts, which he detested. When he expressed any disagreement, she responded, "But don't you want to look nice for me? I want to be proud of you when we go out together." And while these were relatively minor issues when considered individually, taken collectively they began to bother Bill.

The differences in their personalities grew more apparent when they took a ten-day trip south, through Michigan. Though he later remembered it as a generally nice trip, an episode in Kalamazoo magnified what were already serious doubts in Kinsella's mind about his choice to be with Barb. Having decided to spend some extra time in town to attend a Seals and Croft concert, they parked their car near a parking meter on a heavily travelled street. While Barb wanted to put money in the meter, Bill argued that "one of the joys of being a tourist is that you can ignore parking meters in strange cities." She told him she thought rules were meant to be obeyed. Kinsella concluded, "Rules are meant to be *selectively* ignored. Rules are meant to be ignored or broken whenever possible."

He had come to the realization that the primary difference between them was that Barb believed in the system whereas he had a complete mistrust of it and felt that rules were largely conceived by inept bureaucrats. He "decided right there, though it would take [him] a couple more weeks to assimilate the information, that [he] couldn't live with some[one] who would put money in a parking meter in a strange city [to] obey the system when it wasn't necessary to do so."

Realizing they were not as compatible as he had originally hoped, Bill was unable to clearly articulate his feelings to Barb. As a result, she was terribly hurt when he told her he "could not see how [they] could make a go of it," and felt that he had led her along falsely, something he argued was never his intention. And while their situation was, by his own admission, "almost perfect"—Barb's ideal life was to stay living near Hamilton where she would continue with her job while he stayed home to write—he simply refused to "be owned by anybody." Their difficulties would appear in some of his later fiction, including "Green Candles" and "Mother Trucker's Yellow Duck."

When Kinsella started the trip back to Iowa, Lee, who "was all smiles and 'I told you so's'" about his friend's break-up with Barb, called Ann to let her know Bill was on his way back there. Ann let him back into her life, and their relationship picked up where it had left off, both of them "wary of commitment, but enjoying each other immensely."

In his final year at Iowa, Kinsella was awarded a much more appealing teaching assistantship. He took only one workshop course that year, a class led by Elizabeth Cullinan from *The New Yorker*, who he felt offered little in the way of helpful advice towards his writing. As a result, his attendance was sporadic and he chose to not contribute at all to the class. He did, however, continue going to the freelance workshop, and even team taught some class sessions with Clarence Andrews. And although Andrews was unable to secure money from the university to pay him for his help, he was able to take Kinsella with him to a workshop in Council Bluffs.

Although Kinsella had less time to dedicate to his coursework during this second year, his writing schedule allowed him to complete another collection of stories tentatively titled *Black Wampum*, which was accepted for publication for the fall of 1978. With the completion of his MFA drawing closer, Kinsella sent out résumés to every school he could find in North America offering creative writing courses.

Kinsella took several poetry writing courses during his time at Iowa, which he found helped him "be succinct, and to create good strong images, and similes." By this point, he was confident that he could write and publish poetry if he so chose, but he also recognized that there was very little money to be made in it, "and the world of poetry is even more petty than the world of literature." However, the poetic style he applied to his prose later became his trademark in his baseball stories and novels.

Sally Eaton from Oberon Press called Bill to let him know the publisher had decided to call the new story collection *Scars* rather than *Black Wampum* because Michael Macklem had an exciting idea for the book's cover. Bill agreed to the change; he thought the cover of *Dance Me Outside* was as good as any he had ever seen on a Canadian book. Unfortunately, the cover for *Scars* was not only underwhelming, it was "an exercise in black finger painting on shit-colored cardboard." Though he would later be able to negotiate for more input into his books' layout and artwork, with only one book to his credit at the time, Bill had little choice but to defer to Oberon's choice.

In October, Kinsella travelled back to Edmonton for a party for *Dance Me Outside*, a book that had earned him several positive reviews and, to his surprise, was selling quite well. Both Shannon and Erin came to celebrate with him. He also gave his first paid public reading, to approximately twenty people at the University of Alberta in Edmonton, reading two of his stories, "Illiana Comes Home" and "Pretend Dinners."

During the Christmas break in 1977, Bill and Ann decided to drive to California—they were planning to visit her friends and, for the first time, Bill was to meet her family. After surviving a terrible blizzard in Wyoming, spending some time relaxing in Las Vegas using coupons and discount meal vouchers to compensate for their graduate student budgets, and visiting Ann's friends in Salt Lake City and Los Angeles, they drove north to Davis, California, to spend New Year's Eve with friends. When Ann phoned her parents, Sam and Corene English, to arrange for them to meet Bill, Ann's "religious fanatic mother decided she was too morally outraged to meet [him], so Ann drove up and spent a day with them," leaving Bill back in Davis with her friends.

This first experience with Ann's mother set the stage for what would be an often rocky and tempestuous relationship between Corene and Bill. Describing her as someone who "could be a prototype for a religious hypocrite," she was apparently "raised by a tyrannical father [and] allowed religion to rule and ruin her life . . . [thinking] she [was] superior to anyone who [did] not share her particular delusions." The only consolation for Kinsella was "that she [had] allowed herself to have a miserable life. For someone so plugged in to god [sic], she [was] really a terribly unhappy person." In contrast, Bill enjoyed Ann's father, Sam, "a truly happy-go-lucky fellow," whom Kinsella felt "suffered a good deal, most of [it] caused by his wife and her tyrant father," both of whom "looked down on Sam because he wasn't successful enough, and like good Christians everywhere, both father and daughter made sure Sam knew just how much contempt he was held in." Despite the glaring differences between Ann's parents and Bill, his growing affection towards their daughter helped them find some level of kinship.

Ann had undergone a significant amount of therapy to help her, as Bill put it, "understand and deal with her mother's idiotic views of the world." Ann herself had left the Baptist faith and had become Episcopalian—viewed by Kinsella as "the most wishy-washy of religions." Despite the break from her religious upbringing, however, Kinsella felt that Ann "had been brainwashed too much to get away completely from the sinister purveyors of the supernatural."

Nearing the end of his time in the Writers' Workshop, Bill decided to use a copy of *Dance Me Outside* as his thesis, one of the requirements for graduation, as it was all original work and he had already been notified that *Scars* was to be published the following year. What continued to frustrate him, though, was that, in his eyes, "anyone who put in two years got a degree," and some of his peers in the program "used the same material they used to get into the workshop to get out" with little, if any, revision. He claimed to have seen "stories that were ripped to shreds in workshop used in a thesis, completely unrevised." This, he felt, "cheapened [his] degree, which [he] found particularly unacceptable."

The second requirement to complete the program was an essay in which the candidates discussed how they would design and teach the workshop if they had an opportunity. Kinsella submitted a first draft that he had composed directly on the typewriter, with no editing at all. His ideas were ones he felt would strengthen both the program and its graduates. Kinsella's plan was to have each class member assigned to read various literary magazines and report back to the class with written summaries to verify they had actually read the assigned work. The greatest flaw in the program in his estimation was the overwhelming number of the students who "were completely unconversant with contemporary American literature. They were writing but were reading 200-year-old books and had no idea what they were competing with." Compounding his frustrations was his belief that the program's instructors had no real marketing knowledge beyond the mainstream magazines in which so many of them published. His most important idea, however, was that he "would expect *production* from workshop students—that [he] would work with them hard instead of letting them do nothing for two years." At first he concluded the ideas he presented in this essay were never read, let alone considered, though he later suspected someone had read them and had taken offence as it was several years before he was offered any type of teaching position at Iowa. Meanwhile writers he considered less successful had been granted faculty appointments.

While back in Edmonton in October of 1977, Bill travelled to interview for a teaching position at the University of Calgary. The position called for the candidate to teach fiction writing and basic English courses, similar to what his assistantship at Iowa had involved. In March of the following year, the university offered him the position, scheduled to begin in July, with his teaching duties starting in September. The salary was $18,000 a year, far more than he had ever earned before. Though he would have preferred a job in the United States, he knew that creative writing positions in Canada were few and far between and that there were easily a few hundred other people who would gladly take the position were it offered to them. Although they had no plans at that time for marriage, when he accepted the job, Bill asked Ann to come with him to Calgary. By that point, Mickey had let him know she was filing for divorce.

With a contract signed and while waiting to graduate, Kinsella continued writing steadily, awaiting the release of his second collection of stories. Then Ann became ill. En route to Boston in May for some work related to *A-Cross*, a quarterly magazine she edited, and to lecture at a local seminary, Ann called Bill one evening. He described it as "a rather strange and incoherent phone call," but Ann was a high-energy person and so he initially gave the call little thought.

The following evening, however, he received a message from a Boston area hospital where Ann had been admitted as a patient. Upon returning the call, he was notified that Ann was kept for observation because she was "in a highly disturbed state" but had disappeared in between the hospital's initial call and when he returned their message. The doctor inquired about her medical history, trying to determine if she had any mental disorders or history of drug use. After an hour, the doctor called Bill back to let him know Ann had returned to the hospital, still highly agitated and incoherent, and was currently under sedation. They had also spoken with Ann's parents and discovered that her mother had suffered from similar episodes in the past. Kinsella was told that such events were caused by a chemical imbalance and had been discovered to be hereditary. Based on the symptoms and all relevant indicators, the medical staff determined she was suffering from a manic episode.

Realizing someone had to deal with the situation and because he was much closer to Boston than they were, Bill called her parents and offered to go. After what he later described as "a brief, strained conversation with Ann's mother, where [they] compared notes on what [they] knew," Bill made arrangements for a colleague to cover his teaching assignments and flew to Boston to be with Ann and search for her car, which she had abandoned during her breakdown.

Arriving at Logan Airport, Bill took a bus to the city's edge and then a taxi to the hospital to see Ann before checking into a nearby hotel. Ann was heavily medicated, and while she did recognize and know him, she was unable to give him any information about where her car was or what had taken place. The following morning, Kinsella went to the Cambridge Police as Ann had originally been picked up in their jurisdiction, but they were "surly and completely uncooperative," and were unwilling to tell him if they even had the car in their possession. When he phoned Sandy Boyd, the woman whose class Ann was to have lectured, he was told that after having had several incoherent phone calls with Ann on the evening of her episode one of their group had found the car. Bill went across town to retrieve the car and returned to the hospital to be with Ann.

The next day Ann had improved and was somewhat coherent, even asking to see Boyd and some of her other friends. Ann's ex-husband, Harold, whom Bill had called the evening before, stopped by to check on her and to offer Bill a place to stay while he was in town. Apparently, as she was slowly losing control, Ann had called most of the people she knew who lived in the Boston area.

By the third day, Ann's improvement was so great that the hospital decided to release her to Bill's care. While still under the effects of the medication, she was quiet and rational as they made "a horrible, three-day drive back to Iowa City," with Kinsella suffering from a cold, which was compounded by side effects from his cold medication that made him unable to sleep.

Upon their return to Iowa, they contacted the Community Mental Health organization, though they found it of little help beyond distributing medication. With classes ending and his thoughts turning towards Calgary, Bill's next few weeks were a nightmare as the stress of his own situation was exacerbated by concerns about Ann's unstable mental health. Rather than improving once they were back in Iowa City, Ann's condition continued to worsen. The usual treatment for manic episodes was lithium carbonate, which helped balance the chemicals in the patient's system. And though it was effective, it took up to thirty days for the lithium to build up in the blood, and Ann was unaware of this at the time.

Bill was under an obligation to return to Canada as he prepared for the impending move to Calgary, so Ann's father agreed to drive in from California. Seeing his daughter's condition when he arrived, he had her admitted to University Hospital in Iowa City. Meanwhile, Bill spent most of June moving his things to Calgary and finding a place to rent beginning in August.

Kinsella had been contacted by the University of Calgary administration informing him that their British literature professor had quit and asking him if he would teach a section in the fall. Later saying he "would have taught brain surgery in order to get the creative writing job," he agreed to the request. Soon recognizing it as "a terrible and stupid imposition" on him, Bill found himself spending more time on that course than on any of the creative writing and composition courses he had originally been hired to teach.

On the return trip from Calgary to Iowa City to spend time with Ann, Kinsella's car lost power as he was pulling off the freeway, just making it to a car dealership in Ellensburg, Washington, before it quit entirely. As it was a weekend, he had no choice but to wait until the start of the following week for the car to get fixed. During the unplanned stop, with time to think about his life situation, he came to the realization that he "was truly in love with Ann and wanted to marry her." They had regular conversations when he called her from the road, and even over the phone he was able to recognize a marked improvement in her health. In their most recent conversations, she seemed more coherent and cheerful, more like the Ann he had known before the episode in Boston. Unfortunately, Ann's father was doing everything he could to convince his daughter to have nothing more to do with Bill. And Kinsella admitted that, had he been in Sam's position, he "would have probably done the same thing," and described Sam as "a gentleman" with whom he "never exchanged a cross word" during the entire time they knew one another. Having two daughters of his own, Bill recognized Sam's protective fatherly instincts and appreciated the concern towards Ann and the need to ensure her mental health was stable before she made any important life decisions.

The day Bill returned to Iowa, Sam left to go back to California. Kinsella proposed, but Ann turned him down. In spite of that rejection, however, their relationship continued, and Bill was confident they would remain together. In fact, as she continued recuperating, they took a week-long trip to Minneapolis to watch a series of baseball games.

In another trip to Canada from Iowa, before moving to Calgary, Bill arrived in Edmonton the night his daughter Erin was admitted to the hospital and he was able to meet his first grandchild, Jason Kirk, just a few hours after he was born. Erin and her boyfriend, Darryl, were living in a trailer in a small town about fifty miles east of Edmonton, and the new grandfather outfitted them with a washer and dryer as a gift before returning to Iowa to finalize his move north of the border.

Kinsella left Iowa to visit friends and make his way north to Calgary in time to beginning teaching at the beginning of August. Ann had agreed to marry him within a year, but she had left to spend time with her parents in California and to continue recuperating. The couple spoke regularly and had decided to wait until Bill had been teaching for a year in Calgary before they planned to get married in June of 1979. In the meantime, Bill turned his attention to settling into his new life in Calgary and the teaching job awaiting him there.

6

Desolate U.

When he relocated to Calgary at the beginning of August, Bill moved into a room at the boarding house where he had rented space during his visit earlier in the summer. He soon discovered his landlady would present some unique challenges. During his earlier visit in June, there had been a small dog running around, but he noticed it was no longer there when he moved in. When he asked about the dog's whereabouts, his landlady burst into tears and informed him that Chico had died a short time before.

Kinsella innocently inquired, "Why don't you get another dog?"

"Oh, I couldn't do that," she responded. "Chico was a Mormon, you know. He'll be waiting for me on the other side."

Chico was buried in the backyard and Bill's landlady had put up a white plastic fence around the grave and had planted plastic flowers on top of it.

After he settled in, Bill's new housemates, two Chinese engineers, warned him that each of the preceding boarders had stayed only a brief time. The landlady explained to Bill that one of the former boarders was a lover she felt had treated her poorly. Soon after, for a reason he never understood, she told Bill that she was going on an extended vacation and would, therefore, be closing down the house. He took a room at a nearby house owned by a professor from the French Department.

Arriving on campus ready to begin his first full-time teaching position, Kinsella was assigned an office on the fourth floor of Calgary Hall, one floor below the English Department's offices. With a full teaching load awaiting him, he quickly settled into preparing for the first semester's courses. Although he took the job for its creative writing elements, he was assigned, as are many first-year professors, a section of English 201, which he referred to as "bone-head English, composition for students who are only let into university because management is greedy for students." He later reflected that "at least 75% of my bone-head students should never have been allowed with[in] ten meters of a university. Half of them were functionally illiterate."[1] In addition to the burden of teaching the composition course, he also had to contend with the course in modern British literature, for which he had spent a considerable amount of his summer preparing. Although the class was small, most of the students were English majors, and he found many of them knew the material better than he did.

The highlight of his first semester was his English 469 course, Fiction Writing. Years later, after quitting teaching to write full-time, Kinsella reflected that it "was probably the best class I have ever had." The approximately fifteen students who were enrolled were more than ready to be taught and had been waiting for an instructor to be hired. The lively classes helped lift Kinsella's spirits and over half of the students would eventually have material published.

In addition to his teaching responsibilities, and spending "far too much time in the unimportant courses," Bill carved out time to work on his own writing, including rewriting a short story he had started while still in Iowa, one he'd titled "Shoeless Joe Jackson Comes to Iowa," as well as "The Runner," "Indian Struck" and other Silas Ermineskin stories.

Unfortunately, as is often the case with new faculty members, Bill was required to serve on "all the shit jobs as far as committees are concerned." Among his committee assignments was the extra-curricular committee, tasked with meeting the needs of visiting writers and lecturers on campus and setting up open house activities, which he called "a stupid and archaic tradition of opening the university to the great unwashed for one Sunday in March." Besides keeping him from his writing and teaching, Kinsella viewed the committee work as one of the worst jobs on campus. And though he was also appointed to serve on the library committee, he admittedly "didn't do anything." Years after he had left the school, Kinsella realized, "if [he] ever had any illusions about academic life, all were dispelled at the first faculty meeting. At University meetings, pettiness is raised to an art." Never one for mindless administrative politics or process, he quickly began learning to navigate his way through such expectations.

Within his first few days on campus, Kinsella noticed that many of his colleagues viewed him as an academic oddity, since his field of expertise was outside the realm of traditional academic research and presentation. As he settled into the new office, several people dropped by to greet him and introduce themselves. Numerous times he was asked, "And what is *your* field of research?"

"I don't do research," he happily responded. "I'm a fiction writer."

He immediately felt his prestige level drop "to somewhere between the janitor and the lady who sold coffee at the snack bar." Whether they actually felt superior to him or if the feelings of inferiority were self-imposed, he claimed to still be able to "see the looks of incredulity on the faces of some of [his] fellow professors."

Early on he met Rudy Wiebe, a writer-in-residence who was on sabbatical from the University of Alberta in Edmonton. Wiebe had an interest in Bill's writing and even visited his classes, and initially they were on friendly terms. Years later, however, Wiebe would become one of Bill's most vocal critics, lambasting him for what Wiebe felt was Kinsella's appropriation of an Indigenous voice in his works.

Ann came to visit for most of October. By this time, she had decided they could get married in Iowa during Bill's Christmas break. And while the news was very much welcomed by him, it also meant adding wedding planning and getting Ann's documentation together for her to come to Canada to his growing to-do list for the fall term. During her visit, they found a local bookstore, the Black Ostrich, which had an adjoining tearoom. With the idea of developing something similar to the Iowa City Creative Reading Series, they arranged to start a reading series at the store in January after returning from their wedding. Perhaps most importantly, however, it was during this visit that the couple went to Edmonton, where Bill introduced Ann to his mother, Aunt Margaret and both his daughters. With the wedding moved up to December, Bill found them a large basement suite on 24th Avenue just a few blocks away from campus.

It was a hectic first semester in Calgary for Kinsella. Beyond adapting to a new job, making wedding plans, preparing for courses he felt woefully inadequate to teach, dealing with committee assignments and adjusting to teaching writing classes with far too many students to be effective, his second collection of short stories, *Scars*, was released late in 1978 near the end of his first term. Of the sixteen stories in the book, a dozen had already been published in literary journals. And like *Dance Me Outside*, published a year earlier, the stories were all narrated by Silas Ermineskin and explored many of the same types of issues— the racism, marginalization, substance abuse and assault that were too often a part of life on reserves.

Scars afforded readers the opportunity to examine how Kinsella's style and approach to his characters had evolved, even in the short time since *Dance Me Outside* had first appeared on bookshelves. Reg Silvester noted the significance of the book's title: "*Scars* comes after the wounds have healed. It belittles white guilt and offers a possibility of reconciliation between the races which now must occupy this continent together with no humiliation to either side."[2] And while many writers used their fiction to proselytize a certain position or ideology, in *Scars* Kinsella explored the tensions created between the cultures on the reserve without championing a specific side. His ability to address controversial topics, Silvester continued, enabled Kinsella to manoeuvre "difficult territory with definite grace . . . [he] stops short of anti-feminism the same way he stops short of racism. And writing about modern-day Indians in any realistic way, especially imitating their speech pattern, runs the risk of being called racist." Some readers found his descriptions offensive, questioning whether a white man could accurately write about the Indigenous experience, while others saw his attempts at addressing racial tensions as a way of promoting unity: "The stress that exists between races is a definite tool in Kinsella's writing kit. But instead of using it as a wrench against one side or the other, he uses it to help both groups."

Though many readers had been drawn towards the humorous tone of Silas's voice in the first collection, some critics, such as Alan Ricketts, viewed *Scars* as "a more somber and less joyful book than *Dance Me Outside*,"[3] and Kinsella himself as a writer who "has the facility of the serial writer to retell the same story repeatedly." Still others, like Steve Weatherbe and Rick Spence, though appreciative of his ability to write humorously about serious topics, suggested an area he "should stay away from is satire. His serious stories are not without humor. His satirical ones fail dismally."[4] And Kinsella's approach of compiling stories he had already published in magazines and journals with no revisions, something he continued to do throughout his career, had already started to concern some critics as they felt it hindered his narrative potential, with Ricketts commenting, "The serial mode suggests that Kinsella is already trapped in the restrictions of reworking without advancing."[5]

In general, though, the collection was reviewed positively, and Bill's stories were recognized for humanizing a people often overlooked by the government, police and whites overall. Walt Kellythorne wrote, "What emerges most clearly about the Indians in *Scars* . . . is that— contrary to racist opinion and government practice—they are people first, Indians after. It's to Kinsella's credit that he's managed to characterize the two aspects of these lives in terms that makes them instantly recognizable to anyone with a shred of humanity."[6]

With the Hobbema stories gaining a wider audience across the country, Kinsella continued developing new ideas with Silas in mind, though he was also writing other types of stories and editing ones he had started during his time at the University of Victoria and the University of Iowa.

As soon as the first semester was finished, having asked a colleague to enter the last of his course grades for him, Kinsella left for Iowa City, where he had to get a marriage licence and a blood test before the wedding could take place. He spent the week before the wedding with Ann, and they welcomed some of her friends from California into town and made final preparations for the ceremony, to take place on December 30, 1978.

Since Ann's Episcopal congregation had no organ, they were to be married at the Gloria Dei Lutheran Church in Iowa City. Many of their Iowa City friends attended, and Bill's best man was his friend Tony Bukoski from the Writers' Workshop. Following a small reception, the newlyweds left that evening in a blizzard that had settled in earlier in the day, driving as far as Ankeny, west of Des Moines, where they spent their first night together as a married couple.

The next morning, they continued west in heavy snow and bitterly cold temperatures, making it as far as Fargo, North Dakota. Staying the night at a cheap motel, they had to wake every two hours to start Ann's Datsun to keep it from freezing up. Since Bill could never seem to get the car to start even in good weather, it was left up to Ann. Waking the next morning to a temperature of 35 below zero, they crossed into Canada and stopped for the evening. Ann was able to locate a cord to plug the car in rather than repeating the previous night's ordeal. Making it back to Calgary the following day, the couple settled into their new suite and prepared for another semester and a new life together.

Back on campus, Bill threw himself into his work, spending his own money to print posters for the first edition of the Calgary Creative Reading Series (CCRS) he had arranged to host at the Black Ostrich Book Store and Tea Room. He also had the first of what was to become a long-running series of confrontations with administrators when Hal Dahlie, the department head, complained to Bill that his grades in the previous semester's English 201 class were too high, something Bill agreed to address in the upcoming term.

And while he had never been a part of any type of religious tradition and had been professing to be an atheist for years, Bill began attending various churches with Ann, who had developed an idea to write an article on churches in which she would "[rate] them like a restaurant reviewer."[7] Meanwhile, with the memory of Ann's episode in Boston still fairly fresh in his mind, Bill began writing "For Zoltan Who Sings," based on her experience in the hospital.

During the second week of January, the first ever meeting of the CCRS was held with Bill as the featured reader, followed by an open reading for the public. *Scars* was already getting good reviews and the reading drew about thirty-five people, which was a tremendous success for the inaugural event. Bill was disappointed that only two members of the faculty from the school attended, reinforcing his belief that his colleagues viewed creative writing as inferior to academic pursuits.

Soon after arriving back in Calgary after the holidays, Bill went to the hospital to visit his colleague in the department, Judy Sloman, who was recovering from an operation. Ann also went to sit with Judy for several hours over three different days, and while Bill saw this as the humanitarian gesture it was intended to be, it also led to his "first dealings directly, other than the idiocies of a faculty meeting, with petty and suspicious academic minds." Though his colleagues in the department asked several times about Judy's condition, Bill later understood that the inquiries were "not out of concern for her, but just out of meanness." He felt his wife was doing a job none of them would do by going to visit with Judy, providing her comfort and companionship, but he sensed that, because he and Ann were new to the university, "it was somehow deemed inappropriate" by those in the department.

By late January and only one semester into his teaching career at the school, Bill decided he would never make a career of teaching in Calgary. Since the start of the spring term, Ann had been attending Bill's classes, and the students often commented on how much they enjoyed her presence. While praising the course to another professor in the department, a student mentioned Ann's involvement and Dr. Dahlie called Bill in soon after to inform him that Ann was not allowed to sit in on the class unless she was officially registered. Bill later viewed this as "the most pathetically obvious gesture to censure Ann for visiting Judy Sloman." However, he realized that the department chair was technically right and within his power to keep Ann from class. Bill's students were less understanding and he "had to practically physically restrain several of [them] from taking a delegation to Dahlie's office." All in all, Kinsella saw it as yet another incident that "just magnified the mean spirit and small minds that control academia."

Kinsella still managed to block off time most days during the term to dedicate to his own writing and revising. By February he had completed the manuscript for *Shoeless Joe Jackson Comes to Iowa*, his first collection of stories not set on the Hobbema Reserve, and prepared it for submission to Oberon Press. Meanwhile, he continued developing new Hobbema stories, recognizing he had built an audience that enjoyed Silas Ermineskin's voice and the hilarity of Frank Fencepost. In an effort to expose more readers to his work while simultaneously increasing the exposure of the reading series, he read at their regular meetings and at events held on campus. He had begun earning small stipends for his appearances, including one scheduled for that April in Saskatoon where he was to take part in a panel with his mentor, Bill Valgardson.

As the spring term drew to a close and Kinsella began planning for the summer, he found another reason to leave the university when he was informed that, unlike almost every other university he was aware of, professors at Calgary did not have summers off. The school's policy was to allow one month for vacation and another for research work, but for the remaining weeks, faculty members had to remain in Calgary, though he could see no reason for this. Even after leaving academia, his anger had subsided very little when he stated, "I have [no] ties here—never plan to develop any. . .[I] stayed away longer than allowed, but had to lie about where I was and what I was doing. The people in charge at Arts & Science are truly assholes."

Ann's health once more began to take a turn for the worse, though Bill did not realize to what extent at the time. After her manic episode in Boston the previous May, Ann had been taking the lithium carbonate prescribed to her to help control the attacks. The doctors, however, "told her that since she was over 30 when she suffered her first episode that the likelihood of her having a second episode was only about 25%." As a result, she made the decision to stop taking the medication. And while Bill described his wife's personality as "about 30% more animated than most people," he later realized he should have noticed around this time that she was sleeping less and working twelve to fourteen hours at a time. Additionally, she had been making plans to leave Calgary to attend Claremont School of Theology in the fall of 1980. She began describing to him her long-term goal of being a travelling minister in a mobile home, and Kinsella noted later that these plans were an indication that her mental state was not as stable as they had hoped.

Just days after submitting the final grades for the spring term, Bill and Ann left for a trip that would eventually take them to New York City (for the first time for Bill), after a visit with Oberon Press in Ottawa and a Writers' Union of Canada meeting. On his second day in New York, Bill made the trip to Yankee Stadium where he hoped to still be able to buy tickets for the day's game for him and Ann.

Arriving at the ticket window, he overheard the clerk telling people the only seats left were those far out in right field. When his turn came, Kinsella simply laid down his credit card and told the cashier, "Two of the best you have available." Not even bothering to look at the tickets, knowing what he had heard the other fans being told, he made his way back to the car and complained to Ann about the seats they were stuck with. Ann, meanwhile, looked at the tickets and told him, "I don't think these are in right field." Looking at the seat numbers on the tickets, Kinsella realized the seven-dollar tickets were right behind home plate.

Bill later recalled seeing Yankee catcher Thurman Munson nearly face-to-face when he came back towards the stands to catch a pop-up. Tragically, Munson would die in a plane crash later that summer. The scene at the ticket window and the experience of seeing Munson catch in 1979 were later incorporated into *Shoeless Joe* as Ray Kinsella treks from Iowa to New Hampshire to kidnap J.D. Salinger, stopping along the way to watch a game at Yankee Stadium. Bill also developed the story "The Night Manny Mota Tied the Record" around a writer who has an opportunity to bring Munson back from the dead just days after the catcher's untimely death.

Bill and Ann realized their good fortune when the man sitting beside them said he had paid thirty dollars a ticket for the seats he had. The Yankees were playing the Oakland A's, a team that would finish last in the American League West, losing 108 games, though this game went into extra innings before the Yankees finally won. Years later, Kinsella recalled that the ballpark "is a beautiful place, but the area where it is located is evil, unsafe to park [a] car on the streets, [and] slums abound." Comparing himself to the little boy in Flannery O'Connor's short story "The Artificial Nigger," he wrote, "I been there once, and I don't ever plan to go back. I feel the same about New York City, period."

With the first year of teaching in Calgary behind him, during the summer of 1979 Bill produced a number of new stories while revising existing ones. Even while travelling, he started and finished a draft of "First Names and Empty Pockets" while revising "Buffalo Jump" and starting "Pigeon Dog" and "Brotherhood of the Burning Bush," which he soon renamed "The College."

On the way back from New York, they stopped in Iowa City to visit their friends at the Writers' Workshop, including Tony Bukoski, who interviewed Bill for a "Canadians at the Workshop" article. Upon returning to Calgary, Bill was notified that "Fata Morgana" had been accepted by the *Journal of Canadian Fiction*. He was also asked if he would consider writing a movie script for the John Bishop Ballem novel *The Judas Conspiracy*. Meanwhile, Michael Macklem at Oberon announced he wanted to release a book of Bill's stories with the eight he already had on hand and one or two new stories, which had, at that point, yet to be written. Although Bill had already sent him various shorter pieces to use in between each longer story, Oberon had chosen to not publish them. These shorter pieces, however, were later compiled into *The Alligator Report*, published in 1985.

Back in Calgary, Bill spent much of his time writing and trying to ignore the fact that another school year would soon be upon him.

In early August, during a trip to California, he began making notes for a story based on Thurman Munson's death in the plane crash. That evening, he attended a game at Dodger Stadium and witnessed Manny Mota tie the record for pinch hits with the 144th of his career. He combined the two, using what was becoming the trademark magical realism of his baseball fiction, in "The Night Manny Mota Tied the Record," later published in *The Thrill of the Grass*, his first collection of short fiction dealing specifically with baseball, in 1984.

In late August, Kinsella was paid for the movie option on *Dance Me Outside*. Though his percentage was just a few hundred dollars after splitting the payment with Oberon, it did give him reason to believe that his work would eventually be developed into a screen production. Don Haldane, who took out the option, had never before made a film, although he had directed television commercials and several episodes of *The Beachcombers*, a Canadian comedic drama television series that Kinsella described as one "that would surely rank near the top ten of everyone's 10-worst-shows-ever-on-TV," though it would run for nineteen seasons.

Haldane held the movie option for two years, and according to Bill did nothing substantive with it during that time other than having at least two scripts written, neither of which was considered acceptable. After two years, Haldane claimed his contract with Oberon gave him rights in perpetuity. Meanwhile, several other companies had expressed interest in the rights. Oberon made the decision to take Haldane to court, beginning a process that would drag on for nearly three years until a judge ruled in the publisher's favour, saying the contract was inadequate and that both parties should make an attempt to settle the dispute themselves.

During this time, Don Haldane visited Calgary, going to dinner one evening with Bill and Ann. Kinsella was not impressed with him or his idea to distribute the movie in England where, Haldane noted, they liked stories about Indigenous peoples. Adding further insult, Haldane suggested the idea of having Marlon Brando make a cameo appearance in "Ups & Downs," in which his character would ask Frank Fencepost and Silas Ermineskin, "Do you have a reservation?"

Haldane hoped it would also be the movie's title as it was to largely be based on that story, which Kinsella considered "the least successful in the collection."

When the fall term started in 1979 Kinsella once more found himself teaching British literature, a course in which he was "intimidated by older students," and still felt utterly incompetent as an instructor. The most frustrating aspect of the course, however, was that reading to prepare for the class allowed him very little time for his own writing. His disappointment grew when only twenty students showed up for his creative writing course, and the group did not seem nearly as talented as the previous year's students. Compounding his problems was that he had been assigned to yet another committee, giving him the dubious distinction of being "on the two shit-job committees."

On September 16, Ann returned home after midnight from a trip to Denver. Kinsella later remembered this as being the start of "the worst month of [his] life." He noticed immediately that his wife "was very agitated and it was obvious she was heading for another manic episode." And though her mood had obviously changed while she had been away, she refused to go to a doctor, and appeared better by the following afternoon when Bill left to teach his British literature course. When he returned home, though, Ann was gone. Two friends, Bill and Eleanor Coburn, met Bill at his house to begin searching for her, just as she appeared on her own, in far worse shape than she had been the night before.

Ann agreed to go to the hospital, although she wanted to eat first. Following dinner at a nearby Chinese restaurant, she was checked into the hospital where, immediately upon her arrival, "she let go and went completely berserk." Kinsella remembered later, "It was as if she had been keeping control of herself by force of will." Her condition was so severe that the doctors "gave [her] enough tranquilizers to stun an ox, and only then did she go down at all."

Not knowing what her status would be for the foreseeable future, Bill contacted her religious studies professor to inform him she would be absent from class for at least a month. He also let the continuing education program know that she was not going to be able to teach a class for them as she had hoped. While he was visiting with her the day after she was admitted, Ann was able to recognize him but not much else. He was, however, able to have a productive discussion with a psychiatric assistant, telling him what he knew of her condition and of the episode in Boston the year before.

For the next several days, while Bill was occupied with administrative details for the upcoming CCRS meeting, Ann's condition worsened. Not only was she denied release to go to an exhibition of painter Allen Sapp's work they had made plans to attend, but she was drawing murals on her bedsheet in the hospital, babbling the entire time. Bill contacted Ann's mother, only to discover "Ann had already phoned her—and goodness knows who else." He made sure to explain to the hospital staff that Ann should not be allowed to make any long-distance telephone calls, "because she [would be] apt to call these religious maniacs in the East who [were] at least 50% responsible for her condition." Kinsella began having chest pains that weekend, and the following Monday he went to the doctor for an electrocardiogram and blood pressure check-up. Not surprisingly, the doctor told him it was stress related, giving him a prescription to calm his nerves.

In the midst of the crisis Bill received his copy of *Aurora: New Canadian Writing*, in which Morris Wolfe's introduction praised Kinsella's contribution to the collection, "Shoeless Joe Jackson Comes to Iowa." And towards the end of September, Kinsella finished "The Night Manny Mota Tied the Record," though he later marvelled, "I can't imagine how I ever managed to write a word during this period." The day he completed the draft, September 28, was the first time Ann was allowed out of the hospital since she had been admitted eleven days earlier. The freedom, however, was short lived as Bill had to take her back the following morning. She seemed to have channelled her energy towards convincing the staff she was in a condition to leave, then fell apart once she left, unable to keep up the false pretence. After another week, she was allowed a pass to leave with her husband, though he recognized that she was still not well.

After some improvement, Ann was able to have Thanksgiving dinner with Bill and some friends, but her mental stability quickly deteriorated. Just two days later, however, the doctors felt she was well enough to allow her to attend the CCRS readings with Bill. By October 12, more than three weeks after she was first admitted to the hospital, Ann was released and able to go back home. Though not completely back to her vivacious self, the lithium was starting to take effect, helping restore her personality to a more normal state.

As Ann's health improved and Bill continued teaching and working on various committee appointments, both jobs he grew to loathe more each day, the couple found a welcome distraction in Allen Sapp's paintings. Having been fans of the Cree painter for some time, they bought their first original work for $950 (although Kinsella later said "[he] didn't like [it] very much"), at an exhibition where people got into fistfights to get at the paintings when the doors were first opened. Kinsella's interest in Sapp's work would grow over the years to the point where his home was filled with nearly two dozen Sapp originals.

By the start of his second winter in Calgary, Kinsella could hardly stand the thought of continuing to live there. In fact, he had started referring to his employer as "Desolate U." Calgary, he adamantly professed even years after moving to a more favourable climate, "is absolutely the worst place I have ever lived. It is a completely soulless collection of concrete boxes." He believed most of the people living there were, like him and Ann, only there "because a good job [was] available and [they were] counting the days until [they] could get away." By now the plan to move to California in the upcoming spring was no longer realistic due to Ann's illness. However, they had hope that, should she be able to stay on her medication, she might be able to avoid ever having another episode.

As the fall semester drew to a close and a new decade appeared on the horizon, Bill continued writing and reading his works whenever and wherever he could get an audience. Unfortunately, he continued to find most of his colleagues in the English Department unsupportive of his literary endeavours. After Bill requested a day off so that he could do a reading at the Northern Alberta Institute of Technology, the new department head expressed his dissatisfaction.

Bill privately vented, "These small-minded academics don't consider a reading career-related, but any one of them could get a *week* off, no questions asked, to read a paper somewhere, but fiction writing is not considered the same. If it weren't for us, these petty types wouldn't have any novels with which to play the Lit-Crit game."

With Ann's health problems and the rigours of his job, Bill's writing output dropped off considerably, and he often went weeks at a time without writing fiction. However, he found out in late November that a new collection of his stories was to be published. The collection, which he had originally hoped to call *First Names and Empty Pockets*, was set for publication in the fall of 1980 under the title taken from the story that would, within just a few years, forever change Kinsella's life and reputation: *Shoeless Joe Jackson Comes to Iowa*. Just over a week later, Oberon called expressing an interest in doing another collection of Silas stories in the near future.

On December 30, Bill's first anniversary with Ann, they were in California for the Christmas break. Kinsella reflected that 1979 had been a "pretty good year except for Ann's illness, but we should never have to go through that again." He went that day to hear Ann sing at church, and his optimism for the future was tempered by what he called in the same diary entry a "terrible service, mean, ugly choir, sanctimonious bastards all." He closed the year out by completing another short story and relishing being able "to pick oranges for breakfast every morning while everyone in Calgary [was] up to their asshole in snow." His literary career was just days away from taking a turn he could never have envisioned.

7

"If You Build It . . ."

Upon returning to Calgary from California, trading copies of his books in exchange for the cab fare from the airport, Bill arrived home to find among the mail that had piled up a letter on Houghton Mifflin Company letterhead. The letter's author, Larry Kessenich, was an editorial assistant. Part of his job involved searching out new writers and pitching their works to the editors. His hope was to find obscure, unsigned writers he could recommend, giving him some credibility on which to build his own reputation.

Kessenich scoured trade magazines looking for leads on relatively unknown authors. One such publication, *Publishers Weekly*, reviewed books before their actual release date, providing readers and industry insiders a glimpse of forthcoming works. While reading through the magazine one day in December 1979, Kessenich came upon a review of *Aurora: New Canadian Writing 1979*, in which Kinsella's story "Shoeless Joe Jackson Comes to Iowa" was to appear. The idea of a farmer building a baseball field in his Iowa cornfield to bring Shoeless Joe Jackson back from the dead "struck a chord in my heart," the young editor wrote to Kinsella, perhaps "because I'm a sentimental hero-worshipper."[1]

Without having yet read the story, relying solely on the mention in the review, Kessenich sat down to write Kinsella a letter, assuming "fourteen editors would write to him" upon reading that same review.[2] They did not. Having been unsuccessful in developing his short story "The Grecian Urn" into a novel, Kinsella had as yet published only short stories, the majority of which were his Hobbema pieces narrated by Silas Ermineskin. Unaware of these writings, Kessenich wrote, "It was difficult to tell from the review whether this piece is a short story or part of a novel (though I got the impression it's the latter). If it's a novel, and you are as yet without a publisher, I would be delighted to read it. . . As a matter of fact, I was so struck by the charm and originality of your idea that I would be happy to read anything you might want to send."[3]

Intrigued by the idea of writing a novel, Kinsella replied almost immediately to the inquiry, enclosing with his response a biographical sheet and a summary of his works published with Oberon Press. Both *Dance Me Outside* and *Scars* continued to sell well, and he had two books, *Shoeless Joe Jackson Comes to Iowa* and a third collection of his Silas stories, then under the title *I Remember Horses*, tentatively scheduled for publication that fall. However, in assessing his own work, Kinsella told Kessenich: "I am too literate to be commercial and I have failed at consciously trying to write for a commercial market."[4]

And even though his earlier attempts to write a novel had been unsuccessful, Kinsella remained optimistic in his abilities. He wrote, "I think I can write a novel, but I need to work with an excellent editor who is willing to lead me by the hand, mainly with suggestions of how to expand material so that it has some volume to it." When it came to his stories, Bill Valgardson had encouraged him to cut the first two and last two pages, advice that quickly transformed Kinsella from a writer struggling to get anything published to one who now had two collections on the market and two more soon to be released. Now he wanted to find someone who could help him take his shorter pieces and successfully expand them into novels.

Although he had never met Kessenich, who had yet to work with an author during the creative process, and had only the one letter from him, Kinsella was brutally honest with him: "If you're interested in helping me develop a novel do let me hear from you. I'll have precious little time to work until April as I'm teaching two courses this semester that I am only partially qualified to teach . . . I'll be here in Calgary, the place Eliot had in mind when he wrote *The Wasteland* [*sic*]. . ." The possibility of writing a novel for a major publisher was interesting to Bill, so focused was he on being able to afford to leave his teaching job to write full-time. But committing to a novel could be a financial risk. With several short stories in progress at any one time, he regularly completed a piece within a few days, though most stories took a matter of weeks to revise and edit. If a short story was not accepted for publication, he would only lose a few weeks' worth of work. Knowing it would take several months to write a novel, presumably more as it was his first effort working with an editor, he was concerned that writing something of that length that could still be rejected could cause him to lose out on the money he was making writing short fiction.

In this first letter to Kessenich, Bill jumped at the chance to broaden his canon to include "a collection of baseball stories" to accompany the story to be published in *Aurora* within a matter of weeks. The invitation from Kessenich to Kinsella to develop a novel appears in their early correspondence and offered Bill a lifeline to rescue him from teaching in Calgary beyond the 1981–82 academic year, at which point, he wrote, he and Ann hoped to "go to Iowa City, Iowa, and write for several years" as they already owned a home there and Bill continued to feel a connection to the landscape of the American Midwest.

By the end of January, *Aurora* was on bookstore shelves and in Kessenich's next letter to Kinsella he told him he "was so excited that [he] read the story right there in the bookstore,"[5] although in an interview several years later he admitted that it was because he was "so poor" that instead of buying the book he "went into a bookstore in Harvard Square and read the story."[6] Regardless, the piece exceeded every expectation the earlier review in *Publishers Weekly* had given him, raising his anticipation of working with Kinsella in developing the novel.

"Shoeless Joe Jackson Comes to Iowa" resonated with Kessenich because of the characters, which he said were "so real, so vulnerable, so good, that they remind us of that side of human nature which makes living and loving and striving after dreams worth the effort."[7] After reading just the one story, Kessenich responded that he would "be delighted to give it a shot," noting, however, that while "[i]t would be foolish . . . to approach such a project over-confidently . . . What have we got to lose by trying?"

Encouraged by Kessenich's obvious enthusiasm, Kinsella decided to pursue it. But Bill was not yet in a financial position to abandon his job and when the university offered him a new three-year contract in February, one year more than he had anticipated, he signed the contract, though with the plan of leaving early, by the end of the 1981–82 academic year, "unless greed gets the better of me."[8]

Later that month a $1,500 cheque from Oberon arrived along with a contract for a third book of Hobbema stories already scheduled for publication. Though the collection was submitted as *I Remember Horses*, Oberon editor Michael Macklem proposed changing the title to *Born Indian*, and Kinsella agreed. In fact, he soon planned to write an additional story for the collection to accompany the new title, finishing the piece just days after the contract had arrived. Having been disappointed with the cover for *Scars*, this time he planned to invest in an Allen Sapp painting for the book's cover.

By early February, his goal of leaving teaching to pursue writing full-time seemed more tenable. Oberon announced that *Dance Me Outside*, his first collection of Hobbema stories published three years earlier, had become the company's all-time bestseller and that *Born Indian* was slated for publication the following spring. The next day he received the proofs for the collection *Shoeless Joe Jackson Comes to Iowa* and another letter from Kessenich expressing continued interest in working with him on the novel. Further validation of the quality of his work came when he was notified that his story "Pretend Dinners" had been selected for the *Pushcart Prize Anthology 1980–81*.

Despite his writing success, Kinsella's frustrations with teaching continued. Though he had been promised a second section of creative writing, he was informed—by a book salesman who contacted him about course materials for the next semester—that he would be teaching yet another section of advanced composition. Feeling that he was being "screwed" by the "lying, weasling [sic] bastards" in the department's administration, Bill continued planning his exit from the university and focused his energy on growing the Calgary Creative Reading Series. With over $20,000 in savings, he mused in his diary, "If I can last 3 years will be well set to retire to Iowa."[9]

Bill began developing his novel under the working title *The Oldest Living Chicago Cub*, and obtained several books about J.D. Salinger, whom he was considering as a character. By early March, just shy of one month after receiving Kessenich's letter agreeing to work with him, Kinsella had already completed twenty pages of his first draft while researching Joe Jackson's life and making notes for the rest of the novel. And though his focus had shifted away from writing short fiction, Kessenich notified him that spring that three of his stories had earned honourable mention in the upcoming edition of *Best American Short Stories*.

Always on the lookout for inspiration for his work, Kinsella often read through newspapers and magazines from wherever he was at the time, hoping to find some absurd or fantastic headline or clipping he could develop into a story. Over the previous Christmas in California his in-laws, knowing of Bill's fascination with baseball, had given him a copy of *The Baseball Encyclopedia*. While leafing through its pages he was intrigued by one of the briefest entries in the entire book, the statistical line for New York Giants outfielder Archibald "Moonlight" Graham. The only thing more fascinating than the player's nickname was the fact that he had played in only one game in his major league career, during the 1905 season, and never had an opportunity to bat.

Kinsella wrote a letter to the newspaper editor of the *Chisholm Free Press*, the local paper in Chisholm, Minnesota, where Graham had died in 1965. The paper's editor, Veda Ponikvar, responded to the inquiry, informing Bill that Graham had, in fact, been the town doctor and one of the community's leading citizens before his death.

Intrigued, Kinsella was not yet sure how to best incorporate the former player into his novel's plotline.

Having never before worked with an editor while developing an idea, Bill was not used to receiving criticism of his writing while it was still being composed. Kessenich had suggested to Kinsella that "Shoeless Joe Jackson Comes to Iowa" be the novel's opening pages, with Jackson's appearance on the field happening sooner rather than later in the plot. Bill responded, "I'm going to go the other direction for the time being. Stories of mine which work, do so because of their intensity and I just feel that anything coming right on the heels of [the short story] will be a letdown."[10] His solution was instead to begin with the still unnamed protagonist kidnapping J.D. Salinger before retelling the story of how he heard the voice and built the field for Shoeless Joe Jackson.

After reading this first attempt, Kessenich made "another plea for leading off with [the short story], because I believe that that story is the germ, the strong 'spiritual' center from which the rest of the story will take off."[11] He disagreed with Kinsella's position that any mystery in the book would be eliminated by beginning with Jackson's appearance on the field. Rather, Kessenich saw this as an opportunity "to *maintain* the aura of magic and mystery that will make the novel special." In what would be his most substantive and detailed suggestions for the novel, the young editor proclaimed "that only by writing *up to* the high standards of such an opening" would Kinsella "be able to do a whole novel equal to its magic and humor."

Within three weeks, Kinsella had completely revised the novel's opening pages and sent some sixteen pages of the manuscript to Kessenich for further consideration before Bill and Ann left at semester's end for a trip to conferences and readings on their way to Boston, where Bill and Kessenich would finally meet in person. Immediately upon reading the new pages, Kessenich responded with an enthusiastic, "Yes, yes, yes, yes, YES! This is it! This is the spirit of the Shoeless Joe story, the spirit I hoped you could carry throughout the novel." The magic he felt growing from Kinsella's "love of baseball" and "love of living" is what he believed would captivate readers, with "enough interesting characters and relationships" that the book would become "the WAR AND PEACE of baseball!"[12]

Kinsella continued writing, even while on the road. In fact, several encounters along the way were woven into Ray Kinsella's travels in the novel. After Bill and Ann's muffler needed replacing in Thunder Bay, Ontario, they found themselves in a large roadside motel with prior tenants' food still sitting in the cupboards, very similar to a place Ray stops at in the book. Such incidents not only helped Bill develop his novel—he often claimed the most difficult aspect of writing a novel was having enough to write about after he completed a twenty to twenty-five-page short story—but they provided the realistic flair many readers and critics would later identify as one of Kinsella's strengths.

Having decided to incorporate J.D. Salinger into his plotline, Bill read the reclusive writer's *The Catcher in the Rye* aloud the day he and Ann made their way first to Windsor, Vermont, and then to Cornish, New Hampshire, what Kinsella called "Salinger Country." Unlike many Salinger fans, neither Bill nor Ann was interested in catching a glimpse of the writer; instead, they drove through the towns and surrounding countryside, making notes on the scenery to ensure that Bill's description of Ray's trip to meet Salinger would be as realistic as possible. That afternoon, the couple drove into Boston and got their tickets for the game they were planning to attend with Larry Kessenich. Stumbling upon a parking place just outside Fenway Park, they enjoyed a Greek meal at the Aegean Fare restaurant, both events that were incorporated into Ray's trip in *Shoeless Joe*. Finally meeting Kessenich in person for the first time, Kinsella was struck by the editor's friendly personality and also by his youth. While discussing the novel, Kessenich, whose glowing letter of praise had arrived in Calgary after Bill and Ann had already left on their trip, assured Bill that he loved the novel's opening pages and was excited to see more.

Leaving Boston reassured the book was progressing well, Bill and Ann drove over to Cooperstown, New York, where they toured the National Baseball Hall of Fame and Museum, meeting its official historian, Clifford Kachline. Taking advantage of Kachline's years of experience as a writer and editor for *The Sporting News* and his knowledge as a founding member of the Society for American Baseball Research, Kinsella came away from the visit with some much-needed information he anticipated using in the novel, though he remained uncertain as to how Joe Jackson, Moonlight Graham, J.D. Salinger and Eddie Scissons—a character based on an elderly man Bill had met on the street in Iowa City who claimed to be the oldest living Chicago Cub—would be woven together in the plot.

Upon arriving back in Iowa, Kinsella stumbled upon "A Young Girl in 1941 With No Waist at All," an uncollected story of Salinger's that had appeared years earlier in *Mademoiselle*. Bill was struck by the main character's name, Ray Kinsella, which he soon borrowed for his protagonist's in *The Oldest Living Chicago Cub*. At this point he was also already researching and developing ideas to use in his second novel. As part of this process, giving him a break from revising the Salinger kidnapping scene, Bill spent part of his forty-fifth birthday in May researching the Black Angel statue in Iowa City's Oakland Cemetery and writing "Something to Explain," which was reworked into "Something to Think About" and incorporated into his next novel.

Partway through their two weeks in Iowa, Bill and Ann took what proved to be a fortuitous trip to Chisholm, Minnesota, in search of more information about Moonlight Graham. Arriving in town with no specific research agenda, the couple found what information they could about Graham and the town from the public library before visiting the local newspaper office, like Ray and Salinger would in *Shoeless Joe* and Ray and Terence Mann would in *Field of Dreams*. After meeting with Veda Ponikvar and talking about Graham's role within the community, Bill obtained a copy of the former ballplayer's obituary and an editorial entitled "His Was a Life of Greatness," both written by Ponikvar herself, which included information about his life as a ballplayer and as a doctor. As they prepared to leave her office, Bill asked Ponikvar about finding a picture of Graham in his baseball uniform. Ponikvar pushed aside a fern plant sitting on top of her filing cabinet to reveal the exact type of picture Bill had requested.

He would later keep a copy of this picture on his desk in his office back at the University of Calgary.

Ann was more gregarious than Bill, and so he was more than willing to leave her to interview the townspeople. It seemed to him that "everyone over 25 had a Doc Graham story" as he was, by all accounts, "a marvelous character and a well-loved one." This established a pattern for the non-fiction articles Bill and Ann would work on together in the coming years: Ann conducted the personal interviews and collected information while Bill "just lurked in the background," later incorporating the information into the novel's storyline.

The citizens of Chisholm provided Ann with physical details and personal anecdotes related to Graham, allowing Bill to make his character as realistic and sympathetic as those of Jackson and Salinger, both of whom had far more written about them already. Graham's popularity became obvious to Ann as she took down stories about the doctor's generous nature, his work with the local schoolchildren as their district's physician, and his penchant for buying blue hats, specifically, for his wife, Alicia. But in fact, the only reference to his baseball career in her notes is a brief passage describing the doctor's presentation to a classroom of students. In a self-deprecating manner Graham told them, "You know I used to play ball. I was the most outstanding in school. But I was standing out in the hall. So, if you children want to get out of here, all you have to do is make a lot of noise."[13]

When they returned to Iowa City, Bill and Ann attended a carnival with friends from Bill's graduate school days, Tony and Elaine Bukoski. Walking down the carnival's midway, they were drawn to a sideshow by the barker's call coming over the loudspeaker. Intrigued by the spiel—"Mothers bring your daughters, fathers bring your sons"—Bill returned the next day to copy down the barker's script verbatim. That same week, he visited Tony's house outside Iowa City, interviewing his landlord about corn farming to ensure Ray's comments in the book were credible.

After reconnecting with friends and spending much-needed time in their beloved Iowa, Bill and Ann began driving westward to California, where they planned to visit Ann's parents before returning to Calgary for the beginning of the fall term. Finally off the road for a few days, Bill completed the novel's second section, "They Tore Down the Polo Grounds in 1964," by the end of June. He then took a break from writing, and he and Ann drove to Black Butte Dam, during which time he read the manuscript aloud. It was while reading section two to Ann that Bill realized the quality and power behind his own writing. Years later, he said it was on this drive that he knew the novel would be successful.

Encouraged by the progress he had made on the book since leaving Calgary that spring, Bill pushed forward, working on the novel's fourth section and sending Kessenich a copy of his most recent pages. After two weeks in California, Bill began the trip back to Calgary, dreading the looming academic year. The dread was alleviated momentarily by finding he had received a $2,500 Canada Council grant and $800 from the Canadian Broadcasting Corporation for permission to use "The Killing of Colin Moosefeathers" in an upcoming broadcast. There was also another letter waiting from Kessenich, praising the first 125 pages of the novel. Kessenich was so optimistic about the novel's potential that he had shown the draft to Houghton Mifflin's senior editor, Robie Macauley, who suggested it be recommended for the Houghton Mifflin Literary Fellowship, an award given to relatively unknown writers for a book considered by the company's editors to be distinguished. Previous winners included Robert Penn Warren, Elizabeth Bishop, Philip Roth and Carson McCullers, but none of the thirty winners since the award began in 1935 had been Canadian.[14]

That summer Bill's latest collection of stories was released, and some readers were caught by surprise when they discovered the book had no Silas stories. It was, instead, a collection steeped in magic realism. And apart from the title story, the book included very little baseball. Although he usually tried to detach himself from his reviews, and only rarely responded to them, Kinsella celebrated a review from Canada's premier critic of the time, William French. Though he had not reviewed Kinsella's first two books, French not only reviewed *Shoeless Joe Jackson Comes to Iowa* but also praised it.[15]

Following the first two books of Hobbema stories, French recognized Kinsella "was in danger of being typecast as a short-story writer whose only subject involved the Cree Indians of Alberta gleefully turning the tables on their white oppressors . . . They were well enough done, but there was a feeling after the second one that Kinsella had worked the vein and had nowhere else to go."[16] Noting that half of the stories in the new book are realistic and four of the ten "are fantasies bordering on the surreal," French was impressed by Bill's "remarkable virtuosity . . . in style, subject matter and imagination, [so] that we might almost regard him as Kinsella reborn." Other reviewers also noted the "remarkable change in direction" Kinsella had shown with the new stories, "a branching out from the so-called 'Indian' stories of [his] first two collections." Bill's friend from their Iowa days, Anthony Bukoski, wrote a review stating, "There is no telling where this masterful writer will find the characters for his next book."[17]

There were not many fiction writers who regularly employed the use of baseball in their work, apart from Mark Harris in his novels. Ken Adachi viewed the "Shoeless Joe" story as "elegantly crafted . . . suffused by Kinsella's love for the minutiae of the game. His eye and ear are splendidly at work, and he always provides the sense that baseball is not merely a pastime predominated by the tension, the strategy, the ballet of the infielders, the angle of the bat. It's a way of being, an ethic, a whole outlook on the world, emanating at the same time a sense of quiet, awed pleasure, such as seems almost to have vanished from the world."[18] And while it was, to date, his only baseball story, Jon Whyte was already comparing it to *The Year the Yankees Lost the Pennant*, the 1954 Douglass Wallop novel that was immortalized in the Broadway production and later film *Damn Yankees*. Further, he commented that acclaimed Canadian writer Alice Munro "has a peer in the genre of the short story."[19]

Perhaps the main reason his new collection was more appealing to readers in the United States, however, was the shift in setting away from the Hobbema Reserve. The result, wrote Jerry Wasserman, was an assortment of stories in which the author's "dreamers greatly outnumber his realists but the extraordinary can fully succeed, it seems, only if it is dreamed in the service of an intensely ordinary reality."[20] Turning from the dark humour and often pessimistic undertones of the Silas Ermineskin stories, *Shoeless Joe Jackson Comes to Iowa* represented a shift to a more hopeful, optimistic voice. Combining that optimism with the limitless possibilities he saw inherent in the game of baseball, Kinsella had no way of knowing at that time the groundwork he was laying for the novel. And the reputation he would soon have in the genre of baseball fiction as a result of the book would exceed even his wildest expectations.

That summer Bill was approached by *Saturday Night* editor Gary Ross about writing an article on the drought that was affecting southern Saskatchewan and Manitoba. He and Ann decided to do what they had done in Chisholm a few weeks earlier. Ann would research the material, conducting interviews with people in the area, and Bill would write the copy. Even during their trip to Oxbow, Saskatchewan, Bill continued working on the novel, nearly completing the third section, "The Life and Times of Moonlight Graham." And after submitting the first draft of the drought article, his focus once again shifted back to completing the novel by the year's end.

Following the Oxbow trip, Bill opened a letter from Kessenich explaining Houghton Mifflin's hesitation at awarding the fellowship or even accepting the book for publication until they had a completed manuscript to consider. And while he had to revise the article for *Saturday Night*, an overwhelming amount of his time now was spent working on the book before the start of yet another semester. He completed the third section, based largely on the Moonlight Graham research from earlier in the summer, and mailed it to Kessenich for his consideration. On the same day he completed this section, he developed a plot twist for the fourth section. He would have Salinger admit to giving an interview about the Polo Grounds. Ecstatic that the loose ends in his plot were finally coming together, Bill concluded his diary entry that day with an enthusiastic "YEAH!"[21]

The excitement was quickly dampened when he was notified that his creative writing course had seventy students registered for the fall term. Kinsella declared that the situation was "totally absurd" and that "[t]he bureaucrats here are SO STUPID."[22] Despite trying to frighten as many of them away as possible on the first day, there were still sixty students who decided to stay in the class. And while those in power to make substantive changes to the course were open to smaller class sizes in the lower level courses, they refused to do so with Kinsella's creative writing class. He dreamed of when he could "get away from this idiotic place."

In the semester's third week, he had to respond to a student who had complained to the administration about comments he made in class when he was trying to cut the class size down. Then he was notified that the school would no longer pay stipends to writers who were invited to speak at the Calgary Creative Reading Series events Bill and Ann co-directed. Viewing the decision by the "pernicious assholes" as "totally personal," his anger towards the administration now included the "[f]ucking petty accountant mentalities." However, the proofs for *Born Indian* arrived that fall, helping take his mind off university matters, and he shifted his focus to making the final changes to the book.

Bill had already completed over forty pages of section four of his novel by the end of October, and he committed himself to increasing his quota to ten pages per day until he finished a draft of the section. Even years later, when he was far removed from the rigours of teaching, he marvelled at how he had been able to maintain this while teaching "3 courses and read[ing] the tons of illiterate drivel I had to read." The intense pace enabled him to complete the first draft of his novel by the afternoon of November 11. Recording the exact time, 3:55 p.m., in his diary, he noted that the second section of the novel (the first being the short story "Shoeless Joe Jackson Comes to Iowa") had been started on April 5, slightly more than seven months prior.[23] From when he first began work on the book until he typed the last page of the first draft, Kinsella's novel had taken him almost exactly nine months to write. One week later, the handwritten pages were typed, photocopied and in the mail to Kessenich.

He spent the next few weeks editing the novel, waiting for a contract to be offered, his excitement once again curtailed by the growing angst he felt towards the university and to the Calgary climate. As November came to a close, he noted, "I HATE CALGARY and winter weather," following up the next day, after receiving his heating bill, with "I HATE THIS COUNTRY." In early December, as the semester drew to a close, he again commented on his frustration, writing, "I hate it here."[24] The anger proved valuable fodder for his writing, though. On December 4 he completed the short story "Apartheid," in which he highlighted the dismissive attitude academics in the English Department took towards his creative endeavours. The piece was "very good, but ANGRY," he admitted in his diary, and "[w]ould set off sparks here at Desolate U." He decided he would hold off publishing it until after he left the university—a date that could not come quickly enough.

He finished the year working on various short stories and collaborating with Ann on a non-fiction article. In the previous twelve months he had completed a novel, three new Silas stories, several other short stories, and his first magazine article was set for national distribution. He determined it had been "a good year," noting on his and Ann's second anniversary that he "couldn't ask for anyone better than Ann."[25] In fact, his only complaint at the end of 1980 was that "Calgary couldn't be worse,"[26] a situation he soon hoped to change as he searched for teaching jobs in warmer climates.

Bill rang in the new year by working on "The Moccasin Telegraph," a story he wanted to use as a commissioned piece for the Canadian Broadcasting Corporation. A few days later he was revising and completing "Dr. Don" and "The Ballad of the Public Trustee," stories that would later be included in *The Moccasin Telegraph*. Next he finished work on "Books by the Pound," one of his "Brautigans"—short stories in the style of his favourite author, Richard Brautigan—which would be included in *The Alligator Report* four years later, and began "Mother Trucker's Yellow Duck." He was notified that "First Names and Empty Pockets" would be included in the upcoming *Best Canadian Short Stories 1981*. The added exposure could only help sales of his newest collection of Silas stories, *Born Indian*, released in March by Oberon. Bill was happy to see his newest book adorned with an Allen Sapp painting he had purchased for that reason.

After so many stories told from Silas's viewpoint, certain readers may have expected stale clichés and reused storylines. But John Cook recognized the latest collection's value: "After three collections the stories seem to have reached a point where the reader might legitimately ask if there has been any real development in the characters or in Kinsella's vision. . . In spite of my reservations, I find [Kinsella] a storyteller who delights."[27] But Cook also noted that the Ermineskin stories, however humorous, were "wearing a bit thin, and Kinsella needs to free himself and his characters from a bondage that is comfortable, profitable, but in the end deadly." Kinsella had long ago committed himself to making money from his work, though, focusing more on telling stories for profit than on pleasing literary critics or academics. As long as his books continued selling, he didn't care what the critics thought.

Some reviewers began to question a white author writing humorous stories in an Indigenous voice about life on a Canadian reserve. Erling Frus-Baastad noted that Bill "works with several levels of humor. . . I am certain [he] was fully aware of the target he would become after daring to publish stories about Indians. I am glad that didn't stop him."[28] Others were far more critical, including one writing in *Maclean's*, a popular national magazine. During his annual summer trip with Ann, Bill read Mark Czarnecki's review, which he noted had "all the sensitivity of a backhoe."[29] Despite describing the stories as being "cleverly written in a freewheeling style," Czarnecki claimed, "the crude articulation of stereotyped emotion glossed over with aw-shucks moralizing . . . adds up to submissive politics and punching-bag art," detracting from racial conflicts, which he felt were more deserving of serious consideration. Familiar with the two earlier collections of the Silas stories, Czarnecki noted that the format of this book was "questionable". Since many of the stories had previously been published in magazines, as stand-alone pieces, the "genealogies, marriages, professions and so on have had to be re-established each time."[30]

Mike Walton wrote that it was time for Kinsella "to clear off the Indian reservation. This is his third collection of short stories about growing up, living and dying Indian on the Hobbema reserve in Alberta and, frankly, kemo sabe, three's a crowd."[31] Judith Russell was even more direct with her thoughts on the potential controversy regarding cultural appropriation, stating, "I suspect that both as a white [person] and as a writer he is intelligent enough to realize that any analysis of Indian character from a white viewpoint would be lame, if not ridiculous."[32]

In spite of such criticism, the collection was generally well-received by an audience that had come to expect Silas, Frank and the other Cree on the Hobbema Reserve to recognize the humour in the absurdities of the white politicians, police and other bureaucrats they dealt with while also undermining the white people at every possible opportunity. In fact, Ian McLatchie went so far as to single out the story "Weasels and Ermines" as "one of the more impressive pieces of short fiction to appear in Canada in recent years."[33]

Although he had worked with Larry Kessenich throughout the novel's development, Houghton Mifflin had yet to offer Bill a contract for the manuscript. Confident that the book was going to be successful, he began researching other publishers. Encouraged by Kessenich's suggestion he might be awarded the Houghton Mifflin Literary Fellowship, in early February Kinsella submitted the manuscript of his novel for consideration for the Seal Book Award. Started four years earlier in 1977 with the goal of publicizing a Seal-Bantam paperback imprint, the award was an annual competition for the best first novel by a Canadian writer and came with a $10,000 cash prize and another $40,000 in guaranteed royalties. Perhaps more important than the money, however, was that the book would be published in hardback by McClelland & Stewart in Canada; Little, Brown in the United States; and Andre Deutsch in Great Britain. Subsequent paperback editions were to be released by Seal Books in Canada, Bantam Books in the United States and Corgi in England.[34] Winning the award would immediately give Kinsella's novel worldwide distribution, and give Kinsella further validation of his efforts over the past decade, as well as an opportunity to finally leave Calgary. When submitting the manuscript for the award, Kinsella renamed the novel *The Kidnapping of J.D. Salinger*, hoping the judges "would want something racier or more commercial."[35]

He was shortlisted for the award, but did not win. In fact, no award was given that year as the judges failed to agree on a winning novel; Kinsella was told the British judges did not want his book to win because of the baseball in it. On the same day he was given the news regarding the Seal Book Award, he was also informed that he had not been nominated for the Governor General's Award that year. He had not necessary expected to be, but was still disappointed when he saw the list, believing *Shoeless Joe Jackson Comes to Iowa* was a much stronger book than the works from the three finalists—Susan Musgrave, George Bowering and Kinsella's former professor from Victoria, Leon Rooke. These disappointments were tempered somewhat by an offer from McClelland & Stewart to publish his novel, with a $10,000 advance.

The next day Kinsella received a telephone call from Larry Kessenich and Robie Macauley telling him that Houghton Mifflin also wanted to publish the book. With offers from two major publishers within a twenty-four-hour period, Bill placed a call to Nancy Colbert, a Toronto-based agent, to see if she had an interest in representing him as he moved forward in the process. He had negotiated his first four collections of short stories on his own with no outside representation, but recognized that his earlier deals with Oberon had given the publisher significant control over the rights to his material. By the next day, Colbert had agreed to represent Bill in discussions with Houghton Mifflin and with McClelland & Stewart; she also made arrangements to send renowned editor Nan Talese at Simon & Schuster a copy for consideration. The next day, General Publishing expressed interest in the novel, giving Bill at least three publishers who wanted the rights to the manuscript.

Fortunately for Bill, the loss of one award made way for him to win the award that helped bring his work to a much wider audience. In mid-April, Larry Kessenich called to notify Kinsella that, after much consideration, he had been awarded the Houghton Mifflin Literary Fellowship worth $10,000. And though Kinsella was appreciative, he privately remarked that it was "a real anticlimax, as they have been speculating about it for eight [months]."[36] More than the cash award, he wanted to sign with an American publisher as it would provide him access to a wider audience, something that had been lacking with Oberon, which generally limited him to Canadian readers.

Soon after posting the final grades for his classes that spring, Bill attended another Allen Sapp exhibition, where he added to his small but growing collection of the painter's work, buying a piece called "Going Home." At the reception, Kinsella and Sapp had several pictures taken together. Kinsella had been recognized as a voice for Indigenous Canadians through his Silas Ermineskin stories and Sapp's paintings brought to life many aspects of the Cree culture. At one point, the normally quiet, shy Sapp leaned over to Kinsella, saying, "I expect our souls are gone by now."[37]

With the novel out of his hands, Bill turned his attention to other projects and the summer ahead. Anxious to leave Calgary and begin their summer travels, Bill and Ann loaded their car and left for Toronto, where they met Nancy Colbert and discussed the novel's title. Having encountered some reluctance from Houghton Mifflin about the original working title, *The Oldest Living Chicago Cub*, Bill suggested a simple revision borrowing from the original story title, *Shoeless Joe Jackson Comes to Iowa—The Novel*.

In mid-May, after Bill arrived in Boston to sign his contract with Houghton Mifflin, Larry Kessenich informed him that J.D. Salinger's lawyers had contacted the publisher threatening legal action for libel should his name be used for a character in the final draft. After careful consideration, Houghton Mifflin's legal team concluded there was no merit to Salinger's argument as it was based on the idea that Kinsella's representation portrayed him in a false light. Kinsella appreciated Salinger's ability to "[make] himself conspicuous by hiding . . . every-time someone mention[ed] his name he threaten[ed] a lawsuit, which [had] kept him in the public eye,"[38] despite him not having published a story since 1965. Assured there was no legitimacy to any case Salinger might file, Kinsella signed the contract, officially committing the novel to Houghton Mifflin.

With his first novel slated for release sometime in 1982, he had already started revising the second, *The Grecian Urn*, which he soon changed to *Honk If You Love Willie Nelson*, showing the first seventy-five pages to Kessenich during the Boston leg of the trip. By the end of the summer, he had completed over 250 pages of it.

After spending nearly a month in Iowa City, Bill and Ann began the drive back to Calgary, stopping to visit Ann's parents in Orland, California. Though he still thought highly of Ann's father, Sam English, the tension between Bill and her mother, Corene, had become even more pronounced. Despite sharing the common wish of wanting the best for Ann, Corene's strong religious convictions made it nearly unbearable for Bill to be around her for any extended period. After Ann and Corene had an argument over family finances, Bill privately concluded, "[Corene] has to go over the same point-less ground on each of Ann's visits . . . [Corene] is a model for a religious hypocrite [and] thinks because she has a particular fantasy about the supernatural that she is better than anyone else in the world. In reality she is petty, unpleasant and thoroughly unlik-able."[39] Bill's frustration with Christianity was present in his novel, in the character of Annie's mother, described as someone wearing "silver-rimmed glasses flashing glints of disapproval at everything in sight . . . When there were lulls in conversation she read her Bible, sneering a little in her perfection."[40] Annie's brothers are even named after the four gospels in the New Testament—Matthew, Mark, Luke and John.

While attending a church service with Ann's family one morning, he heard a sermon that angered him. Later he noted "that SOB [minister] sure knows how to make me mad   talked about God's protection—someday they'll catch on the christians get killed as often, get just as sick as non-christians." Though he considered the minister "a reasonably nice man when not involved with religion," this sermon "was a prime reason" Bill joined the American Atheists. Fed up with "the whole group [of] dumb, mealymouthed [*sic*], hypocrites" in the church, he "felt [he] had to make some effort to fight the spread of religion and its infiltration of everyday life."[41]

In 1981, a labour strike lasting nearly two months deprived baseball fans of almost 40% of the regular season games. Perhaps the only consolation from the strike was "The Thrill of the Grass," a story about baseball fans' disillusionment because of the strike and the last story in a collection of the same name that would be published three years later.

As another academic term loomed on the horizon, the copy-edited pages for the novel, now called *Shoeless Joe*, arrived for Kinsella's approval. Despite finding the editor "very picky—sometimes trying to make bland hamburger out of steak,"[42] Bill was largely satisfied with the revisions and within a matter of days was ready to send it back to the publisher. In late September he received a visit from Nancy Colbert, who was excited about the possibilities for a film adaptation of *Shoeless Joe*, and by an encouraging letter from Larry Kessenich expressing how thrilled his colleagues at Houghton Mifflin were with the novel. Bill began sketching out notes for another baseball novel set in Iowa, one that would rely even more on the magic realism for which *Shoeless Joe* would soon be known.

When the cover art arrived in early December, Bill was not impressed: "very artsy, but lacks color, [and] would not attract me to pick it up."[43] He would have preferred an illustration of a baseball signed by Jackson, Graham and Salinger. Still, he was encouraged to learn the sales department was so enamoured with the book the company had raised the number of copies in the first printing from 10,000 to 25,000, though he also privately noted that "they should be" excited with the book as he was confident in its ability to resonate with readers. As the year ended, he looked back on what he had accomplished: "Lots of publicity. Lots of travel. Lots of love." And, in a rare moment of tender reflection, he closed out his diary with the simple wish: "All my years should be this good."[44]

He began 1982 writing at a feverish pace, completing over forty-five pages in the first two weeks alone, but was soon consumed with media interviews and other obligations for the release of *Shoeless*

Joe, now just weeks away. Still unsure if the novel's success would be enough to allow him to leave teaching, he continued applying for jobs. He got an interview with the University of Houston, hoping that, regardless of what happened with the book, he would finally be free from the miserable weather and academic pettiness he felt had dominated his life in Calgary for the previous four years.

Already confident in the novel's potential and with Houghton Mifflin's staff doing everything in its power to ensure its commercial success, Bill's hopes were further buoyed as early reviews began appearing in newspapers and trade publications across the United States and Canada. Charles Gordon wrote, "Kinsella's dreams and nostalgia could be the year's best writing."[45] Another, Jack Hodgins, wrote, "*Shoeless Joe* distinguishes itself not only by the energy of its prose and the entertaining developments of its plot, but also by the way in which it reveals itself to be a story about writing stories, about the concerns of the spirit, about the need for wonder."[46] Gwendolyn MacEwen said the novel "is a winner [. . .] because it's inventive, unpredictable, and completely entertaining. It says as much about the nature of human imagination and the role that magic plays, or should play, in our lives." MacEwen's was also one of the first reviews to address the participatory dynamic between the novel and its readers and explained that each reader has "been invited to the game, and it's up to each one of us how much of the spectacle he wants, or dares, to witness."[47]

Kinsella found himself already being compared to writers who had years earlier set the standard for serious adult baseball fiction. By May, just weeks after the book's release, Michael J. Francis wrote that it had "the quality to thrust itself into [the] fast company" of Bernard Malamud, who wrote the 1952 novel *The Natural*, and Robert Coover, who wrote 1968's *The Universal Baseball Association, Inc., J. Henry Waugh, Prop*, the standards against which all subsequent baseball novels had been measured.[48]

Up to now, readers who enjoyed Kinsella's works had done so primarily through the voice of Silas Ermineskin and had not had the opportunity to see Kinsella establish a setting that was not the

Hobbema Reserve. To those familiar with the place Bill had come to love and call home during his time there, Iowa leapt off the page, becoming as much a character as Ray, Graham or Salinger themselves. On a local Iowa radio broadcast on KCCK, the announcer proclaimed that Bill's book "captures the colors and sounds of the midwestern landscape, makes readers want to walk out into the cool fields of evening and watch fireflies flicker above the corn. *Shoeless Joe* is a tribute to baseball and the beauty of Iowa, a graceful first novel deserving of readers and recognition."[49]

Though Bill still had nearly a full month until the spring semester at Calgary ended, the novel's release in April added additional stress as he and Ann planned for their annual cross-country road trip much more methodically and intentionally than in previous years, working non-stop with Houghton Mifflin's marketing department to allow Bill maximum promotional exposure. They would visit as many radio stations, newspaper writers, bookstores and baseball stadiums as they could cover over the course of their three-month excursion.

Ann's organizational abilities and attention to detail helped ease much of the strain Bill was feeling. She had a mechanic confirm that her orange Datsun, nicknamed "the Great Pumpkin," was "good for another 12,000 miles," despite having nearly 145,000 already on its odometer. She approached Bill about having "a poster or two on the car" as a means of attracting attention and promoting the book en route.[50] With his approval, she purchased paint and shellac and attached publicity flyers from Houghton Mifflin to the car's fenders. Along the back panel on the passenger's side of the car she painted the words "Kinsella. Author on tour" in bold letters. Coordinating the tour with publicists in Boston and Toronto, and with Bill's agent, Nancy Colbert, Ann told her husband all he would be required to do was "roll over and play alive."[51]

With four weeks until the tour was scheduled to begin, Ann had already made one thousand copies of a promotional flyer she had designed, complete with early newspaper reviews, photographs and an in-house memorandum from the publisher, to be distributed along the way. Not wanting to fall behind in her networking while they travelled, she mailed some 300 copies of other promotional materials to numerous outlets along their planned route, hoping to secure as many interviews and signings as possible.

As the reality of the trip grew more daunting, Bill was contacted by *TV Guide*—the editor was interested in assigning him at least one article for a future edition, which would expose an entirely new, larger market to his work. And with the official release days away, Bill and Ann were delighted when his agent informed them that the book's Japanese rights had been sold, paving the way to an audience that would come to revere *Shoeless Joe*.

Juggling his academic workload with his planning for the Calgary release party and subsequent tour, Bill was stretched thin, and media obligations and interviews consumed more time as the spring wore on. He would be the cover story for an early summer edition of an Edmonton magazine and an interview guest with the Canadian Broadcasting Corporation. The Canadian release party was scheduled for April 15, one week before the American release. Just days before the party, *Quill & Quire* ran a profile on Bill in which he described himself as a North American writer as opposed to strictly a Canadian writer. Unfortunately, and much to Bill's frustration, the author of the piece changed "North American" to simply "American" writer, and he worried this would offend loyal Canadian readers of his work. Although the quote was mentioned from time to time years afterwards, it had no significant impact on either his sales or his popularity in Canada.

While Ann prepared the Great Pumpkin for the upcoming trip, Bill kept adding to his workload, agreeing to go co-teach some thirty-six high school students in Whitehorse, Yukon, with George Bowering and Rosalind McPhee at the end of April. Though he still expressed his frustrations about academic life, opportunities to work with new writers on specific aspects of their craft was the one part of teaching he enjoyed and was something he was regularly invited to do following the success of *Shoeless Joe*. When Ann suggested different ways of workshopping with the students during the two-day seminar, Bill informed her that he would not do writing exercises of any kind. Admiring her husband "for not taking the easy way and entertaining the hopes of every *would-be* writer," she privately noted, "That's his way of not prostituting the art [and] craft of writing—by not making any part of the process seem easier or more attractive than it is, but working from the point-after creation vs. the point-before."[52]

Nancy Colbert notified Bill the day before the book launch party that her plan was to auction the paperback rights with an opening bid of $15,000. Unfortunately, in the same conversation she also had to tell him about a review by Ian Pearson scheduled for publication in the following week's issue of *Maclean's*. The review was riddled with inaccuracies and misinformation; Pearson erroneously stated that Ray and Salinger make the trip back to Iowa with Moonlight Graham's grandson rather than with the younger version of Graham himself. The poorly written review would not be published until after the book's release, and so Bill and Ann, for a brief time at least, focused their energies on the launch party in Calgary the following day.

Leading up to the launch, Ann had taken out advertisements in various papers and undertaken an impressive word-of-mouth campaign hoping to maximize the exposure of the book's first day on the market. Bill conservatively estimated only thirty-five people would attend; Ann, however, was convinced her efforts would garner far more than that. As was often the case when the couple disagreed over some fact or possible outcome, they agreed to a small wager. If more than forty people attended, Bill agreed to pay Ann a dollar for each person beyond that. If fewer than forty attended, Ann would pay him the same amount for each person below that. Bill happily lost the bet when some ninety people came out for the launch.

Introducing Bill that evening, Ann acknowledged the intimacy of the moment with so many family and friends in the room, saying, "It compares [...] to saying goodbye to one of your children who has decided that it's time to leave home [...] Just as some people look at your [child] and try to imagine what sort of home you raised the kid in, people look at an author's book and try to imagine what sort of a world he thinks this is."[53] Ann acknowledged that her husband was "not ashamed to say he hasn't fallen in love with [Calgary]," though, she told the crowd, "he does feel close to a number of the people here [including] students and former students, colleagues, fans and encouraging supporters."

A few days before they were scheduled to begin what would eventually be a three-month tour across much of Canada and the United States, Pearson's review was published in *Maclean's*. According to Ann, it seemed "as if [he] read very hastily—and jacket copy primarily." By the end of the day, both Bill and Ann, along with Nancy Colbert, had crafted responses to the magazine. The frustration the review brought was eased somewhat by a *Publishers Weekly* profile Larry Kessenich sent to them, along with the news that Houghton Mifflin's sales staff had already placed orders for 15,000 copies of *Shoeless Joe*. The company's hopes were that the accompanying *PW* review would lead to even more sales as the book tour gained momentum over the summer.

Ann began packing the Datsun two days before the trip was to start. Supplies included autographed copies of *Shoeless Joe* to trade for unsigned copies between Calgary and Toronto. Bill had also decided to sign ten copies of each of his Oberon books to sell at events or to trade for services en route, something that he often did in an effort to both gain new readers and cut costs while travelling.

On April 26, the long-awaited tour began, a trip that, although it would bring them back to Calgary at summer's end for another year of teaching at "Desolate U," signalled the beginning of the end of Bill's time as a professor. For while he had been offered a new contract with full tenure by the university that spring, virtually assuring he could continue teaching as long as he liked, Kinsella had surprised the administration weeks earlier by not only declining the offer, but by notifying them that the 1982–83 academic year would be his last with the school. Between his savings and the Houghton Mifflin fellowship, he decided that he had enough money to begin writing full-time.

Leaving Calgary, the couple drove towards Toronto, making stops for interviews and signings in Regina, Saskatchewan; Winnipeg, Manitoba; and various small towns in between. During a stop at Candlewood Books in Brandon, Manitoba, they sold five books from the stock packed in the Great Pumpkin as the bookstore had already sold out of its initial order from the publisher. Ann figured the wave of sales was the result of a glowing review in the *Winnipeg Free Press* earlier that day. Only three days into the trip, all of the Oberon books had already been traded or sold.

As Ann drove east, Bill flew to Whitehorse for the workshop with the high school writers, using the time off the road to work on short stories for his next collection. Much of his free time there, however, was filled with interviews and book signings. Always the competitor, Bill noted in his diary that, at the writing conference's conclusion, he "must have signed 75 books, Rosalind signed a few, [and] George less than that."[54]

When Bill reunited with Ann in Toronto, his schedule was filled with newspaper and radio interviews, even booking future interviews when his commitments grew too numerous to be able to fulfill in one visit to a city. Upon returning to their hotel one day, they were asked by another guest riding the elevator with them, "Aren't you the guy who wrote that book on baseball?"

Taken aback, Bill simply nodded. Ann asked the man if he had seen Bill on TV that morning.

"Yes, and you were a hit. Congratulations," he replied.

Recovering from his initial surprise, Bill finally spoke up to say, "I'm just amazed that people really watch those shows."[55]

Not quite two weeks into the tour, Bill was drawing crowds of nearly 200 people at some stops, his books were selling well in nearly every city along the way, and he was giving interviews to anyone who wanted one. In early May, he was formally offered the opportunity to write a short piece intended for the upcoming summer All-Star issue of *TV Guide*. The $750 paycheque was relatively modest, but the article would put Kinsella's name on a byline seen by some one million readers.[56]

After nearly a week in Toronto, Bill concluded his visit with a radio interview during a Blue Jays game. Despite his interest in radio broadcasting as a young man, he politely declined announcer Tom Cheek's offer to announce a batter, electing instead to talk baseball and his writing in between the on-field action. And while he had kept a rigorous pace of interviews and personal appearances during the previous two weeks, the commitments only intensified when he and Ann arrived in New York City at the start of the tour's third week.

In her personal notes from the trip she had started calling "the Continuing Saga of the Book Promotional Trail," Ann compiled quotes from Bill's conversations with interviewers and fans along the route and from conversations and broadcasts heard during the course of the trip. In New York City, she recorded National Public Radio's Barry Schweid's comment in a conversation with Bill: "So one of the reporters dashed out and bought the President [Ronald Reagan] a copy of your book."[57] By the time they had arrived in Philadelphia two days later, they were informed of a rumour that had started gaining momentum claiming there was no actual writer named W.P. Kinsella; rather, the name was supposedly a pseudonym used by Salinger himself who, after years of not publishing a word and fiercely guarding his privacy, had decided to release a novel without the fanfare that would have undoubtedly accompanied anything with his own name on the cover. Rather than being upset by the rumour, Bill was thrilled by the additional free publicity and the potential sales.

In between stops in Detroit and Madison, Wisconsin, Bill was a guest on a call-in sports talk show on a Milwaukee radio station to pitch his book and talk about baseball. He took a call from a fan who told him, "Here's a scenario for your next book. God wants the Chicago Cubs to win the last pennant before Armageddon."[58] Two days later Bill sat down and began writing the first page of "The Last Pennant Before Armageddon," in which he was able to build on the legendary streak of failures throughout the Cubs' history while subtly mocking evangelical Christians. That evening, Bill and Ann attended a cocktail party where the general manager of the Madison Muskies minor league team entertained the audience with the story of a minor league team in Texas where a player who had been released shot the general manager's dog. Bill would later work this into the short story "How Manny Embarquadero Overcame and Began His Climb to the Major Leagues." Meanwhile, *Shoeless Joe* had been sitting at number one on the St. Louis bestseller list for four straight weeks, due in no small part to local radio personality Jack Carney, who spent nearly two hours on the air with Bill helping promote the novel.

Although they had not visited a major literary city since leaving the east coast, by the time the couple reached Illinois near the end of May, Bill had already had over fifty print media reviews and interviews in various outlets. As they arrived in Chicago, the closest large city to the book's Iowa setting, the publicity reached its highest point to date with six appearances scheduled the first day in town. And when they briefly returned to St. Louis, longtime Cardinals radio announcer Jack Buck interviewed Bill on KMOX, further establishing the book's popularity in the Midwest market.

When Bill and Ann arrived in Iowa City, some seventy people, including many friends from Bill's time in the Writers' Workshop, came out to hear him read. The couple took a two-week break from touring, and Bill reconnected with the idyllic landscape he had come to love and which had become a focal point of his novel. In fact, the locale would serve as the backdrop for three more baseball novels and numerous short stories in the coming years. More importantly, perhaps, the break from travelling gave Bill an opportunity to write.

While in Iowa he completed "Barefoot and Pregnant in Des Moines" in addition to beginning several more stories, while Ann worked on improving the house on South Johnson Street. In the last few days before beginning the trip west to visit Ann's parents, Bill wrote "The Job," another of his growing collection of "Brautigans," and began another short story, "Driving Toward the Moon," both of which made their way into separate collections published in 1984 and 1985. While Bill was still in Iowa, Nancy Colbert phoned to inform him that the paperback rights to *Shoeless Joe* had been sold to Ballantine for $15,000. Bill complained about the 50% due to Houghton Mifflin, what he privately called a "real rip off,"[59] believing he was due 90% of the sale, minus the fees paid to Colbert. His frustration towards the publishing industry was building.

Taking advantage of being back in Iowa, Kinsella spent time in the University of Iowa library poring over material and taking notes for his next novel, to be set almost entirely in the state. He took copious, detailed notes on the state's history and the history of the 1908 Chicago Cubs, who would play a prominent role in the book's plot.

Less than three months away from the start of the fall semester, Bill had been holding onto the hope that Colbert would be able to sell the movie rights to *Shoeless Joe*, thereby providing a substantial enough income for him and Ann to leave Calgary on the sooner side. Unfortunately, at the end of June, it had become clear that a deal was not going to be finalized in such a short amount of time, and he resigned himself to the fact that he would "be back at Desolate U" in the fall.[60]

When Bill and Ann arrived in Orland, California, in the middle of July, they received news that a *New York Times* review of *Shoeless Joe* had been delayed due to a lack of space, and that there were over 19,000 hardback copies of *Shoeless Joe* presently in stores. Assuming the forthcoming review would only help sales, there was growing optimism that the book's 25,000 first printing would sell out. Because of the novel's success, publications began contacting Bill hoping he would contribute something with a baseball connection. While on the road, he was approached by *SPORT* magazine, whose editors wanted him to travel for a week with the Montreal Expos for an article on the team. And while the success from *Shoeless Joe* caused people to associate Kinsella's name with baseball, he had, as yet, met very few baseball players. He declined the offer, choosing instead to finish the book tour by driving up the west coast back to Calgary. Though he was usually happy to talk about baseball, its popularity and its shortcomings, following *Shoeless Joe*'s release, he found himself puzzled by editors who thought, simply because he had written a novel with baseball players as characters, that he would want to write non-fiction articles on the game. However, he did agree to write a 1,500-word article for *TV Guide*'s World Series issue in October, choosing to focus on the hot dogs being served at ballparks, rather than writing the article for the All-Star issue.

Bill and Ann spent the waning days of their summer trip conducting the last radio and newspaper interviews in Oregon and

Washington and attending the Oregon Shakespeare Festival. They arrived home in Calgary on August 1, and though Bill was not looking forward to the upcoming school year or his last winter in Calgary, he was encouraged by the large volume of fan mail that had accumulated in his absence and the steady stream of positive reviews that continued to appear.

For the first time since selling his restaurant over a decade earlier and committing himself to finishing his creative writing degree, he was confident in a future in which he would be able to write full-time, with the luxury of an income that would allow him never to return to the classroom unless it was on his own terms.

8

Goodbye, Desolate U.

F resh off the success of his summer promotional tour for *Shoeless Joe*, and having already announced he would not come back to the university after the upcoming school year, Bill returned to Calgary, if not happy about his return to the classroom then at least happy knowing his time in what he had begun calling "Depression City" was limited.[1] Soon after arriving back in Canada, he received a letter J.D. Salinger's lawyers had sent to Houghton Mifflin claiming the author was both "outraged and offended" at his last name being used in *Shoeless Joe*, threatening legal action should Kinsella attempt to "extend or expand this misappropriation, including by exploitation of the book or idea in any other media or other areas of endeavor . . ."[2] Viewing the letter as nothing more than "legal noise," Bill paid little attention to the threat. He predicted that Salinger's response to the book, once made known to the public, would likely only serve to sell more copies of the already popular novel.[3]

Bill's upper-level creative writing course looked as though it "might be fun for [the] first time" in more than three years.[4] However, the most positive thing he had to say about his composition course was the students were "no more illiterate than usual."[5] Seeing the first snow begin to accumulate in mid-October that year, he lamented, "Now I know why I hate Calgary so much. I would rather be poor in a decent climate."[6] His outlook brightened somewhat when, that same day, a fire started in Calgary Hall, where his office was located. Bill and a colleague watched, giddy with the possibility of the building burning to the ground. In the end, classes were cancelled for two days, but Bill wished the fire had done more damage.

That fall Kinsella was already anticipating the release of his next book. Originally called *The Sundog Society*, now titled *The Moccasin Telegraph*, it was another collection of Silas Ermineskin stories to be published first in Canada and then in the United States the following year. It would be the first collection of his stories published in the U.S. Further complicating the relationship between Bill and Oberon was the fact that Nancy Colbert, his agent, had assumed the responsibility of negotiating his book contracts. Learning from the legal mess between Oberon and Don Haldane over the film rights to *Dance Me Outside*, Kinsella wanted to avoid similar issues with future books.

Recognizing the success Kinsella had recently achieved and realizing his working with a literary agent would mean someone with more experience was overseeing the contractual side of the relationship, Michael Macklem wrote Bill in August, appealing to the early days of their relationship and reminding him of the ways Oberon and Kinsella were able to help each other. Grateful to have heard from both Bill and Ann earlier in the summer, Macklem expressed relief, albeit sarcastically, in knowing Kinsella was still very much alive and writing Silas stories. The publisher's frustration was largely because he felt he and Bill no longer communicated about topics related to the stories Kinsella wrote, things Macklem felt were easily "lost in this harsh modern world of literary agents and lawyers— what a far cry from the innocent world in which you and I started a few years ago and in which we both got on so well and did so well for each other."[7]

Though Nancy Colbert was looking out for her client's best interests, Macklem felt as though she was preventing a contract for the new collection from being signed. He told Kinsella, "Nancy Colbert tried to hold back the book as a weapon in case our lawsuit against Don Haldane failed; then she started to hold it back to force her appointment as our agent, all of which seems pretty irrelevant to what is our first priority, namely to get the new book into production."

He warned Bill that Colbert's behaviour could end up making not only her agency but also her client look bad. In an effort to entice Kinsella into signing the contract in time to publish the book the following spring, Macklem offered to let the author choose the title and the form for the new collection before closing with a more confrontational tone than perhaps he intended: "Why don't you take the reins in your own hands and make some decisions? Let's get on with it. We're wasting time; we're wasting precious work. These stories are being held in a drawer. That's no place for them."

No longer as innocent and naïve as he was when he first signed an Oberon contract six years earlier, Bill responded, voicing his concerns about the film and television rights, and letting Macklem know he had confidence in Colbert's ability to negotiate the contract as she had far more experience in this area than did the publisher. *Shoeless Joe* had brought him success and the luxury of knowing other publishers were now interested in his fiction. He assured Macklem, "I want the book to get rolling too. Although we have considerable interest from other publishers I prefer that Oberon publish *The Moccasin Telegraph*, as you say people have come to expect my work to appear under the Oberon trademark."[8]

The tension between the two parties became more strained when, two weeks later, Nicholas Macklem, Michael's son, who also worked in the company, responded to the letter Bill had sent Michael: "I'm sorry you were frustrated by my father's letter [. . .] but I think that both he and I are beginning to get seriously frustrated [. . .] Like everyone else, we could use some good news these days, and there's no better news at Oberon than a new Kinsella book. I can't for the life of me see why there shouldn't be one and I hope you can't either."[9] In the end, Bill opted to sign with Penguin to publish the new collection. Adding insult to Oberon's injury was the fact that Nicholas Macklem was attending one of Bill's readings in Ottawa when Kinsella announced to the crowd that *The Moccasin Telegraph* would come out with Penguin.

Bill was informed just before Christmas break that *Shoeless Joe* had been optioned for a year with an $8,000 advance against $100,000 on the first day of filming and 5% of the film's profits. Though he remained frustrated at the ongoing film rights dispute involving Oberon, Don Haldane and Norman Jewison, who would become the film's executive producer, he was optimistic about the possibility of his novel making its way to the big screen. The following day, Nancy Colbert called to inform him that he would receive $14,000 in royalties from Houghton Mifflin.

In the new year, Kinsella was suffering from increasingly elevated blood sugar. In an attempt to treat the issue himself, he began a more strictly controlled diet to maintain lower levels. And while a subsequent visit to a diabetes clinic confirmed his numbers were higher than they should have been, doctors did not yet feel he needed to control the issue with insulin. In March 1983, Bill was informed that he would soon be announced as the winner of the *Books in Canada* First Novel Award. Unfortunately, the diabetes diagnosis kept him feeling low, both physically and emotionally.

In spite of his health issues, he continued to fit as many public appearances as he could around his required teaching schedule. He was invited to do readings across Canada, giving him opportunities to not only meet his fans, but to read new stories so he could gauge the public's interest in them. And while he enjoyed the invitations to read and sell his works, not all events were equally successful. One event, he privately fumed, had "THE WORST CROWD I HAVE EVER READ TO. About 18 people with all the animation of parking meters . . . including a male librarian who couldn't say my name."[10] He would later set out ground rules for events he was invited to:

1. I insist that your local libraries, or school libraries stock at least 75% of my books, all of which are in print . . . Check to make sure my books ARE available—the Indian stories are very often stolen from libraries.

2. Promotion. The most serious problem I encounter is that an organization will go to a lot of trouble to book an appearance, then relax and do nothing, assuming a crowd will automatically appear. A LARGE CROWD REQUIRES WORK. If you're not prepared to work please don't invite me. I insist that your organization guarantee a turn out of at least 50 people. My experience is that any town, no matter how small, can get 50 people together on a few hours notice for a shower, curling banquet or prayer meeting—I deserve at least a similar amount of attention [...]

3. Schools. I DO NOT BABYSIT. I will read and answer questions in front of any number of INTERESTED school children. Those students MUST be exposed to my work. They should be read at least one story of mine and have some idea of who it is they are going to see.

4. Accommodation. I have to reluctantly refuse to be housed in private homes, because I have been repeatedly frozen and housed in criminally substandard conditions. I prefer to eat in restaurants; please check with me if you plan a private dinner as I am diabetic and have many diet restrictions.

5. If these requirements frighten you off, good, we probably wouldn't have gotten along anyway [...][11]

As his time at the university drew to a close, Bill's health was his primary concern. Though he had dealt with a variety of health issues dating back to his childhood, some serious enough to have required lengthy hospital stays, he blamed his diabetes and stress levels on working in what he felt was a thoroughly unbearable environment over the previous five years. Specifically, he faulted the university's administration for being more concerned with the bottom line than they were with the quality of education students received.

Towards the end of the semester he was finally provided a platform to publicly air his grievances, in an interview with Tom Keyser of the *Calgary Herald*. Seeing it as a chance "to get my revenge on the assholes at U. of C.," Kinsella held back little as he vented about the university, its administration and academia in general.[12]

Viewing the administration as having more of an interest "in cramming as many illiterate students into university at whatever cost," rather than focusing on the quality of higher education, Bill asserted such an approach "makes a mockery of whatever education system there may be."[13] More specific to his own teaching interests and area of specialization, he had felt for years that those in positions to make substantive changes had repeatedly lied to him about having an interest in developing a creative writing program. Instead of teaching creative writing, Kinsella argued, "[t]hey gleefully allowed over 20 students, over 50% of whom were functional illiterates to register in my third year writing class, which I was forced to teach for two years."

Perhaps most frustrating, however, was his perception that the administration felt it had control over the faculty even when school was not in session. Feeling he had been lied to upfront, when he wasn't told he could not leave campus for the entire summer, Bill felt harassed. Privately, he focused his anger on the "pernicious, nitpicking, petulant faculty members [who] have made my life miserable," noting the relief he anticipated on leaving Calgary and contemplating "ways to do this incompetent university and this hateful city as much damage as I can."

Bill shared many of these thoughts with Keyser, and the response to the published interview was almost immediate. Department chair James Black took particular issue with Kinsella's comments about "plastic Calgary," with his notion that the adage "If you ain't dead, you ain't read" was being used to determine which authors' works were taught in the department, and Bill's references to "bonehead" students. He wrote a rebuttal in which he accused Keyser of having been manipulated by his soon-to-be-former colleague, whom he viewed as "an impressible spinner of yarns."[14]

Kinsella penned a response defending Keyser, whom he felt had been the target of Black's anger. Noting that Keyser "is a responsible journalist," Bill took full responsibility for his original comments, writing, "Black's ire should be directed toward me and not the *Herald* journalist."[15] He went on to amend what had been attributed to him in the original article:

> First, my mention of "If you ain't dead, you ain't read," was in referring to my own work, for while my books are taught widely in U.S. universities, they scarcely had the binding broken here at the U. of C. Second, I cannot understand Black's outrage at the term "bonehead" English. For no matter what euphemisms the English department may disguise them with, the two 200-level courses I taught were "bonehead" English. These courses were peopled mainly by students attending not because they wanted to but because they had to. Fully 50% of those students were so ignorant of basic writing skills they should not be allowed within 10 miles of a university [. . .] Third, let me say there are indeed bright and dedicated teachers in the English Department. But being bright and dedicated doesn't exempt them from being stymied at every turn by the stultifying bureaucracy. The bright people know who they are. Others, who choose to be offended by my comments, richly deserve to be.

In a final affront to Kinsella, a letter from Black was waiting for him after a promotional trip to Toronto, voicing the department chair's displeasure at Bill's absence while still under contract. Days later, the two men had a confrontation, at which time Black expressed his anger towards Bill's interview in the paper. And while he disliked confrontational situations, Bill felt he stood his ground.

The Moccasin Telegraph, his fourth collection of stories told in Silas Ermineskin's voice, was released that spring. The initial printing of 10,000 copies sold out in just nine weeks, further establishing his place in the Canadian literary canon. The collection explored the very real issues of drug addiction and alcoholism, attempts by the Cree people to reclaim their identity from the encroaching white world, Indigenous peoples being defined and confined by cultural and racial stereotypes, the feelings of inferiority promoted by religious groups coming to the reserves, and the continued oppression of Silas and his fellow Cree by the Canadian government, most often seen through interactions with the Royal Canadian Mounted Police.

However, Silas's reputation as a writer in these stories presented him with a new set of challenges not seen in the earlier stories he had narrated. In "Strings," for example, Ellsworth Shot-both-sides, who has been charged with murder and whose wife and children left him, tells Silas, "I read your book [...] I liked it," before giving him some of his own work to read.[16] Although Ellsworth relates to Silas as a Cree living on the reserve, he sees Silas's growing fame as a storyteller as a way of avoiding the traps of drinking and using drugs, telling him, "You got everything going for you." And while Silas has been able to use his stories as a way to cope with the harsh life on the reserve, the frustration and marginalization are no less real for him than for Ellsworth or any of the others who are subjected to living there.

In the earliest detailed examination of Kinsella and his collective work, Don Murray observed that "[t]he rough edges of the narrator's prose add to the authenticity of the tales, and Silas's growing Indian 'savvy' combine with his wit and candor to make him a fine straight man for his brothers as they con the officious or self-seeking white men who once conned them out of their native lands and rights."[17] *Publishers Weekly* also recognized the realism in the stories, praising the opportunity for readers to "feast on the exotic names alone" as "these small chronicles ring with authenticity."[18]

This fourth collection of Silas stories was eagerly anticipated by readers, primarily in Canada, who had developed an appreciation for the unique style and subjects Kinsella offered. Jay Carr saw the new book as Kinsella showing he was "well on his way toward carving out a tremendously compelling and unique piece of fictional turf. His Indians are like none you've ever met in the pages of a book."[19] For Americans only now being introduced to Kinsella's Hobbema stories, reviewers prepared them for the blend of humorous situations and sombre topics. Linda Leppanen noted, "A few of the stories are packed with laughs, but others are painfully sad because of their honesty" while recognizing the collection "is filled with disappointments,

John, Mary Olive and Billy Kinsella pose for a photo outside their home in Darwell, AB. With no other children to play with and homeschooled until age ten, Bill credited his imagination to the time spent alone as a child. PHOTO COURTESY OF SHANNON KINSELLA

While a student at Eastglen High School in Edmonton, Bill was discouraged by his counsellor from pursuing a writing career, something for which Bill never forgave him. PHOTO COURTESY OF SHANNON KINSELLA

Although Bill was never a serious athlete, his interest in sports could be seen throughout his life, as when he competed in local badminton tournaments during high school. PHOTO COURTESY OF SHANNON KINSELLA

He looked happy on the day of his wedding to Myrna Salls, but Bill later said the best things to come from his first marriage were his daughters. PHOTO COURTESY OF SHANNON KINSELLA

Near the end of his life, Bill noted he was most proud of raising his two daughters, Shannon (right) and Erin (bottom). PHOTO COURTESY OF SHANNON KINSELLA

A long-time fan and collector of Cree artist Allen Sapp's work, Bill first met the painter in Calgary in April 1981. Their friendship grew and eventually Bill wrote the accompanying text for a book of Sapp's work, *Two Spirits Soar*, published in 1990.
PHOTO BY DR. ALAN GONOR, COURTESY OF LIBRARY AND ARCHIVES CANADA, E011198110

Ready to launch his book tour for *Shoeless Joe* in 1982, Bill stands behind Ann Knight's Datsun, which was decorated specifically for the trip. PHOTO COURTESY OF LIBRARY AND ARCHIVES CANADA, E011198109

Bill had some happy times with his third wife, Ann Knight. They met in Iowa in 1976—just before Bill's career as a published author began—and were together until their separation in 1993 and divorce four years later. Upon Ann's 2002 death, Bill's daughter Shannon said, "Ann took a little piece of all our hearts with her." PHOTO COURTESY OF LEE HARWOOD

Although his time in Iowa is best known for inspiring the setting of *Shoeless Joe*, Kinsella memorialized Oakland Cemetery's Black Angel statue and its legend in his second novel, *The Iowa Baseball Confederacy*. PHOTO COURTESY OF LEE HARWOOD

Although he confessed he couldn't play the game well, Bill stepped in to bat at the *Field of Dreams* film set in Dyersville, Iowa, a site he would often visit with students from his summer classes at the Iowa Summer Writing Festival. PHOTO COURTESY OF LIBRARY AND ARCHIVES CANADA, E011198115

On the *Field of Dreams* set in the summer of 1988, Bill stands with his wife, Ann (left), actors Kevin Costner (centre), Gaby Hoffmann (child in front) and Amy Madigan (second from right), and the movie's screenwriter and director, Phil Alden Robinson (right). Bill was a full-time writer by the time *Field of Dreams* was released in 1989, and the movie made his work recognized around the world. PHOTO BY MELINDA SUE GORDON, COURTESY OF UNIVERSAL STUDIOS

Many of Bill's story ideas originated from places he visited or people he knew. This picture was taken at Gyro Park in Prince George, BC, where he developed the idea for his short story "Searching for Freddy." PHOTO COURTESY OF LEE HARWOOD

Going beyond simply reading his stories to the audience, Bill often gave his book events an air of performance theatre. PHOTO COURTESY OF LIBRARY AND ARCHIVES CANADA, E011198113

heartache and patois. It is a community that will touch your heart and remind you of the plight of the North American Indian."[20]

And while the new book enjoyed largely positive reviews in both Canada and the United States, some critics began taking issue with problems they saw in Kinsella's stories. Wendy Roy criticized him for leaving "gaps in the reader's knowledge of the character,"[21] a result of the stories having been published independently before being compiled in the collection. The result was, for some readers, a fragmented collection that assumed prior knowledge of characters and events in the current stories. Others saw unevenness in the book, often as a result of Kinsella's attempts at using humour to expose the serious issues confronting the marginalized people on the reserve. Barbara Rose, for instance, said, "Kinsella seems uncertain of his intentions . . . The critical element [. . .] rapidly disappears; the comedy degenerates into slapstick . . . Kinsella wants to criticize those who are unconcerned with the degrading plight of the Indians while showing what a jolly time they can have. Unfortunately, the two do not always mix," concluding by explaining that his comedy "does not convey a sense of necessity and lacks the conviction that the only other method is pointed denunciation."[22]

But the most serious critique came from those who had begun questioning Kinsella's use of the voice of the eighteen-year-old Cree, Silas Ermineskin, suggesting that a white writer using the voice of an Indigenous person living on a reserve amounted to, at best, cultural appropriation and, at worst, blatant racism. Though it wasn't the first time someone had raised the issue in his fiction, a largely positive review in the *Alberta Report* that summer included a sidebar titled "A call for repentance." It described a reading Bill had given at the annual meeting of the Alberta Conference of the United Church of Canada only a month earlier. The day after he had entertained the crowd with selections from his Silas stories, a resolution was proposed to the group condemning the works' "racist attitudes." The motion asked the delegates in attendance to repent "because we have participated in and encouraged the spread of racist attitudes."

The motion was never voted on, but Stan McKay, the UCC's coordinator of the National Native Ministries Council and Cree himself, said he personally did not find the stories offensive, going as far as to suggest, "I like to think I can laugh at myself."[23] And though such opposing voices were still very much in the minority, the issue would gain momentum with every new Silas story Bill published. At this point the majority of reviewers, however, saw his stories as a way of bridging the gaps between cultures, with Paul Pintarich asserting Bill "takes the simple, everyday incidents of contemporary Indian life and transforms them into tales comparable to parables of other cultures," using humour not as a way of insulting Indigenous peoples' plight but because humour, "often the best antidote for peoples who live perpetually in society's hard times," combines with suffering to "find common ground."[24]

By mid-summer, Bill and Ann had made the transition to their new home in the coastal British Columbia town of White Rock, a place that gave them the opportunity to live near the beach and in a milder climate than they had lately been used to. Though it may have been coincidental, Bill's blood tests that spring, taken the day after moving out of his campus office, indicated that his blood sugar was getting under control and his overall health was better than it had been in some time.

Finally able to focus solely on his writing, for the first time in his life, Bill continued working on his next novel—another baseball project that Larry Kessenich would also edit—and on more short stories involving baseball. He also began exploring genre fiction, which he'd never tried apart from a failed attempt at writing a Harlequin romance with Ann while living in Iowa. That winter, after reading Stephen King's *Cujo*, Bill contemplated writing a horror novel of his own. Curious about King's formula for success, Bill sat down with his copy of the book, reading it analytically, hoping to discover what made it work. And though he was unable to find a way to make King's horror approach fit his own work, it was one of many times when Bill combed through other popular writers' books in an effort of better understanding his craft and pushing himself to improve his own writing.

At the start of 1984, the royalties coming in from various projects ensured Bill and Ann would be free from financial concerns for the foreseeable future. Now, perhaps more than ever before in his adult life, Bill Kinsella felt he controlled his own course in life, finally fulfilling his dream that had been so flippantly dismissed by a guidance counsellor thirty years earlier.

That year his first collection of baseball short stories was released. Realizing that virtually nobody else was writing short fiction about baseball, and that only an occasional baseball novel had been released, Bill made a more concerted effort to fill what he saw as a gap in the literary market. Though the title story in *Shoeless Joe Jackson Comes to Iowa* had paved the way for his success with the subsequent novel, it was not until he was working on his second collection with Penguin, *The Thrill of the Grass*, that he began intentionally developing shorter works dealing with the game. The new collection of stories was released shortly before spring training began that year in February.

And unlike his previous collections, this book included an introduction, one in which he outlined the "little morsels of himself" that often served as catalysts for the stories.[25] The cup of cherry blossoms he gathered from the streets of Victoria for his daughter; the bird he killed as a boy and brought to his mother; the humiliation he suffered from a carnival barker; the vivacious, supportive, red-headed wife, and more all find their way from Kinsella's life into these stories. In "Bud and Tom," for example, the unnamed narrator begins the story claiming to have no fear of death for the simple reasons that, at ten years old, he had survived a near death experience that began as a case of strep throat and, as a fourteen-year-old, he had watched his Uncle Bud die suddenly in front of him at the kitchen table while playing cribbage. Both stories were taken from Kinsella's own life, though neither was known to anyone outside his immediate family and close friends. And though the narrator in *Shoeless Joe* and his father and twin brother shared Kinsella's surname, in "How I Got My Nickname" Bill inserted his own name into the story for the first time, retelling how William Patrick Kinsella had been given the nickname "Tripper" by Leo Durocher and the Brooklyn Dodgers during the 1951 season.

While such events from his personal life often acted as inspiration for his work, he did not view his fiction as being remotely autobiographical. "I've always felt that my life was uninteresting, so I created interesting lives in my writing."[26] However, quick to remind his readers that a successful writer needs to "liven up the dull, [and] tone down the bizarre until it is believable," he also admitted to weaving in "symbols, ironies, Biblical and mythological tales retold," while keeping to his primary purpose of entertaining his audience.

All eleven of the stories in the book had baseball in them. Some, like "How I Got My Nickname" and "The Baseball Spur," were told by narrators whose only connection to the sport was that they were fans of certain players or teams. Others, such as "Driving Toward the Moon," "The Last Pennant Before Armageddon" and "The Firefighter," focused on those who played or managed the game, though most of Kinsella's characters are affiliated with minor league players. The collection, with stories ranging from fantastical to sentimental to melancholy, allowed Bill to address specific issues within the game, some serious and others part of baseball legend. "The Thrill of the Grass," for example, is the story Bill wrote in the summer of 1981, during the baseball labour strike. The story's unnamed narrator visits a ballpark late at night to lament the loss of the game when he comes to see the artificial turf as an offence to the memory of the grass fields of his youth. "It was an evil day when they stripped the sod from this ballpark . . . rolled it, memories and all, into great green-and-black cinnamonroll [sic] shapes, trucked it away,"[27] he tells us, as he begins plotting to replace the artificial surface with real grass, enabling the game to reclaim its roots. Inviting other equally passionate fans to participate each night, the narrator and his compatriots' subversive acts serve as a way of undermining the owners and players. The characters felt both groups had lost touch with the game's romantic elements, and the fans now reclaimed the game for themselves. Kinsella's commentary on the game and the ways in which fans are often ignored by both players and owners resurfaced during the 1994 labour strike, when he vowed never to pay to attend another game for as long as anyone who was involved in the dispute was still playing.

In "The Last Pennant Before Armageddon," Kinsella incorporated the prophecy the caller had made during the radio interview in

Milwaukee while he was on the book tour for *Shoeless Joe*. He assigned the quote to Al Tiller, his fictional manager of the Chicago Cubs, who declares that "if the Chicago Cubs win the National League pennant, the world is going to end."[28] The Cubs hadn't won a World Series since 1908 or a pennant since 1945, and Cubs fans often thought of themselves as being cursed. The story provided fans with an explanation: a higher power was against them. In subsequent years, whenever the Cubs showed any hope of making it to the postseason, Kinsella's story would once again resurface as a prophecy of what would happen should the Cubs make it to the World Series.

Most critics and the public immediately hailed the varied, whimsical collection a success. Paul McKay recognized the author's love for the game and "his candid, affectionate eye picks out the funny, raunchy, poignant and absurd cast of characters who make up the fabric of farm-team baseball."[29] And Ken Adachi saw the stories not as baseball tales but as "folklore, fact and magic, nostalgia and sentiment; and they are all an attempt to grasp the roots of the human condition."[30] Elsewhere, the book was described as a group of stories that "deal with love as well as loss and desperation, emotions that often hover around baseball itself,"[31] tales that "are not so much about baseball as they are about dreams, love, loneliness, jealousy, and other themes."[32]

Other reviews singled out specific stories for consideration, though not all could agree on the stories' success. "Bud and Tom," for instance, was mentioned as one of the best stories in which Kinsella "artfully conveys the magnitude of the feud and the importance of baseball in men's lives,"[33] but was equally criticized for "[striking] out as a drab experiment in jumbled naturalism."[34] And though his best stories in the book were described as "wonderful stuff," John Keres was critical of his attempts to use the game so directly, referencing such stories as "whiffs" rather than home runs.[35] The title story, for example, was described by Keres as being "as boring as watching Astro-turf not grow." And Susan Monsky complained the stories were all too similar in nature, saying "over and over again, Kinsella yearns for the good old days of the game," noting that the author's overuse of the game grew tiresome: "Baseball as a vehicle, baseball as a metaphor: sometimes a baseball is *just* a baseball."[36]

In spite of some of the more critical commentary, baseball fans began recognizing Kinsella as a writer who could incorporate the game into his work and non-baseball fans were drawn to his ability to create likeable, sympathetic characters who struggled with life issues not dissimilar from their own. And while Elliot Krieger viewed the collection as "one of the few successful fiction books about baseball,"[37] Gail Hand concluded, "You don't have to like baseball to love W.P. Kinsella."[38]

Bill continued his practice of simultaneously balancing several projects, but shifted his focus more towards finishing his first draft of his next novel, *The Iowa Baseball Confederacy*, which Larry Kessenich had told him had tremendous possibility. By the start of the summer of 1984, Bill was, by his own estimates, 95% complete with *The Fencepost Chronicles*, 85% finished with *Honk If You Love Willie Nelson*, 80% finished with *The Iowa Baseball Confederacy*, and at least 60% complete on two other projects.

In an effort to implement a more regimented approach to his writing, one that allowed him time to both write and revise existing drafts, Bill began composing at least four pages of text, or editing the equivalent of four pages, for two consecutive days before taking a day off to catch up with correspondence or other personal matters. This allowed him to average eighty pages of creative output each month and was less intense than his old approach of working seven days in a row before taking a day off.

Under his new system, he soon finished the first draft of *The Iowa Baseball Confederacy* and was only a few pages away from completing another collection of Silas stories. Then, in September, Bill and Ann received a call from Ann's mother with the news that Ann's father had died of a massive heart attack while travelling with friends to a meeting. Bill had always enjoyed his father-in-law's company, and considered him "a good-hearted, loving man, who [. . .] made the best of a barely tolerable situation for the last forty years."[39]

Just weeks after Sam's death, Bill was copying the manuscript of *The Iowa Baseball Confederacy* to send to Houghton Mifflin when he heard that one of his literary inspirations, Richard Brautigan, had died. Brautigan's suicide shocked Kinsella—the troubled writer was not yet fifty years old, just four months older than Bill himself. Over the next several days it emerged that Brautigan had died alone, with perhaps as much as five weeks passing before his body was discovered.

Coincidentally, just three days before Brautigan's death was announced, Bill had signed a contract with Coffee House Press, an independent publisher in Minneapolis, for a collection of the stories he called his "Brautigans." And while some of the stories had been previously issued in literary magazines and journals, Kinsella selling them two and three stories at a time whenever possible, their unique styling made it impossible for them to be included alongside his other types of stories. The stories, which he later described as "fanciful," "magical" and having an "unusual point of view,"[40] were an openly acknowledged tribute to his favourite writer.

Within a month of submitting the manuscript for his second novel, Bill received a lengthy letter from Larry Kessenich in which the editor praised the first 200 pages but suggested several edits to the last 150. Kinsella began revising the story the following day. As the year drew to a close, Nancy Colbert called Bill with the news that Houghton Mifflin, pleased with the changes he had made to the manuscript, was prepared to publish *The Iowa Baseball Confederacy* with a $20,000 advance. At Bill's subdued response, Colbert said, "I wish Ann was on the line; she at least squeals a little at good news."[41] Though he was pleased with the news and with the money, Kinsella privately mused, "It's about fucking time; I deserved this to happen to me 20 years ago."

In 1985, closing in on his fiftieth birthday, Bill had finally reached a level of commercial and financial success he could have only dreamed about just a few years earlier. He thought back to the years spent working in sales, driving a taxi and building his restaurant, realizing how many more books he could have written if he had started his writing career earlier in life. Privately, he noted that, had he written one book a year starting at age twenty-five, he would have had forty books completed by age sixty-four. Instead, he calculated he would need to complete two books per annum to meet this goal by 1997—though he'd reached that pace since leaving Calgary.

Bill had begun completing books at a faster rate than his publishers were able to release them. He vacillated between making the edits Larry Kessenich suggested for *The Iowa Baseball Confederacy*, compiling and organizing another collection of Hobbema stories to send Nancy Colbert, and working on numerous other short stories. As his productivity continued at a fever pitch, he was asked to contribute his biographical information for inclusion in the *Canadian Who's Who*, something he felt would "be worth a few thousand 'I told you so's'" to those who ever doubted in his ability to achieve the level of success and notoriety he had come to know.[42]

Multiple studios had expressed interest in the film rights for *Shoeless Joe* once the previous contract from the year before expired, and that spring Colbert negotiated the option to 20th Century Fox for $50,000 towards a $250,000 purchase price should the film go into production. Following years of frustration in dealing with the movie rights for *Dance Me Outside*, Bill was one step closer to seeing his work being produced by a major motion picture company.

The day after his cheque arrived, Bill spoke with the movie's screenwriter and director, Phil Alden Robinson, a thirty-five-year-old whose prior film credits included co-writing *Rhinestone*, starring Sylvester Stallone and Dolly Parton, and both writing and directing *In the Mood*, a comedy starring Beverly D'Angelo and Patrick Dempsey. Robinson struck Bill as both pleasant and competent, traits that he had found lacking in others he'd met within the film industry. And while Bill initially hoped for a better-known name—perhaps his favourite director, Robert Altman—he later acknowledged the decision to have Robinson direct the film was the right one "because the screenplay was so good and it didn't get changed."[43] Kinsella also appreciated that, though he was not required to do so, Robinson stayed in regular contact during the writing process, letting him know what changes were being made. The result was that Bill was thrilled with the screenplay and the finished product, feeling that Robinson had "captured the essence of the novel."

After more than six years of marriage to Ann, the pressure from her to attend church was beginning to bother Bill more than it had in the past. He loved her and the relationship they had, but found it nearly impossible to "face those sanctimonious losers," and considered the entire experience "absolutely degrading."[44] Their arguments happened often enough to create a tension just below the surface of their otherwise happy relationship. Perhaps more than anything, Bill was frustrated by how Ann's Christian friends seemed to view him, and he never felt completely at ease with them as a result. Begging off from attending a church dinner with her one evening, he remarked, "Being with religious people is like being with parents, you can never be yourself, plus there is a smugness about every one of them, a condescending sense of superiority, which the more they try to hide it, the more it shows."[45]

The tension did not have an impact on his writing that summer, though, as he shifted back to working on baseball stories for a collection he planned to send Colbert in the fall. And while it would not be published for more than a decade, he began writing *If Wishes Were Horses*, a novel that would eventually incorporate two of his most recognizable protagonists from earlier works, Ray Kinsella from *Shoeless Joe* and Gideon Clarke from *The Iowa Baseball Confederacy*. In August, Coffee House Press published Kinsella's eighth book in nine years, *The Alligator Report*—his "Brautigans."

The Alligator Report includes both a dedication to Brautigan and an introduction in which Bill says he is unable to "think of another writer who had influenced my life and career as much."[46] Five years before, Bill had written a fan letter to Brautigan, and he closed his introduction to the quirky collection with it. Though he never received a response to the letter, Bill told the tortured writer about his own emerging career and recognized the influence Brautigan had on him getting to that point.

Reviewers of *The Alligator Report* were taken with Kinsella's range and his ability to adapt his writing style. Describing Bill's unpredictability, notable critic William French wrote, "If he's trying to impress us with his versatility, he succeeds," though French went on to say that "what he demonstrates most forcibly, despite his bizarre imagination and manic sense of humor, is his limitations."[47]

And though Paul Craig argued that Kinsella "does a better job with the sometimes similar subject matter"[48] than Richard Brautigan himself did, French was not so kind, arguing, "I'm not so sure Brautigan would be flattered."[49] Even the letter Bill had written to Brautigan in December 1980 was not spared critique. Cary Fagan called it "a rather pretentious celebration of Kinsella"[50] and Bronwen Wallace went so far as to claim, "Once you've read the fan letter . . . things slide rapidly downhill."[51]

The collection included stories vastly different from anything else Kinsella had published up to that point, and readers were unsure of what the shift in style signified. The issue for Thomas Woods was that Kinsella's "expansive, casual, almost rangy style, so suited to his longer stories, is not suited to the short, surreal Brautigan-esque pieces" in *The Alligator Report*. Woods hoped the collection represented less of a permanent shift in Bill's craft and more of "an accidental detour in an erstwhile satisfying journey through the world as filtered through Kinsella's keen perception."[52]

For Bill himself the book was an opportunity to expand his craft beyond the comedic social criticism from Silas Ermineskin and the baseball stories that had earned him his popularity. And the fact that *The Alligator Report* was published by a smaller press meant there was no great pressure to outsell any of his prior books, as no one realistically expected that to happen.

Perhaps more impressive than his prodigious output in 1985—over 1,100 pages of new material—or the dozens of public readings and appearances he made, for the first time in his life, Bill had earned over $100,000. It was validation and a confirmation that he had made the right decision in foregoing a life in academia. Bill acknowledged, as the year ended, that he was "Happy as I'm likely to get."[53]

9

Trouble on the Reserve

In January 1986 Bill and Ann flew to Hawaii, and Bill realized a long-time dream of living, at least briefly, in a warmer climate. During his first week at Waikiki Harbor, he settled in for what would be nearly three full months of living near the beach and writing. Drawing inspiration from his search for a condominium on the island, Bill began writing "Lieberman in Love," a short story about a middle-aged man who falls in love with his realtor while soliciting romantic advice from a prostitute with whom he is involved.

At the end of January, Phil Alden Robinson wrote a letter notifying Bill that, despite the screenwriter's love for *Shoeless Joe*, there was simply no way to keep the entire novel's storyline in the film as doing so would result in a movie well over a standard timeframe. Bill's succinct response, in the form of a postcard, instructed Robinson to do what needed to be done in order to make the film.

Shortly after, Bill signed a contract for "The Last Pennant Before Armageddon" to be adapted for the stage. Though he had nothing to do with writing the script for that production, he did sign on to be the playwright in residence for the New Play Centre in Vancouver for two months the following spring. His work would involve writing new material and adapting three of his existing baseball stories for the stage.

Coinciding with the start of baseball season that spring, Houghton Mifflin released *The Iowa Baseball Confederacy*. Once again using Iowa as the setting and magic realism as a way of connecting the past and present, Bill based the novel on its protagonist Gideon Clarke's dedication to proving the existence of the Iowa Baseball Confederacy, a league of amateur players from Iowa made famous when a team of its all-stars played the 1908 Chicago Cubs in what was supposed to have been an exhibition double-header. When the first game remains tied and a massive rainstorm sets in, the teams play for more than two thousand innings before the Confederacy all-stars win with the help of Drifting Away, a Native American player. Unfortunately for Gideon, the only other person who had knowledge of the facts concerning the league and the game with the Cubs was his father, Matthew Clarke, killed years earlier when he was hit in the temple by a foul ball at a Milwaukee Braves game. Kinsella incorporated elements of Native American traditional teachings and references to Christian traditions and lore that centred on father-son connections, which, combined with the fantasy aspect of time travel, created a plot that resonated with readers and critics alike.

As the majority of his literary output for nearly a decade had been either his Silas Ermineskin stories or baseball fiction, it may have seemed inevitable for Bill to combine the two topics. Realizing the appeal of the magic realism in *Shoeless Joe*, Kinsella took it to a new level in his second novel. He began, as he had with *Shoeless Joe*, by building on an existing short story. *The Iowa Baseball Confederacy* builds around "The Baseball Spur," a story published in *The Thrill of the Grass* two years before. Placing that story well into the book's third chapter, Kinsella prefaced it with a backstory so readers would understand the conflict confronting Gideon Clarke and used the events in the story as the portal through which Gideon and his best friend, career minor league player Stan Rogalski, are able to transport themselves more than seventy years back in time to 1908.

Gideon is soon watching Stan play for the Confederacy against the Chicago Cubs team of Tinker to Evers to Chance and "Three Finger" Brown fame. There are visits from Theodore Roosevelt, Leonardo da Vinci, and other baseball players and historical figures, and the game soon extends to a contest of literally biblical proportions when it rains for forty days, flooding the town and washing it off the map. The game, Gideon realizes, is actually a contest of wills between the Native American player, Drifting Away, and the tribal grandfathers with whom he is in conflict, fighting to reunite with his lover.

The book received mixed reviews from readers that summer. Some, anticipating a hopeful tale similar to *Shoeless Joe*, were frustrated by the often biting religious commentary and the acerbic tone. Others, however, appreciated the magnitude of the story, and the crossing of historical, cultural and literary boundaries. Certain critics took exception to his subject matter. Beginning with *Shoeless Joe*, Bill had published three baseball books—two novels and one collection of short stories—in four years. Kenneth McGoogan observed that Canadian writers such as Leonard Cohen, Robert Kroetsch and George Bowering had written in the magic realist style but had been "internally concerned with 'Canadian' subject matter," making Bill "an anomaly [who had] 'gone American.'"[1]

Perhaps because of the enormously high expectations set by *Shoeless Joe*, *The Iowa Baseball Confederacy* was, for many, a disappointment. Eric Gerber found the use of fantasy forced, stating, "What was fresh and magical in the first novel, seems calculated and recycled this time out."[2] And Patrick Ercolono felt Bill "[suffered] from the sophomore jinx" with a novel "bogged down by bloodless, lifelessly drawn characters who are hard to care a whit about."[3] And even those like John Gayton, who recognized Bill's ability to convey the story's magical aspects, saw the baseball game itself taking up too much of the novel's plot, more than one hundred pages, making it, as one critic said, "protracted and anticlimactic."[4]

Kinsella remained proud of *The Iowa Baseball Confederacy*, defending its plot and style. Concerning his approach to fiction, he told one reporter, "My feeling is fiction writing is dreaming and creating things. You can dream up things that are much more interesting than real life."[5] To another, he said, "In magic realism, people tend to believe what's happening is real. I write about the power of dreams, and how far you have to go to make them happen."[6]

And many critics concurred, viewing the novel as further evidence that Bill had reached a level unmatched by his peers, with Chris Farlekas writing, "No other contemporary novelist captures the eternal appeal of baseball like W.P. Kinsella."[7] Michael Bandler maintained that the book's success may have been dependent on the "reader's willingness to suspend disbelief, to surrender to the supernatural, to give into the wondrousness of childhood," all things made possible by Kinsella's prose.[8] Perhaps the most glowing endorsement came from noted baseball writer Roger Kahn, who proclaimed, "We are reading a writer here, a real writer, Muses be praised . . . which at once distinguishes *The Iowa Baseball Confederacy* from the glut of anecdote-filled ghosted baseball memoirs."[9]

In any case, Bill's work continued selling well and he remained in constant demand for workshops, book festivals and personal appearances across the United States and Canada.

After the novel was released, he began revising his latest collection of Hobbema stories, *The Fencepost Chronicles*, scheduled for publication later that year. It had been nearly four years since the last collection of Silas stories. Though these stories, like the earlier four books, are told from Silas's point of view and deal with life on the Hobbema Reserve, this book is the first in which Bill intentionally made each story humorous, because he was intent on winning the Stephen Leacock Memorial Medal for Humour. Though the stories are told from Silas's perspective, Frank Fencepost's character takes a more dominant role as he masterminds a variety of schemes to make money and embarrass the white establishment. And for the first time in his short fiction, Bill combined the two genres for which he was best known—humorous Hobbema stories and baseball fiction—into the same story, "The Managers."

Released in Canada in the fall of 1986 and in the United States the following year, the book reignited the cultural appropriation and racism debates that had been gaining momentum among academics and some readers with each of the previous collections. Still, Bill maintained, "I write about people who just happen to be Indians."[10] And as had been the case with earlier collections, *The Fencepost Chronicles* was seen by some critics as being stale repetition of previous works. The loosely connected stories, bound together only by the consistency of characters and settings, were described by Jim Spencer as "hybrid literature . . . a cross between a novel and a collection of short stories. Events don't relate to one another, but the characters never change."[11] And while each individual story was credited for "[standing] on its own and Kinsella's evocative prose and wacky humor held a reader's interest throughout," Fred Liddle criticized the collection as a whole for "[suffering] from a sameness. His characters eventually grow tiresome."[12]

Most troubling, perhaps, was the criticism that went beyond the individual stories and questioned Bill's overall style. Whereas so many of his early stories had been praised for the inventiveness and his approach in dealing with serious issues in a humorous manner, he was now being criticized for not expanding his craft: "Kinsella doesn't seem to be pushing himself here. The result is a minor work that sometimes has a weak charm, but too often fades away to a Cheshire cat grin."[13]

The return to the Silas stories demonstrated once more Bill's ability to defy some readers' expectations, making it difficult to simply label him as a baseball writer or a writer of humorous Silas Ermineskin stories. Critic William French described him as "the most ambidextrous writer on the Canadian scene. With one hand he writes fantastical baseball novels that defy time and logic yet have a curious inner truth. With the other he becomes a Cree Indian and spins comic tales about life on a mythical Alberta reservation. In either territory, there's no one remotely like him."[14]

But easily the most discussed topic among critics was whether or not Bill's stories had long ago crossed the line from witty fiction to offensive cultural appropriation and outright racist narratives. With each book of Silas stories following the release of *Dance Me Outside* in 1977, Bill's critics spoke out more emphatically about his use, as a white man, of an Indigenous voice to tell the stories and whether or not he had, intentionally or not, crossed the line into disrespectful and blatantly offensive pieces that disregarded the plight of the Indigenous people on Canadian reserves.

Jim Spencer noted, "W.P. Kinsella walks the fine line between racism and humor that marks most ethnic jokes. His Indians are not people but types. That they bring laughter instead of outrage testifies to Kinsella's deft touch."[15] And Frank Moher recognized that a new collection of the Silas stories would "no doubt stir up new charges of racism against its author for writing outside his own culture," but seemed to forgive any racism, whether intended or not, by explaining, "That's what happens when a book is as honest as it is funny. And *The Fencepost Chronicles* is very, very funny."[16]

Michael Dorris wondered whether the line between good-natured fun and mean-spirited lampooning was something Kinsella had begun crossing in this collection: "There is no doubt that Kinsella wishes us to laugh *with* the Cree Indian characters as they spoof and overturn the pomposities of government bureaucrats, Royal Canadian Mounted Police, Christian missionaries, and university do-gooders, but does he invite us to laugh at them as well?" Dorris more pointedly asked readers if they would "tolerate so well a book about those same characters if they were blacks or Jews instead of Indians" and if "the self-deprecating jokes that people, or family members, make about themselves and at their own expense, [are] really quite so funny when told by an outsider to other outsiders who don't know the rest of the story?"[17] Similarly, while noting the stories as a whole are "all good fun," William French admitted he could not "escape a nagging feeling that this isn't really the way it is on reservations, even in Alberta, and that Kinsella may be doing the Indians a disservice by pretending it is."[18]

Yet many continued to view Kinsella's as a voice for and not against Indigenous people. Rather than seeing Bill as lampooning the fate of the Cree on the fictional Hobbema Reserve, Paul Pintarich said, "Kinsella makes the point that these people who have been humiliated for generations have regained, through humor, their pride, a modicum of acceptance and a wry kind of existential *joie de vivre*."[19]

Fred Liddle saw Bill's newest book as humorous, although "one soon recognizes his empathy for the reservation Indians. Stripped of dignity by government bureaucrats, they survive with cunning and wits."[20] With Kinsella's reputation as a humourist extending into the United States by this point, American critics like Norbert Blei had begun seeing his work in the broader spectrum of American literature: "While the growing body of modern American literature concerned with the North American Indian continues to enhance our experience with their culture, one is seldom amused by the ways of life depicted. But Kinsella . . . often goes for the laugh and succeeds brilliantly, tellingly, much in the way of a modern Mark Twain and often (deservedly) at the expense of the white man."[21]

In November, Bill was notified that Houghton Mifflin would release *The Fencepost Chronicles* in the United States the following year, bringing another collection of Silas stories into the American marketplace, the second collection to be released in both Canada and the United States. Additionally, the company was planning to publish his next collection of baseball stories, *The Further Adventures of Slugger McBatt*.

As the year drew to a close, Bill's career continued its upward trajectory. In 1986 for the first time he had published two books—*The Iowa Baseball Confederacy* and *The Fencepost Chronicles*—in the same year. And though his diabetes continued troubling him at times, he and Ann were financially secure. With multiple projects already under contract, the momentum in Kinsella's career and the optimism in his personal life remained unabated.

Bill began 1987 at work on *If Wishes Were Horses*. The novel's protagonist, Joe McCoy, a former major league pitcher, lives in parallel universes. Kinsella inserted two existing characters, Ray Kinsella (from *Shoeless Joe*) and Gideon Clarke (from *The Iowa Baseball Confederacy*), to help establish the story's narrative. He would have a completed draft ready to send Nancy Colbert later that spring, but the book would remain unpublished for nearly another decade. As would be the case with *Butterfly Winter* and *The Winter Helen Dropped By*, Kinsella held onto manuscripts for a decade or longer before they were finally under contract and released by a publisher. In some cases, the manuscripts languished for over twenty years before release.

The Fencepost Chronicles found new life in 1987 when it was released in the United States, within weeks of another new collection, *Red Wolf, Red Wolf*, a sampling of short stories that didn't fit into either the baseball or Silas Ermineskin categories. For only the second time in his writing career, Bill included an introduction for his collection. As he often spoke out against those who wrote autobiographical fiction, he acknowledged in the introduction that two of the stories in *Red Wolf, Red Wolf* contained elements of his own life, including a visit he once made "to a mental hospital outside Boston to rescue a friend who had a breakdown while on a business trip."[22] And he credited his Yugoslavian grandmother, Baba Drobney, for his storytelling ability. The grandmother and the story about her were, in fact, entirely made up, though for years afterwards, reviewers would describe the influence Baba Drobney had had on her grandson's life. Bill's explanation to readers for why he used so little autobiography in his work was simply, "I always maintain that my life is too dull to write about."

Red Wolf, Red Wolf was his first foray with a mainstream publisher into writing short stories that did not fall into either of the two approaches with which he was usually identified. The result generated high praise from friends and family, including his oldest daughter, Shannon, who felt it was the best collection he ever wrote. Kenneth McGoogan said it included "some of the finest stories Kinsella has ever written" and that he had "learned to control his great gift for metaphor, which now intrudes only rarely."[23] Others thought the book ranked "among the best of Kinsella's prodigious output"[24] and that Bill had explored "the sort of disenfranchisement experienced by ordinary folk populating the short fiction of such diverse American writers as Bobby [*sic*] Ann Mason, Raymond Carver and Andre Dubus."[25] Being recognized as an American writer and not only a Canadian writer legitimized the notion Bill had years before when he described himself as a "North American writer."

Ken Adachi, however, observed that, in this book, Kinsella "makes the mistake of trying to will himself into the psyche and the diction of his narrators and, because he doesn't seem to know much about them, he shrinks his characters down to minimal clichés."[26] And when examined in comparison with his previously published works, the book was considered by Mary Walters Riskin as "a disappointment."[27] Burt Heward, however, thought the stories were more sophisticated and mature than previous work, "echoing such writers as John Updike, Mordecai Richler and Philip Roth."[28]

Comparing the collection with *The Alligator Report*, William French thought Bill was trying to demonstrate "that he can write other things besides whimsical tales about Indians in Alberta and fantastical inventions about baseball, on which his reputation rests," with the stories revealing "a commendable understanding of ordinary humans and their sometimes baffling behavior."[29]

Until this collection, much of Bill's criticism of officials and institutions like religion and government lording over the people was limited to the stories set on the Hobbema Reserve, while baseball offered a glimpse of an idyllic world in which fallen characters could find redemption and achieve some type of forgiveness or reconciliation. In *Red Wolf, Red Wolf* French saw Kinsella asserting his own worldview more emphatically than he had before, a worldview that seemed to be "anti-middle class" as "he views members of that group as passionless, overly concerned about security and . . . bored silly. His sympathies are with the lovers, the risk-takers, the anti-establishment individuals who swim against the current." This was the attitude Bill had shown for years in his personal life. He was a man who had left academia in frustration more than four years earlier and whose office for years had a sign on the wall asking visitors, "Have you told a bureaucrat to go to Hell today?"

Kinsella's reputation as a storyteller, particularly with his Silas Ermineskin stories, continued growing—his statement from Oberon early in that year indicated that *Dance Me Outside* had sold over 25,000 copies and showed no signs of slowing down. And though the accusations of appropriation continued after *The Fencepost Chronicles* appeared in the United States, some within the Indigenous community embraced what Bill was doing in his stories. One such supporter was Art Beaver, a student at Trent University, who called Bill that spring to convey how much he enjoyed the stories, specifically those in *Dance Me Outside*, and how, as an Indigenous person himself, he felt as though he had lived with the characters on the fictional Hobbema Reserve.[30]

The appreciation Bill felt from his fans was reciprocated when he was accepting an award in Vancouver that spring: "For a writer appreciation completes the artistic process. And I thank you for that. Appreciation is also a 2-way street, and I'd like to thank the readers who go into bookstores and buy my books. You keep me off the streets and allow me to fulfill a lifelong dream of earning my living as a storyteller."[31] Soon after, the Canadian Booksellers Association named him Author of the Year. Then he was notified he had made the shortlist for the Stephen Leacock Memorial Medal for Humour. His response, based in no small part on the fact he had written *The Fencepost Chronicles* with the specific intention of winning the award, was, "I'd fucking well better be."[32] Weeks later, his plan was realized when he won the Leacock and the accompanying $3,500 prize. Given the nature of the award, he was somewhat amused when the media awaiting him in Prince Rupert, British Columbia on the day of the announcement, appeared to have no sense of humour. After he told the reporters that winning the award "was right up there with the time my [high school] class voted me most likely to be murdered," they asked him what school he attended and what year he graduated.[33]

In 1987 Ann's mental health took another turn for the worse. That summer Bill determined that she had once again started skipping her medications after she began "writing some very strange stuff."[34] Blood tests revealed that her lithium levels were low and she was admitted to Vancouver General Hospital for psychological assessment before being transferred for more extensive testing and treatment. She was discharged after a lengthy stay, but the experience reminded them both of how fragile her mental wellness was.

At the end of the summer, Bill started yet another project, what would become perhaps the most autobiographical of his novels to this point. It began as the story "Truckbox Al's Big Break," but within three days of writing it Bill had started making notes for transforming it into a novel to be called *Box Socials*. Kinsella's humour had most often been seen in his Silas Ermineskin stories, while his baseball fiction was known more for its sentimentality, focusing on the protagonists' attempts to reconcile themselves with some past failure or misgiving. Years earlier, when describing his use of humour as it specifically applied to the Hobbema stories, Bill explained that he saw three broad categories of humour: blatant, absurd and innocent, the last being "where the narrator doesn't realize he's funny."[35] Viewing his own style as either innocent or sometimes blatant, Kinsella finally decided to write a humorous baseball novel. *Box Socials* was a semi-autobiographical narrative in which an adolescent boy, Jamie O'Day, tells the story of living in western Alberta, a setting based on Bill's own childhood experiences in Darwell nearly half a century earlier.

And while part of its plot focuses on a young man from the community having an opportunity to play in an all-star game in Edmonton's Renfrew Park, *Box Socials* is less about baseball and more about Jamie O'Day's innocent observations of growing up in a largely immigrant population. It is also the first of Kinsella's novels to incorporate a humorous voice. O'Day makes fun of the absurdities and human fallibilities Kinsella himself often found funny. At fifty-three years old, Bill had, for the first time, started incorporating many of his own life experiences from his formative years on the farm into his fiction.

Working most of the year under the assumption that the film version of *Shoeless Joe* was moving forward, Bill received a call in October notifying him that 20th Century Fox was no longer interested in producing the film. Then, four days later, Phil Robinson contacted him to say the script had been sold to Universal. Though the script had been written at 20th Century Fox, when studio president Larry Gordon left the company, he was able to take a few select projects with him, including the script for *Shoeless Joe*. Gordon and Robinson were able to pitch the script to another company, but the studio that decided to film it was responsible for negotiating a deal with Fox for the movie's rights. After considering options from several studios, they ultimately decided on Universal. So confident was Robinson in the film becoming a reality that the studio had started scouting possible locations for filming, including farms in southern Ontario, Illinois, Wisconsin and Iowa. Knowing the novel would undergo various changes and adaptations, Bill was still surprised when Robinson informed him that J.D. Salinger's character had been changed into Terence Mann, an African-American countercultural writer to be played by James Earl Jones. When the script arrived a few weeks later, Bill was moved to tears by how well the adaptation was written. His exuberance only grew when the cheque for $180,000 arrived weeks later, assuring him the film had entered production.

Despite the struggles he and Ann faced while dealing with her mental health issues that year, Bill's productivity flourished and he had another collection of baseball stories slated for release. He had added writer-in-residence for the New Play Centre to his résumé, with three one-act plays set to debut the following spring, just in time for the beginning of baseball season. The plays were based on three of his baseball stories in *The Thrill of the Grass*—"The Valley of the Schmoon," "The Night Manny Mota Tied the Record" and the title story. And though he had no way of knowing the film's impact at the time, it would soon secure his place in American popular culture in perpetuity.

10

"... He Will Come"

Ever since *Shoeless Joe* had been published, six years before, magazine editors and media outlets had been contacting Bill for his thoughts and opinions on all things baseball related. Writing and answering questions about topics ranging from Joe Jackson's continued banishment from the game, as well as the Hall of Fame, ballpark concessions and the prospective outcomes for each season, Bill had become one of the foremost sources on the topic of baseball. But he was hardly more than a casual fan before the novel was published. As he continued writing book reviews, he was often approached about writing reviews for newly released baseball-related books. When approached by the *Los Angeles Times* about reviewing Roger Angell's *Season Ticket*, Kinsella declined, explaining, "I don't feel all baseball writers should review each other's work."[1]

The two writers had a prior history as Bill had offered multiple stories to Angell, who had served as the editor of *The New Yorker*, for years. In late 1978, Bill pitched a draft of "Shoeless Joe Jackson Comes to Iowa," but the story was rejected, despite Angell's interest in its style, because he and his staff found it to be "sentimental and even a little predictable."[2] And when *Shoeless Joe* was released and Bill was on the promotional tour with Ann, the two men appeared together at a bookstore in Chicago. Fortunately for Bill, the store had several dozen of his books in stock. Unfortunately for Angell, his publisher had neglected to ship his new book to the store. Watching Angell complain about having to sign stickers to be pasted inside the books once they arrived, Bill noted, "The joke, I think, was on him—he'd been rejecting my stories for the past 15 years."[3] He was soon being compared to Angell. Denny Boyd thought Kinsella's baseball prose surpassed that of "the American giants, Roger Angell, Roger Kahn, and Thomas Boswell."[4]

Though he was reticent to write reviews of baseball-related works, he certainly showed no sign of slowing down his own output within the genre. Finishing the draft of *Box Socials* at the start of 1988, he soon wrote an introduction for the one-act plays adapted from *The Thrill of the Grass*, which opened to an enthusiastic audience in Vancouver that spring. He also began *The Winter Helen Dropped By*, the second book in the (non-baseball) trilogy he had envisioned just weeks after completing the first book, *Box Socials*.

His reputation as a baseball writer only expanded as his second collection of baseball fiction, *The Further Adventures of Slugger McBatt*, was released in the spring. The book was well received by critics, and even *Maclean's*, which had drawn Bill's ire when it published a negative review of *Shoeless Joe*, had praised it, "the first time those SOBs have ever said a kind word about me."[5] Once again, readers were drawn to his ability to articulate a love for the game that was shared by so many. Stating that "Kinsella's work is grounded in his love for our best game, and he has imagination enough to keep finding in it fresh and surprising possibilities," a review in *Kliatt* boldly proclaimed that the collection, "ranks right up there with *Shoeless Joe* . . . and *The Thrill of the Grass*," calling each book "gentle, funny, and sad by turns."[6]

Kinsella's work had arrived amid a dormant period in serious baseball fiction for adults, and he had found fans of the game hungry for fiction about the game, much like readers of Bernard Malamud and Mark Harris had been years earlier. Bill Ott described him as being "at the top of his form in these baseball-related short stories" as he "[u]nlike many fiction writers, who use baseball as a metaphor for whatever catches their fancy . . . respects the game for itself."[7] Morton Ritts went so far as to claim his stories "lift the sport to the level of myth" and demonstrate "why baseball appeals as much to readers in armchairs as to spectators in the stands."[8] And though Marylaine Block argued "probably no one uses baseball as metaphor better than Kinsella,"[9] others maintained the collection was "sometimes marred by a single nostalgia too exquisite for even die-hard fans,"[10] and that Bill made a habit of "[settling] for glib O. Henry endings ("Punchlines," "The Valley of the Schmoon") and, elsewhere, needlessly inflating his material," though even this critic admitted that the "uneven collection" was "sustained by graceful writing."[11] *Publishers Weekly* called him "a whiz at bringing characters to life, at capturing the emotional bonds that make people cling to and care for each other."[12] Perhaps most flattering for Bill, however, was when *USA Today* reviewed the new collection and claimed, "If the Baseball Hall of Fame can create space for pine tar bats, it certainly should create a Kinsella Reading Room."[13]

Bill's work would soon reach an even bigger audience as, after so many years of discussion and numerous delays, *Shoeless Joe* was finally being filmed. Phil Alden Robinson had settled on Don Lansing's family farm outside of Dyersville, Iowa, as the primary set location, bringing the story back to the idyllic landscape in which it was created. Arriving in Iowa in early June, Bill, Ann and Shannon met the director and the film's star, Kevin Costner, and many of the crew members. Though initially intrigued by the activity on the set, Bill soon grew bored while watching filming in a feed store scene from various angles, each requiring a seemingly infinite number of takes.

The following day, Bill and Ann sat in the sweltering auditorium where the crew was filming the PTA scene in which Annie's character gives an impassioned speech about censorship. Iowa was in the midst of a terrible drought and Bill grew exhausted, from the heat and the process, though he remained impressed at the stamina exhibited by Robinson and the rest of the crew. And though he had no interest in returning to the set for filming, for the remainder of their stay he did enjoy seeing the dailies from the previous days' shooting, providing him a glimpse of what the final product would look like.

Several weeks after returning from the set, Bill, who was always interested in seeing whatever movies were currently in theatres and renting ones friends and family recommended to him, watched *In the Mood*, a film from the previous year that Phil Robinson had directed. Describing it as "awful, like a novel that should never have been published," Bill privately noted he would have had no confidence in the director had he seen the movie earlier. Still, he remained optimistic Robinson was "someone who learn[ed] from his mistakes."[14]

With the filming complete and two novels in progress (*Butterfly Winter* and *The Winter Helen Dropped By*), Kinsella attended the thirty-fifth Eastwood High School reunion, an event that afforded him an opportunity to return to his school having achieved his goal of becoming a successful writer. Most enjoyable, however, was that Bill could share in the successes of his former classmates, whom he reflected, "as a whole . . . were an extremely successful class."[15]

Following the trip to Iowa for the filming that summer and a self-imposed respite from writing in the fall, Bill's output towards the end of 1988 more than made up for the lost time as he completed four more baseball stories in a ten-day period. These pieces, "Lumpy Drobot Designated Hitter," "The Dixon Cornbelt League," "Wavelengths" and "The Arbiter," pushed that year's output of new and revised text to over 930 pages, nearly twenty pages more than the previous year.

With the film adaptation of *Shoeless Joe*, still without an official title, due in theatres the following spring, and his best financial year ever coming to a close, Bill started what would become a tradition until his death more than twenty-seven years later: writing an annual "self-serving" letter in which he provided an overview of his year, both personal and professional, and commentary on anything political, religious or social that had happened to irritate him during the previous year. Realizing that his life had become so busy that he could not possibly write to everyone individually, he explained to his friends and family, "I've decided to write a stretch-letter, a one-size-fits-all letter."[16] But rather than replicating the types of holiday letters often sent, ones that told of only the positive things in a person's life, his own desire was "to see an honest Christmas letter, you know the kind you never receive:

> George has had two affairs so far this year, and as always we're only staying together because of the children, the little bastards. George Jr. spends all his time in his bedroom watching pornographic videos. I'm still embezzling money from the beauty parlor where I work, and though George's father was able to spend the holidays with us, one of the conditions of his parole was that he not go within two blocks of the day care center.

While he may have relished the idea of a brutally honest letter, a letter that his friends came to anticipate each year, Bill admitted his letter would be as self-serving as any, allowing him to promote his work and share the previous year's successes. He used the first letter to acknowledge the role Ann, his wife of ten years, had in his life, as she "continues to smooth the way for me in many ways, as she has done so wonderfully in the past, and to generally make the world a better place." In addition to her church work and volunteering to sing for people unable to leave their homes whenever possible, Ann continued updating an extensive bibliography of Bill's work and related reviews and biographies. For the first time in their relationship, the couple collaborated on a project, *Rainbow Warehouse,* a book of poetry Ann was editing, which had been accepted for publication in 1989 with Pottersfield Press, a small Nova Scotia imprint.

Though Bill had composed poetry sporadically for years and felt he could have published many collections before then, he maintained that making more money as a fiction writer prevented him from becoming a poet. *Rainbow Warehouse* included fifty poems, eighteen of which were written by Ann, and featured artwork on the cover by Bill's best friend, Lee Harwood. No longer in a position where he felt every book needed to sell more than the previous one, Bill found the poems allowed him the chance to explore a genre he enjoyed, which readers would not expect from him, and provided Ann a platform from which to publish her own work.

The poems vary in subject and length but are often reflections on Bill and Ann's time together. "Roadsongs," for example, is subtitled "vignettes from a 1982 book promotion tour" and recounts many of Ann's memories from the thousands of miles they logged promoting *Shoeless Joe* throughout Canada and the United States. Some of Bill's poems, like "Vows" and "One Generation," are dedicated to family members. The only poem Kinsella's fans might have been able to attribute to him had his name not been included with it is "Casey at the Bat—1988, or On First Looking Into Casey's Homer," a parody of Ernest Lawrence Thayer's classic "Casey at the Bat." Although the collection provided a new creative outlet for Kinsella, it was largely overlooked, as most of his fans preferred the genre to which they were accustomed.

For Bill, 1989 began with the excitement of the upcoming release of the still-untitled movie and a new collection of Silas Ermineskin stories, *The Miss Hobbema Pageant*. But the ulcers that had plagued him off and on for years had begun troubling him again, and when Ann began another spell of intense writing, it signalled to her husband that she had stopped taking her lithium regularly. As they prepared for their now annual trip to Hawaii, however, her health improved and Bill was able to resume his regular writing regimen.

Upon returning from Honolulu after their three-week vacation, Bill and Ann received a message from Phil Robinson, who informed them that the film would be called *Field of Dreams*. A month later, the director called with encouraging news from an early screening—he had been told Steven Spielberg and Amy Irving, Spielberg's wife at the time, were both moved by the climactic scene with Ray and his father tossing a baseball between them. Though still weeks away from the official premiere, both Kinsella and Robinson were encouraged by the reaction.

With the movie slated to open in Dubuque, Iowa, on April 20 and at a Vancouver screening the following day, Bill spent much of the month doing interviews across the United States and Canada. He was excited to share an early screening with his closest friends and family, including his daughters, Shannon and Erin; Lee and Maggie Harwood; and Spider and Jeanne Robinson. An early preview on April 12 moved Bill to tears. He was touched by seeing his own work on the screen and impressed by Phil Robinson's adaptation of the novel.

Though he had been doing book tours and promotional appearances regularly for more than a decade, the release of *Field of Dreams* kept Bill busier than he had been even during the promotional tour for *Shoeless Joe* seven years earlier. During one trip to Toronto he was featured on a CBC-TV segment, spoke to four classes at a local school, and was accompanied by a film crew to Exhibition Stadium, where he watched a Blue Jays game. Unfortunately, the trip was marred by a nasty fall while leaving the venue. Tripping over a brace sticking out from a fence, Bill fell in the parking lot and landed on his face, requiring him to visit the emergency room that night. Despite cracking his cheekbone, he kept his commitments the following day, as he had a full docket of interviews scheduled. And while he had to later threaten legal action against the team to recoup his medical expenses, he also began making plans for a short story about a fan who takes on all the injuries of his sports hero.

Even though much of the spring was consumed with film promotion, Bill was also preparing to see *The Miss Hobbema Pageant* released in the United States, his twelfth book in as many years. Published in Canada the year before, the book had started generating more controversial reviews, with some claiming the stories were little more than manifestations of Kinsella's racism.

By the first week of May, *Field of Dreams* had already made nearly $9 million and would be on over 400 screens by the middle of the month. When he went to see it himself for the second time, Kinsella enjoyed it even more than during the preview. Finding himself overwhelmed with publicity commitments and preparing for his next book to hit the shelves, Bill took a prolonged break from writing in May, a rare disruption in his normally rigid work schedule. In early August, after a summer filled with more screenings and interviews, Robinson called to let Bill know of the studio's post–Labour Day push to publicize the movie even more and of the plans for a worldwide opening by the year's end.

One of Bill's great pleasures in having the film in theatres was being able to share the success with his friends and family and those who had, in their own ways, helped him achieve the acclaim he had earned after so many years of working. Described by her granddaughter as someone who was "well-read [and] could write up a storm herself . . . a great teacher," Bill's mother, Olive, struggled to understand his ability to make a living solely as a writer.[17] Olive and Aunt Margaret had a better grasp of Bill's popularity and success after seeing the film. And in August, Veda Ponikvar from the *Chisholm Free Press*, the woman who helped Bill and Ann with so much of their Moonlight Graham research years earlier, sent him a letter with a story from her newspaper. The film's impact transcended those close to him as well, as he received a fan letter from former Lt. Col. Oliver North, who had gained fame for his role in the Iran-Contra affair that spring. The impact on popular culture was apparent to Bill when he opened the newspaper on August 26 and saw that Charles Schulz's entire *Peanuts* comic strip was based on *Field of Dreams*. It was not long before iconic lines such as "If you build it, he will come" and "Is this Heaven?" began making their way, in various incarnations, into the American lexicon.

The film's success not only helped increase *Shoeless Joe*'s popularity, but also helped soften the negative publicity that had come when *The Miss Hobbema Pageant* was released. Although many critics praised the collection for its humour, biting social criticism and portrayal of life on the reserve, it also received more negative backlash than any of the earlier collections had, with most of the dissenting voices focusing on the ways Bill portrayed life for the Cree people, his appropriation of the Indigenous voice for his own benefit and what some went so far as to claim was overt racism.

Some critics noted that the popularity stemming from Kinsella's baseball stories might have begun to be overshadowed by the charges levied against his Silas stories. Greg Heaton said, "[Kinsella's] five Ermineskin books have earned at least as much popularity as his baseball stories and a lot more controversy," and referenced what had become Bill's standard response to such accusations: "He's not a racist, he's a storyteller."[18]

For years, Bill had claimed his Silas stories were about a marginalized people who dealt with oppression from the government, religion and police. Many of his most vocal critics, like Heaton, however, had started to question that thinking, including one who wrote:

> ... if it's true that Mr. Kinsella's stories are universal, in that they do not depend on their characters being Indian, then why doesn't he write about naïve, unschooled white people, instead of picking on natives, a group trying hard to shed these stereotypes? And why does he make them speak in that ridiculous Tonto patois? The only answer is a paraphrase of the author: he is a storyteller, not a social reformer ... Storytelling, it would seem, is its own justification.

Sarah Harvey concluded that "Most of the humor that comes from Frank [Fencepost] is racist and sexist, and he has become a tiresome character."[19] But Joan Donaldson saw Bill's characters and the minimal background information he used as an indication of his strengths as a writer: "Despite a lack of research into native culture, Kinsella deftly creates a fictional world so convincing that apparently even his readership is surprised to find he is Caucasian."[20]

In addition to critics from the literary world, those inside Bill's former life as an academic had also started to voice their concern about the stories. The most vocal and adamant critic was Rudy Wiebe, a professor at the University of Alberta, and someone Kinsella had first met soon after arriving in Calgary in the fall of 1978. Wiebe maintained that Bill was guilty of cultural appropriation, using his interpretation of First Nations voice, customs and stereotypes to offend Indigenous people under the guise of humour. In the most controversial and vocal criticism of Kinsella's works to date, Wiebe went so far as to suggest residents living in Hobbema on the actual Ermineskin Reserve sue Bill "for using their name, and to claim his royalties as damages."[21]

Kinsella's outrage was immediate and he responded through the media, pointing to Wiebe's "nerve to advocate where I could locate a novel, especially from someone who professes to proclaim free speech" and calling his former colleague a "sanctimonious, humorless academic, feeding at the public trough." Wiebe, however, felt that Kinsella's stories only reinforced "the negative stereotypes already plaguing [Indigenous people]" and that "a writer must write responsibly. He has the social responsibility not to slander people."

Bill's response to Wiebe's criticism left no room for uncertainty regarding what he felt about both the attack and Wiebe personally. The day after the initial comments were published in the *Edmonton Journal*, Bill was a guest on a CBC radio show where he voiced his outrage that "a petty, sanctimonious little academic like Rudy Wiebe . . . would have the nerve to tell me, or any living writer, what to write, or where to set stories. It is even more surprising because academics often pretend to be in favor of freedom of expression."[22] The following morning, on a separate show in Calgary, Kinsella continued his rant, fuelling a debate that would remain in the media for weeks to come.

And such criticism was not limited to academics who took offence to the stories. After many years of Kinsella claiming the response from Canada's Indigenous population was largely positive, some in the community had begun voicing their opposition. Marilyn Buffalo McDonald, a Hobbema resident who had served as Advisor on Native Affairs for the University of Alberta, was quoted in an *Edmonton Journal* review, calling Kinsella's latest book "insulting and pornographic" and amounting to little more than "one white man's twisted fantasies."[23]

In an open defence of Kinsella published in the *Edmonton Sun* following the comments by Wiebe and McDonald, Graham Hicks proclaimed such attacks came "from that holier-than-thou crowd cloistered in academia, in government-subsidized self-interest groups and journalism."[24] The stories' universality, he said, lay in the fact that they are about "wonderful, larger-than-life characters who have very funny, very touching adventures," which could be set in a "small village in the Philippines, Peru or Itchy Bottom, Sask. It's a place where everybody knows everybody for life, where faults are glaring and usually accepted." And while those speaking out against the stories often used the Frank Fencepost character as the prime example of the supposed racism running rampant on the pages, Hicks argued "thousands upon thousands of lively Canadians—black, white and brown—behave and talk like Frank."

But the most emphatic part of Hicks's commentary came when he addressed Wiebe and McDonald by name, claiming they "do not understand that Kinsella's Hobbema tales, by not haranguing, lecturing or selling guilt, do more to improve the public perception of Indians than hundreds of tomes subsidized by Native Affairs or Canada Council . . . [his critics] miss the deep compassion and heavy humor of a populist writer like Kinsella—who communicates so much better with the average Canadian reader than that smug, isolated critic."

And while more critics than before seemed willing to address the potential racism, some of these same critics saw the controversial style as allowing readers to reconsider their own thinking and attitudes towards Indigenous people. "Kinsella blatantly perpetuates some native stereotypes," John Holman noted, "but at least he gives faces. There is some truth in his stories and it can't be denied . . . [his stories] make us think of our own frailties and strengths, and once all things are considered, how equal we all are."[25]

Amid this debate, Ann's manic traits had once again began to manifest themselves. Upon her return from a trip to Seattle in November, Bill noticed the change in her behaviour. Hoping it would pass once she was home, he worried as he watched her mood deteriorate to the point that he had her admitted to Peace Arch Hospital in White Rock, where she stayed for nearly three weeks before being allowed to leave on brief furloughs home.

Even with the backlash towards his work from critics like Wiebe, however, Bill saw the situation's silver lining as the controversy had generated free publicity. Responding to the latest wave of criticism towards his work, Bill said he had considered Silas Ermineskin and the other Cree characters retired, but the most recent controversy had inspired him to release at least one more collection of their escapades, saying, "We can't keep enough books in the stores, and it's all thanks to Rudy Wiebe."[26]

11

"Nowhere to Go but Down"

I n January 1990, days before leaving for a six-week vacation to Hawaii, Bill Kinsella gave an interview during which he was informed of the existence of an "Indian group [that] is looking for ways to stop me writing any more Hobbema stories."[1] Suspecting Wiebe had some involvement in orchestrating the movement, Kinsella privately fumed about the "petty sons-of-bitches" while recognizing, "When you're #1 you have to take some shots."

Bill left the controversy behind during his and Ann's annual escape, but his notoriety resulted in an invitation to a session of the state Senate while there, where he was introduced and presented with a certificate of merit. And never one to miss an opportunity to read his works or sell his books, he used part of the vacation to read to a large audience at the University of Hawaii.

Impressed with Phil Robinson's adaptation of *Shoeless Joe*, Bill and Ann were thrilled when *Field of Dreams* was nominated for three Academy Awards: for Best Picture; Best Writing, Screenplay Based on Material from Another Medium; and Best Music, Original Score. Still, Kinsella was disappointed that the film's three most notable actors—Kevin Costner, James Earl Jones and Burt Lancaster—were shut out entirely in their respective acting categories. Building on the movie's success, both the British and Japanese paperbacks used Costner's picture on the book's cover, connecting the novel with the film for readers.

Bill returned from Hawaii only to leave a few days later for another round of readings and book festivals. Due in large part to the renewed interest in *Shoeless Joe* following the success of *Field of Dreams*, Bill would present at over fifty public readings in 1990, keeping him on the road for nearly five months in total. And though he enjoyed the opportunity to read to and interact with fans, he confided in his closest friends and family that he might start cutting back, so he would have more time writing at home.[2] In spite of the rigorous pace, Bill continued revising *If Wishes Were Horses*, which he hoped to send to Larry Kessenich later in the spring.

The publicity intensified once more in March when *Field of Dreams* failed to win any of the Academy Awards for which it was nominated. In spite of that, the attention the film's nominations brought to Bill's writing led to a phone call three days later from Bill Thompson with Briarwood Writers' Alliance, who represented, among others, fellow Canadian writer Margaret Atwood. The Massachusetts-based Thompson told Kinsella that he would be able to ensure even more readings, particularly on university campuses. Knowing the value such opportunities would present for increased sales, as well as giving him venues for reading new material, Bill recognized it may well have been "one of the most important phone calls [he] ever received."[3]

On May 25, the day he turned fifty-five, Bill travelled to Sudbury, Ontario, where he was presented an honorary degree from Laurentian University. And while his own experience as an academic at the University of Calgary had not been especially positive, Bill was impressed with the humour he found at Laurentian: On the certificate were printed the words "IF YOU BUILD IT HE WILL COME" in Latin. Despite his disdain for academic life, Bill could now officially be introduced as Dr. William Patrick Kinsella. Not long after that, his mentor, Bill Valgardson, called to inform him that his alma mater, the

University of Victoria, had decided to confer an honorary degree on him the following year.

In July, Bill noted upon getting a cheque for over $92,000 that he used to make only $2,400 for an entire year. Unfortunately, his enjoyment of this success was tempered by physical issues, as his stomach ulcers started flaring up again.[4] The stress in his life was exacerbated that summer when his mother, now eighty-seven years old and still living with his Aunt Margaret, suffered a serious stroke. After several weeks in the hospital, Olive remained in precarious health and her mind had deteriorated to the point that she could no longer remember if her son was even in the room, or if he had been there previously. Though she would live for another eight years, by early winter her mind had slipped so much that, even though she remembered neighbours from Darwell over forty years before, she began mistaking Bill for her late husband, John.

While dealing with Olive's deteriorating condition and fighting his own health issues, Bill was committed to a book tour that fall for the U.S. release of *Red Wolf, Red Wolf*, taking him to Dallas, Shreveport, Minneapolis, Lexington and several other cities and reservations across the country.

Just days after returning from the *Red Wolf, Red Wolf* tour, he attended the launch for *Two Spirits Soar*, a book about the work of his favourite artist, Allen Sapp. In his first foray into non-fiction, Bill had written the copy, telling the story of Sapp's life and artistic career, and of the influence the painter had on Kinsella himself. Bill and Ann had acquired an impressive collection of Sapp's work over the years and loaned eight of their paintings for the grand opening of the Allen Sapp Gallery in North Battleford, Saskatchewan.

In the fall of what he would later describe as "the year being famous caught up with me,"[5] Bill flew with Ann to Barbados to begin a two-week cruise back to Los Angeles, visiting Aruba, Panama, Costa Rica and Mexico. And though the vacation gave him a much-needed break, a new two-book, $60,000 contract for *Box Socials* and *The Winter Helen Dropped By* ensured that he would continue writing for the foreseeable future. While he looked forward to the new books, his ulcers and diabetes made 1990 his least productive year in at least a decade and a half. Knowing the demands on his time were unlikely to ease in the coming months, he privately noted that he would "have to concentrate on compartmentalization, which is how I managed to turn out such a volume of work in the past. I *must* set aside time to write and then put everything out of my mind and write. Writing *must* be first priority. Everything else *can* be done after my writing is accomplished for the day." With a renewed commitment to the process that had proven so successful in the past, Bill closed the year with fifty pages of another new novel, *Magic Time*, completed.

After years of spending an extended part of their winters in Hawaii, Bill and Ann chose to stay closer to home that year, visiting Palm Springs, California. Settling first into a motel in January, the couple soon bought a small condominium close to the downtown area, giving them a getaway where Bill could concentrate on his writing during winter visits. By this point in his life, Bill had grown to love the warmer weather and southwestern climate so much that he began proclaiming the only thing keeping him from becoming a United States citizen, a benefit of his father's own citizenship, was the fact that Canada had universal healthcare, something that had become increasingly important to both Bill and Ann. Indeed, Bill began worrying himself sick again that spring when Ann began acting agitated, insisting her husband attend "a second-rate evangelical crusade" in Palm Springs.[6] Though he conceded in an effort to appease her, it did little to ease his mind about her mental state. Following a doctor's visit the next day, they were relieved to find her lithium levels were within the acceptable range, though Bill still harboured serious concerns.

Following what he felt had been a disappointing year as far as his creative output was concerned, Kinsella committed himself to finishing two novels in the coming year. The first, *Magic Time*, was another baseball story set in Iowa. The second book, *Conflicting Statements*, was a mystery thriller, Bill's attempt to establish himself in another genre.

In late spring, he mailed the manuscript for *Box Socials*, which had been complete for some time, to his publisher. Considering he had already won the Leacock Medal and had gained a reputation in both Canada and the United States for his humorous short fiction, it was not insignificant when Bill told friends that the story was "the funniest book I've ever written."[7] He began focusing his energy on completing the *Conflicting Statements* manuscript, which he still hoped to have done by year's end, and working on *Magic Time*. Perhaps his greatest challenge, however, was achieving balance between his personal life, his professional obligations and his determination to maintain his reputation in the literary world.

Though he had received numerous awards and honours in recent years, the honorary doctorate he received from his alma mater, the University of Victoria, that spring held a special place for Kinsella, allowing him to share his success with former professors and mentors, including Bill Valgardson and Robin Skelton, both of whom were influential in his early career. Never one to pass up the opportunity to needle his friends still teaching in the university setting, Bill told a crowd at a reading before the ceremony that he preferred driving a taxi to teaching in academia because "you meet a better class of people driving cab."[8]

And while he didn't miss the politics and pettiness of teaching university, Bill was pleased when his success as a writer provided him the opportunity to teach creative writing workshops, the only part of the profession that ever held any interest for him. In early July of 1991, he returned to the classroom, just for a week, at the Iowa Summer Writing Festival, hosted by the University of Iowa. With only one class to teach, Bill was able to provide the class with an intimate, hands-on approach to their craft, something he had always felt was sorely lacking at Calgary.

For the first time since the filming of *Field of Dreams* three years before, Bill returned to the Lansing family farm in Dyersville, Iowa. Following the film crew's departure in 1988, Don Lansing, whose family had owned the farm for years, kept part of the baseball field on his property rather than plowing it up to plant corn. His neighbours, Don and Rita Ameskamp, had returned to farming their portion— left and centre fields. When life began imitating art and fans began showing up to visit the site just weeks after the film's debut, the Ameskamps decided to return their portion to its place in the outfield. And though some may have been put off by the site's commercial feel, Bill was thrilled to see it become a tourist attraction. In fact, he thought the Lansings should charge set price for admission rather than allowing people to come for free and offer a donation.

Early that fall, *Box Socials* was released in Canada, though the U.S. release would not be until the following spring, in time for the start of baseball season. Though his baseball stories were always more popular in the States anyway, the book's Alberta setting and humour would resonate with his Canadian audience, making it his first novel to have obvious crossover appeal.

Following *Field of Dreams*, readers were greatly anticipating the release of *Box Socials*—it was the first baseball book from Bill since *The Further Adventures of Slugger McBatt* in 1988, a year before the movie premiered. And while no actual baseball appears until more than 200 pages in, one of the main storylines in the novel is based on Truckbox Al McClintock, a young man from a small town approximately sixty miles west of Edmonton and who has a tryout with the St. Louis Cardinals in the mid-1940s.

For years Kinsella had alternated between "nostalgia-soaked tales in which simple values, baseball and a death of idealism combine to make unlikely dreams come true" and "deliberately [exploiting] racist and sexist stereotypes for dramatic effect" in his Silas stories. One reviewer saw *Box Socials* as a "[switch in] focus to life in a non-native northern Alberta backwater in the 1940s," which combined "a syrupy ode to times past with an often scathing portrait of small-town small-mindedness."[9]

The story provided Bill an opportunity to explore gender roles and observations about the diverse immigrant population from his boyhood. And while the minute details and eclectic characters provide an entertaining glimpse of a bygone era, the book was criticized for lacking "a central character or story line strong enough to make its assorted parts into a coherent whole," with the chapters resembling "the patchwork quilts common in the communities like

Six Towns: the whole is colorful and homey, but is manufactured from odds and ends, rather than the maker's finest cloth."

And though *Box Socials* contained far less baseball than Kinsella's previous two novels, the game's role as a subplot was recognized by James Roberts as "central to the story, since it provides a focus around which all the other stories revolve."[10] The book, however, was not intended to be another baseball novel in the vein of *Shoeless Joe* or *The Iowa Baseball Confederacy*; rather, it was meant to be a comedic story, an approach Kinsella had yet to showcase in his novels.

By this point Bill's fiction had generated a body of academic work worldwide. Dating back to his time teaching in Calgary, he was sent copies of papers from high school and university students who explored various critical approaches to his short stories and novels. In 1987, Don Murray, an associate professor in the English Department at the University of Regina, published the first book dedicated to Bill's life and growing literary canon. Though fewer than seventy-five pages total, Murray's book combined several hours' worth of interviews with Bill alongside critical analysis of all his published books to date. In the spring of 1992, an entire conference was held dedicated to scholarly examinations of Kinsella's writing, sponsored by Quad City Arts and five Iowa colleges—Augustana, Black Hawk, Teikyo Marycrest, St. Ambrose and Scott Community. Bill was named the fifth biennial Super Author in Residence. The W.P. Kinsella Conference, subtitled "Fields & Dreams: Merging Realism and Fantasy in the Work of W.P. Kinsella," included traditional academic scholarship, a screening of *Field of Dreams* as well as multiple presentations by and readings from Kinsella himself.

At the conference Bill acknowledged incorporating some of the very types of symbolism he chastised academics for focusing on, saying, "I am an old-fashioned storyteller. I try to make people laugh and cry. A fiction writer's duty is to entertain. If you can sneak in something profound or symbolic, so much the better."[11] By the fall, the scholarly examinations of his work grew to include studies from the graduate level, including a thesis from a student in Germany. And while he still felt academics tended to overanalyze books rather than allowing themselves to be entertained by them, such scholarship indicated that his work had found a wider readership and was being considered as literature among scholars at the university level, something that, while he did not often agree with it, Bill appreciated.

By the end of the year, *Box Socials* had sold well and had received largely positive reviews in Canada. And while his creative output had doubled that of his disappointing production a year earlier, Bill still lamented that he'd only worked well that year in Palm Springs. Returning there for the early part of 1992, Bill and Ann joined a Scrabble club, immersing themselves in a community dedicated to playing the word game the couple had enjoyed together for years. Though he became an accomplished player years later, Bill found his involvement with the group that winter embarrassing at times, when pitted against their superior ability.

As always, the time away from Canada rejuvenated Kinsella, and he prepared for a fifteen-city tour Ballantine had planned for the U.S. launch of *Box Socials*. With over 80,000 copies already on the shelves, he was optimistic about its chances of success. The positive reviews from major outlets like the the *New York Times* and *Library Journal* further lifted his spirits as the junket began.

Unfortunately, the tour's hectic pace, one that would take him from Arizona to Louisiana, Indiana and Washington, left him exhausted well before the second leg, which would take him to Washington, D.C., New York City, Boston, Detroit, Chicago and Dallas. With media commitments all day and public readings scheduled in the evenings before departing the following morning for the tour's next stop, Bill soon lost his voice and began feeling miserable. He made a particularly frustrating visit to the Canadian Embassy in Washington, D.C., where he was to be honoured. It began with no one meeting him at the airport, then arriving at the Ritz-Carlton to discover that the embassy had cancelled his reservation and had to rebook him at a smaller, more uncomfortable hotel in town. After an early morning apologetic phone call, he was finally given a room at another luxury hotel before reading to a large audience at the embassy. When the embassy attempted to apologize to Bill by sending him fresh flowers and two bottles of wine, his frustration had reached its limit. He was allergic to the flowers, and requested they be delivered to a local hospital, and he didn't drink.

After the book tour ended, Bill was free to finish working on *Magic Time*, his fourth baseball novel. Unfortunately, his work was interrupted by his concern for Ann who, once again, began appearing erratic. He hoped it was merely the result of her writing long hours preparing the exhaustive annotated bibliography of his entire literary canon, as well as a compilation of any reviews of his works she was able to procure. By the end of the summer, however, it had become apparent that her behaviour was more than likely the result of her missing her prescribed dosage of lithium.

In addition to his concern for Ann's health was the unease he felt when visiting his mother in late August to celebrate Aunt Margaret's birthday. After a trip to the Darwell farm at Ann's insistence, he visited Olive only to discover she thought her husband, dead for nearly four decades, was living by himself out at the farm.

That fall, after signing a contract with Southern Methodist University Press to publish a first U.S. edition of *Shoeless Joe Jackson Comes to Iowa*, Bill temporarily moved to Victoria where, after nearly a decade away from academia, he returned to the classroom as a visiting professor, teaching two courses in advanced fiction writing. While he had found the lower-level writing and literature courses and the committee assignments at Calgary to be mundane, he now discovered, when obligated only to teach more competent creative writing students, that he enjoyed being back in that environment. The teaching commitments and increased travel, however, contributed to what he declared was his "least productive year as a writer in the last 20."[12]

That winter, Bill and Ann prepared for their annual White Rock Writers Club Christmas party at the home in South Surrey, right near White Rock, that they now shared with Shannon. But the day of the party Ann's mental health once more threatened to take a serious turn. Returning home from church after Sunday services, she uncharacteristically attacked Shannon and a friend for inviting dates to that evening's festivities. Ann had always had a close relationship with both Shannon and Erin, and Shannon had mentioned to her father on multiple occasions that she often wished Ann had been her mother. And though Ann later admitted she was wrong, Shannon and her friend took their dates out for dinner, despite Shannon having prepared much of the food for the party that night.

The guests that night included close friends Carolyn Swayze and her husband, Barry Jones; editor Gary Ross; writer Douglas Coupland, and Coupland's guest, an emerging writer/poet, Evelyn Lau; and longtime friends Spider and Jeanne Robinson. And though the party eventually ended without any major incidents, despite the fact those close to Ann could tell her mental state was in question, it would play a pivotal role in Bill's life years later.

The following morning Bill began driving to Palm Springs, where Ann would join him days later. As soon as she arrived, Bill realized her mood was bordering on out-of-control, though he couldn't see why as she had been taking her medication during the previous months. When it became obvious she was in need of psychological help, he arranged for plane tickets back to Vancouver so they would not run the risk of her being hospitalized in the United States at $1,200 per day.

Ann was admitted to the hospital a day after they arrived back in Canada. After spending a week and a half in the hospital, she received an overnight pass to come home, though Bill noticed she was still exhibiting a more active personality than normal. Still, she was discharged completely on January 1, 1993. The stress and nervousness surrounding Ann's health, however, left Bill struggling to write.

While *Box Socials* was selling relatively well, though nowhere near the levels of his previous novels, Bill completed his next book, a collection of baseball short stories, *The Dixon Cornbelt League*, which was his first compilation of baseball fiction in five years. And, as usual, he was balancing other projects in progress, this time working on *If Wishes Were Horses*. His reputation in the baseball fiction genre was solidified that winter when he noted in his diary, "I'm truly famous. I was a $500 question on *Jeopardy* last night."[13]

That spring, after years of witnessing Ann's mental health struggles, he acknowledged to himself that he had been fighting a melancholy feeling for several weeks, which led him to take Prozac for a brief time. Though depression wasn't something that ran in his family, he had begun to recognize mood swings and depressive feelings that had never before been so pronounced.

With *The Dixon Cornbelt League* soon to be on bookshelves in Canada, Bill's professional life was going well, though his sales in recent years failed to match those from just a few years before. His personal life, however, had begun to show signs of unravelling. The strain of Ann's ongoing mental issues, coupled with his frustration at her not wanting to stay on her medication, had led him to begin questioning the stability of their marriage of more than fourteen years. Meanwhile, he had developed deeper friendships with two women—Evelyn Lau and Barb Turner. Lau, author of the memoir *Runaway: Diary of a Street Kid*, had attended the annual White Rock Writers Club Christmas party Bill and Ann had hosted the previous December. Though she was thirty-six years Bill's junior, they had corresponded in the months following and met for lunch, attended readings and shared in each other's literary interests. Privately describing Lau as "a remarkable young woman, candid and brave,"[14] Bill was becoming fascinated with her on both a professional and a personal level.

At the same time his relationship with Lau was intensifying, Kinsella also began spending more time with Barb Turner, a graphic designer. They had known each other for nearly ten years, since she moved to White Rock in 1983, and Bill began meeting her for coffee as it provided him someone he could talk to about shared interests and a break from worrying about Ann's mental state. That fall, Ann had begun to focus her energy towards trying to write a novel with such fervour that Bill suspected she might be nearing another breakdown. Waking up at four one morning, she had completed forty pages of the manuscript by the following day, during which time Bill met with Barb twice for coffee and to take walks, distancing himself from Ann.

In September, after years of disputes over contracts and film rights, *Dance Me Outside* finally began filming. And though he received

$25,000 as his share, Bill was frustrated that a portion of the previous option money had been deducted from the principal amount. His anger towards the film industry only grew and he lamented, "Fucking movie business—you shake hands with the bastards [and] they squirt right across the room."[15] The money did nothing to assuage his feelings towards the film, which he felt was poorly written and lacked the humour of his original stories.

For over twenty-five years, Kinsella had written very little other than fiction, with the exception of the few articles on which he and Ann collaborated and the opinion pieces, usually related to baseball, he had written for periodicals. And while he had regularly returned to teach at the week-long workshop at the University of Iowa, Bill often said there was very little that he could do to teach writing; instead, he saw his role as being that of a mentor who could help existing writers hone their craft, much like Bill Valgardson had done to help him at the University of Victoria years before. However, that October, *Writer's Digest* offered Bill a $10,000 advance to write a book focused on writing imaginative fiction, anticipating a 50,000 copy first printing. Though the book was never published, it provided Bill a chance to write about what he felt were the most important aspects of becoming a successful writer, incorporating many examples and anecdotes from his own career.

Before he would undertake the task of instructing others how to write fiction, he was kept busy with book events related to *The Dixon Cornbelt League*, released in Canada earlier in the summer to coincide with the start of the baseball season. His publisher had expressed disappointment in the number of copies *Box Socials* had sold, and there was some question as to whether his decade-long stint as the leading writer of baseball fiction was coming to an end. Bill, however, remained pleased with the book's sales and was undeterred. While his books had for years sold respectable numbers, Bill later lamented that, by the mid-1990s, "[publishers] decided that they only wanted people who sold like Stephen King."[16] *Box Socials* sold approximately 70,000 hardback copies, but the publisher did not want to even read his next book. Bill maintained it "was the beginning of the end for midlist writers like myself."

The stories in *The Dixon Cornbelt League* incorporated elements of fantasy and magic realism, with characters turning into wolves, long dead baseball players washing ashore after fifteen years of being lost at sea, and marginally talented players finding ways to alter their identities to stay in the game. Araminta Wordsworth saw the collection as an opportunity for professional redemption: "W.P. Kinsella returns to top form after the disappointing *Box Socials*, which seemed like a short story bulked out tediously to a short full-length book."[17] And Ken Belson praised Bill's return to magic realism as the stories "retain the appearance of normalcy, but each tale includes a heavy dose of the unpredictable. The yarns he spins are as much fact as they are fancy . . . [and] cover an entire range of emotions."[18]

And while Bob Minzesheimer argued that, when "[c]ompared with *Shoeless Joe* . . . *Box Socials* and *The Iowa Baseball Confederacy*, the stories in *The Dixon Cornbelt League* are more modest pieces of writing," he also maintained, "no matter how bizarre the story, his characters remain defiantly human . . . It's nine innings of magic realism, as if Isabel Allende and Gabriel Garcia Marquez had been hanging around a bullpen swapping stories."[19]

Not everyone, however, felt comparisons to Márquez were justified. Philip Marchand of *The Toronto Star* observed, "The supernatural functions in Marquez . . . as an expression of the strength and unruliness of human obsessions," but noted, "Kinsella's use of the supernatural bears more resemblance to the old television series *The Twilight Zone*."[20]

In spite of the mixed reviews, which were becoming the norm, critics like Jay Stone appreciated Bill's sympathetic characters and found it "genius that he is writing about more than baseball, for he uncovers in the game something of the mystery of life itself."[21] Stone also saw the stories as being "so spare that the tales do not read as short stories" and one said the collection read more like "a notebook for the real book that he intends to write some day." In fact, Bill soon took the book's titular story and began weaving it with other stories, including "Distances" and "Punchlines," both of which were previously published in *The Further Adventures of Slugger McBatt*, and "How

Manny Embarquadero Overcame and Began His Climb to the Major Leagues," included in *The Dixon Cornbelt League*. All of this fed into his ongoing project *Magic Time*, though it would be another five years before the novel was published.

As he promoted *The Dixon Cornbelt League*, the issue of cultural appropriation continued to cast a shadow. Jim Commandant, a Mohawk activist, began voicing his concerns and, as Rudy Wiebe had, called for Bill's Silas Ermineskin stories to be banned due to their lack of cultural sensitivity. Encouraged by Ann to meet with Commandant, Bill sat down with him, making no significant progress towards a solution but offering signed copies of his works at the end of their time together.

The next day, Ann's health took another turn for the worse. A month after that, with Bill now spending increasing amounts of time with Barb, Bill and Ann discussed the idea of a trial separation. They had spent seventeen years together, nearly fifteen years as a married couple. While Bill preferred to separate, Ann made it clear that she was opposed to the idea and wanted to stay with him or pursue a divorce, though she was adamant about wanting reconciliation. Following their talk, he privately mused, "She doesn't want separation. [She wants] all or nothing. So, guess it will be all."[22] Despite their years together, during which Ann had been vital in helping Bill research and market his work, he ultimately decided it was best for them to go their separate ways.

The following day Ann wrote a letter detailing their separation of assets, to which Bill agreed. He moved in with Barb less than a week after deciding to separate from Ann. The result of the stress from another failed marriage was that Bill's depression deepened as the year drew to a close. As he often did when his personal life was in disarray, he focused on his work, this time on the revisions for his next collection of Silas stories.

That winter, in early December, Erin gave birth to another son, Max. And while he was happy for another healthy grandson, he continued longing for a granddaughter—he had so loved watching his own girls growing up.

Despite the problems in his personal life and the downturn in his creative output, he remained optimistic about the possibility of the relationship with Barb and recommitting himself to his writing, setting goals of finishing *If Wishes Were Horses* and *The Winter Helen Dropped By*, and developing new baseball and Silas Ermineskin stories.

Bill asked Barb to accompany him to Palm Springs for the first few weeks of 1994. She was reluctant to travel, though, so he made plans to go by himself. Matters were somewhat complicated as Ann would also be living in Palm Springs for the winter (at a different location), staying in the beachfront condominium in White Rock during the rest of the year. Bill and Ann remained relatively collegial towards each other, even joining Erin for tea when they met Bill's new grandson.

While Bill was interested in seeing where the budding relationship with Barb would take them, his personal life grew slightly more complicated at the end of January, when Evelyn Lau called him late one night, close to midnight. They talked about their shared interests in film and the next day she sent Bill a seven-page love poem. It was both unexpected and, as he mused in his diary, "curious."[23] Meanwhile, conversations with Ann about the status of their relationship proved futile, with no progress being made. Simultaneously, all indications suggested Barb was far more serious about their future together than he had thought as she now mentioned the possibility of visiting him in Palm Springs, upset over how much time Bill planned to spend in California that winter. When she arrived, he was thrilled she had made the decision to come, admitting, "I really care for this woman."[24]

While he was in Palm Springs, Carol Bonnett at HarperCollins called to inform him that a film option had been taken out on "Lieberman in Love," the short story from *Red Wolf, Red Wolf* that Bill had written following his 1986 trip to Hawaii with Ann, about a widowed land developer who becomes involved with a prostitute in Hawaii, a relationship that encourages him to then pursue a romance with a married real estate agent. And though nothing was yet official, Warner Brothers had also been in contact about the possibility of offering a contract on *The Dixon Cornbelt League*.

Though he loathed the winter weather in the north, Bill returned to Canada in the middle of February to receive the Order of Canada. Established by Queen Elizabeth II in 1962, the award recognizes those who have demonstrated "outstanding achievement, dedication to the community and service to the nation."[25] And while he lamented that Ottawa was "too Frenchified" and "many people are rude if you don't speak French,"[26] the achievement further validated his career.

In late February, HarperCollins offered Kinsella a $20,000 contract for *The Dixon Cornbelt League* in the U.S. Unfortunately, the professional success was offset by a heated argument that same day with Barb, who had become critical of him. They made up shortly afterwards, but Bill worried the exchange was a bad sign. Though he was not one who relished public confrontation, he privately noted, "You don't treat someone you care for so unpleasantly."[27] Days later, after a particularly moody outburst from Barb, he wrote, in a rare detailed entry in his diary, "Barb's moods are just too much for me— she keeps making new rules, and I have to screen everything I say in case it offends her, and I still offend her because I have no idea what sets her off. She seems determined to be unhappy, whether it's just a really mean disposition, or whether she's consciously or unconsciously trying to push away anyone who cares for her, life is too short to put up with such erratic behavior."[28] And though they soon reconciled after these fights, the conflicts started happening far more frequently than he was prepared to deal with.

As had often been the case when his personal life was in turmoil, Bill's intense focus on his writing helped him channel his energy elsewhere. Over three consecutive days in early May, he began proof-reading the galley proofs of another collection of Silas stories; worked on revising *Russian Dolls*, a series of loosely connected short stories set in Vancouver in 1979, many of which were written in the style of his Brautigans in *The Alligator Report*; and sent the manuscript for *If Wishes Were Horses* to HarperCollins.

The steady stream of projects, however, could not prevent his issues with Ann from interfering with his work. Following a poorly written review in the *Vancouver Sun*, in which Ann was named as Bill's wife in spite of their separation, she wrote him an angry letter. He was sympathetic, but maintained the fault lay with the writer and not with him, as they had discussed only religion and politics. Three days later, however, Shannon called her father to inform him that Ann had been behaving strangely and that she had announced that she had stopped taking her lithium three weeks earlier. By early June, they had worked out a more formal separation agreement, something Bill had wanted for months as Ann held out hope for reconciliation.

That summer, Bill returned to Iowa City to teach another class at the Summer Writing Festival. He thoroughly enjoyed the experience, though he doubted many of the students would develop into successful writers. Perhaps more importantly, the trip afforded him an opportunity to reconnect with a landscape he had grown to love and a place where he often said he felt more at home than anywhere else he had lived.

Bill also made a significant professional change in the summer of 1994. By late August he had decided to leave his agent of more than ten years, Nancy Colbert, as she had recently relocated to North Carolina. Preferring to work with someone closer to him geographically, Bill signed an agreement with his longtime friend Carolyn Swayze—a novelist, biographer, columnist and lawyer—whom he had encouraged to enter into the literary publishing industry. They officially signed the contract in early September, and Bill left the only agent he had ever had to work with someone who was only just now breaking into the business.

Having published dozens of the Silas Ermineskin stories since *Dance Me Outside* first appeared in 1997, Bill had once thought *The Miss Hobbema Pageant* would be his last collection set on the Hobbema Reserve; however, the controversy from those like Rudy Wiebe had only caused more interest in the stories. The result was *Brother Frank's Gospel Hour*, the seventh Ermineskin collection, published in the early fall of 1994.

Like his earlier Silas collections, the eleven pieces in this book addressed the cultural contrasts between the marginalized Cree living on reserves and the dominant white culture in the rest of Canada. And though Silas still narrated the stories, with grammar and sentence structure that had evolved to show his growth as a writer, Frank Fencepost took a more prominent role in the book, finding new ways to fool the government, the police and the gullible populace of mainstream Canada with his various schemes.

Confronting those who held to the idea he was racist, Bill took the position that his stories "in all cases take the Indian side."[29] Some critics saw what Kinsella envisioned in his works, with one noting how he "makes short work of ludicrous governmental systems," most notably through Frank, who "is an inveterate liar, a con man, a sometime thief and a practically fulltime fornicator." In spite of his unseemly traits, Frank is one "who generally ends up more or less on the side of the angels, at least from the Indian point of view—as are most of Kinsella's characters."

But for some readers, stories like "Conflicting Statements," which graphically details a rape scene, began showing a darker side of life on the reserve and served as examples of why they felt it was time for Bill to no longer write in Silas's voice. Taking issue with Kinsella's own admission that he "[didn't] care to meet very many Indian people [as they] are not going to contribute much to what I write because my characters live in my head," Stephen Rouse of *The Ottawa Citizen* observed, "Judging by the arid inconsistency of the stories in this collection it appears Silas and Frank have migrated from Kinsella's imagination in search of greener pastures," and argued "their departure might leave some money in his publisher's budget for a couple of fresh, talented Native writers."[30] Kinsella, fuelled by the criticism he received following *The Miss Hobbema Pageant*, often relished those types of reviews as they made the commercial success his Silas Ermineskin stories brought him that much more enjoyable.

As had often been the case in recent years, achievement in his professional life seemed to be tempered by chaos in his personal life. Bill got word that fall that Aunt Margaret, now eighty-eight, had fallen off a chair and received several stitches. And his mother, debilitated by the stroke years before, now resided in a long-term care facility in Edmonton, and her health continued to decline. By the fall Barb and

Bill were fighting regularly, with him often complaining about her volatile personality and short temper.

In November, Bill represented the University of Victoria alumni on a two-week cruise, taking him from Miami through the Panama Canal, to Costa Rica and Acapulco. And while Bill and Barb used the getaway to celebrate their first anniversary as a couple, Bill's increasing frustration towards her attitude and angry outbursts left him even more uncertain as to what the future might hold.

By the following spring, the tumultuous relationship had grown even more fractured. Much of their arguing during this period stemmed from conflicting attitudes towards travelling. Bill enjoyed travelling and looked forward to his winters in California, and his writing dictated he be away from home for several weeks or even months of the year, teaching or reading at book events. Barb, however, did not share his enthusiasm, and her negativity towards such trips caused him to lament he was "really annoyed by [her] attitude to travel."[31] Compounding the problem were the times when Ann would call for Bill, and Barb would answer the phone "all snarky as usual."[32]

In early May, while he was preparing for a radio show and reading in Bellingham, Washington, Barb became angry with him, causing him to refuse to travel with her. After this, their fighting soon escalated to the point where her outbursts led to her embarrassing him in public. By mid-summer, what had been a relatively happy relationship months earlier had dissolved into almost constant confrontation.

As the problems between Bill and Barb grew more heated, he began talking more regularly with Evelyn Lau. A call to her in early June, during which he counselled her on problems she was having with her publisher, led to an invitation from her to attend an event at a local bookstore. By the end of July, they had begun meeting for lunch and coffee, discussing both their professional problems and achievements to their personal lives. On September 6, Bill attended Lau's book launch, finding himself increasingly interested in the aspiring writer who was younger than both of his daughters.

Arriving in Palm Springs in late September for a brief visit, Bill realized how much he now enjoyed being away from Canada, as it allowed him to distance himself from Barb. By mid-November, when they would normally be finalizing plans for the winter sojourn south, he informed her that she should not come with him to Palm Springs and that they should end the relationship.

The following day, he began driving to California, and two days later, he was back communicating with Evelyn. About two weeks into his winter retreat, Bill had a lengthy phone call with Lau, one that left him feeling optimistic about their relationship. By the end of the third week in Palm Springs, she arrived for what turned into a two-week-long cycle of writing, playing Scrabble, watching movies and lovemaking. After dropping her off at the airport to return home, Bill wrote in his diary that the time with her was "like a honeymoon" and that he would "really miss her."[33] He was surprised to find that Evelyn was interested in pursuing a more serious relationship and was hopeful that it would last. However, he also recognized the reality of the situation, the most obvious issue being their age difference, and was "prepared to simply enjoy [his] good fortune as long as it lasts."[34]

Nearly lost in the turmoil of his personal life was the publication of *The Winter Helen Dropped By*. When *Box Socials* was released in 1991, Bill envisioned it as the beginning of a trilogy focused on the rural community of his youth, all narrated by Jamie O'Day. It was not until 1995, however, that the second book was published. In the four years between the two novels, Kinsella had published a collection of baseball stories, *The Dixon Cornbelt League*, that had been met with mixed reviews and *Brother Frank's Gospel Hour*, which renewed the cries of racism against him.

Though the narrator in *The Winter Helen Dropped By* is the same as in *Box Socials*, he is growing into an adolescent becoming wise to the world—experiencing the pain of loss, discovering the often grim realities of an adulthood and being educated in sex. Like its predecessor, the book draws from Kinsella's love for storytelling in the Southern literary tradition. Referred to by John Doyle as "all old-fashioned yarn-spinning, lucid but meandering through many side roads,"[35] the book's narrative balances the youthful innocence its narrator possesses with the impending sense of loss everyone confronts while growing up. Doyle speculated that this latest novel "could well be Kinsella's response to the appropriation-of-voice controversy" though it "isn't an apologia for [his] territorial claims."

Like his Silas stories, both *Box Socials* and *The Winter Helen Dropped By* are set in rural western Canadian settings, focus on aspects of small communities and address the difficulties confronting people from these places on a daily basis as they struggle to survive. Unlike his controversial Silas stories, however, with Jamie O'Day Bill drew from his personal experiences, including his being homeschooled, having a lapsed Catholic father and being the only child around for miles. Noting this, Doyle commented that Bill "has a powerful and hypnotic voice and this novel is a novel to savour for its congeniality and artistic integrity."

Not everyone, however, was as welcoming of the new novel, and Colby Cosh asked, "Is he blazing a new trail, or has he lost his way?"[36] Having always been known for his strong characters, even when the plots of his books lacked depth, Cosh saw both *Box Socials* and *The Winter Helen Dropped By* as being filled with characters that "do not all get the respectful and careful development" that had long been a trademark, and went as far as to say, regarding the latest book, "character often seems to verge upon caricature."

The novel opens with Jamie's father telling his son, "Every story is about sex or death, or sometimes both."[37] As the story shows the boy's maturation, it is written in past tense, from Jamie's adult perspective. Paying special attention to the storytelling style in the narrative, Nancy Baele noted its strengths as being "its 1940s feel, its cast of characters . . . and its theme that a sense of history and community comes from the oral tradition of telling and retelling stories,"[38] though concluding that the novel overall was troubled by a fragmented plot that never fully develops.

Now sixty years old, Kinsella had begun to draw more from his personal life, specifically from the years on the farm. Perhaps commenting on the power his words had to outlast his own life, the critics who opposed his Hobbema stories, and anyone who had ever doubted his ability to earn a living as a writer, Kinsella had Jamie's father tell the boy, "What you speak, what you say dies on the breeze, but writing down, Jamie, that's a whole 'nother matter, almost forever. I want you to remember that, son. Writing down is permanent and almost forever."[39] Years later, Kinsella told a longtime friend that this novel was, in fact, the best glimpse into his personal life in Darwell that he had ever published.[40]

Following the book's release, Kinsella began 1996 by focusing once again on his baseball novels, putting the finishing touches on the manuscript of *If Wishes Were Horses*. Weeks after finishing the new novel, he sent another collection of Silas stories, *The Secret of the Northern Lights*, to his agent. The collection was his eighth and ultimately final collection of such stories as he felt he had written all he cared to from Silas's perspective. The following month, he was contracted by HarperCollins to edit a collection of baseball quotations, requiring him to do little more than compile excerpts of quotes from an assortment of players, managers, fans, umpires and writers, and to write a brief introduction for the book.

His relationship with Evelyn had progressed to the point where he had professed his love to her, and he took great pleasure in the late-night phone calls they shared and the poems she faxed to him at all hours. While Bill was spending a month at the Atlantic Center for the Arts in New Smyrna Beach, Florida, where he was the writer-in-residence, Evelyn flew to visit him, accompanying him on a side trip to Disney World, where he noted she was "a perfect companion."[41]

In late March Bill and Evelyn took a trip to Savannah, Georgia, and Charleston, South Carolina. While in Charleston they watched the Academy Awards together in their hotel room. When the award for Best Live Action Short was announced, Bill was stunned to see "Lieberman in Love," based on his short story, win. He had not been notified it had even been filmed, let alone nominated that year, and his shock quickly turned to anger when Christine Lahti and Jana Memel, the film's director and producer, stepped to the podium and "thanked everyone even peripherally associated," but not him.[42]

The following morning, Bill faxed Carolyn Swayze a letter for Lahti, which was immediately released to the media, and which read,

"While nothing can ever be done to right the situation, I cannot adequately express my rage and dismay at being treated so unfairly."[43] The result was a phone call from Memel, who apologized and agreed to issue an apology for the oversight and have it published in *Variety*. These gestures, however, did little to calm Kinsella's anger, both at not being recognized in front of millions of viewers, and at not having his name mentioned for other "Hollywood types" to hear, perhaps causing them to say, "This guy has had three movies made and they've garnered four Academy Award nominations and one Oscar, maybe we should take a serious look at his other books."

Upon returning to his condo in Vancouver later that spring, Bill began planning book events and personal trips with Evelyn for the coming months. Unfortunately, his enthusiasm was dampened when Evelyn called to express concern about their relationship and what might come of it. He understood this, and recognized the likelihood that, as time went on, she would most likely be attracted to someone closer to her own age, admitting, "I, unfortunately, have nowhere to go but down, both physically and mentally. And, I am slowing down."[44] The next evening, Bill joined Barb for dinner, at which time she expressed interest in rekindling their romance, something Bill was not yet ready to do as his relationship with Lau was still in a state of flux.

Later that spring Bill came home to find a note Evelyn had left informing him that she had read his diary and took his failure to mention the time he had spent with Barb over dinner and on shopping trips as lying to her. Rather than being upset about her leaving, Bill's anger was focused more on the fact that Lau had read his private thoughts, something he labelled "a great betrayal."[45] He had enjoyed the romance for the few months it had lasted, but he was seemingly undisturbed by the sudden break-up, acknowledging, "Evelyn is very needy emotionally, [and it] takes an awful lot of energy to spend time with her."

Never one to be alone for very long between romantic relationships, Bill was back with Barb within a matter of days. This reunion was short-lived, however, as he and Evelyn began exchanging letters by late summer. Following another major fight with Barb, Bill spoke with Lau, at which point both expressed second thoughts about their break-up that spring. After Bill broke up with Barb once again, she left an obscene message on Lau's machine, and Kinsella confirmed he had made the right decision for himself. Days later, he and Lau made their first appearance as a couple during a book event they attended, seemingly solidifying their commitment to each other and ending any hope Barb may have had of reconciling with Bill.

In late September, Carolyn Swayze gave Bill the frustrating news that U.S. publishers had rejected both *If Wishes Were Horses* and *The Winter Helen Dropped By*, citing that his book sales had lagged in recent years. While he personally considered the roughly 70,000 hardcover copies of *Box Socials* to be a not insignificant number, it wasn't enough to convince publishers to take a chance on the two new works. For the first time since *Shoeless Joe* was released more than thirteen years earlier, Kinsella's novels were having trouble finding a major publisher outside Canada.

Bill was disappointed, but not entirely surprised by the rejection. Years earlier, he had submitted an early draft of *If Wishes Were Horses* to Larry Kessenich. The story had an even more ambitious plot than either of his first two baseball novels at the time, but the editor was not impressed with the initial draft and did not want Bill hurting his reputation as one of the premier authors in the baseball fiction genre. Kessenich told him, "it's not a successful novel," and though he acknowledged, "There are . . . some very strong characters and scenes . . . even the best of writers sometimes pursue stories that do not work out as a whole, and I'm afraid that's the case here."[46]

Seeing the main characters in the earlier novels as Bill's greatest strengths, Kessenich bluntly informed him, "your protagonists are extremely likeable, whatever their flaws. They are not losers in the way McCoy is." In fact, the editor had grown into his role since first working with Kinsella seven years before as both navigated their ways through the process of writing and editing *Shoeless Joe*, and now suggested Bill publish only his best work and not something that would ultimately fall short of readers' expectations. Kessenich's honest assessment was that Kinsella would be better off forgetting the draft and developing the short story "The Battery" into a larger work, explaining, "I feel that is a story that has the germ of something bigger in it."

Bill, rather than taking offence to the honest criticism from his editor, responded, "I'm not surprised; my feeling was that the second section [of *If Wishes Were Horses*] didn't hold together well."[47] But rather than ignoring one draft for the other, he continued his lifelong approach of never wasting work he had already written. For nearly ten years, be worked sporadically on *If Wishes Were Horses* until its release and began expanding "The Battery" for nearly twenty-five years until it was published as *Butterfly Winter* in 2011.

That fall, still certain his novels were worthy of more serious consideration than what they had been given by American publishers, Bill embarked on a brief promotional junket for *If Wishes Were Horses*, which had been published by the Canadian division of HarperCollins and was, somewhat awkwardly at the time considering all that had transpired, dedicated to Barbara Turner. Though it was his second novel in as many years, it was his first book involving baseball since *Box Socials* was released five years before.

In spite of having written eighteen books—including novels, short stories and poetry—Bill's most well-known work, due in no small part to the film version, remained *Shoeless Joe*. And though he was thrilled to be remembered for the book, he later wished he had written it later in his career, after some of his other novels were published, since everything he wrote after 1982 was compared to the iconic story. Even *The Iowa Baseball Confederacy*, though appreciated for its magic realism and use of the game as myth, was often viewed as not quite measuring up to the standard its predecessor had set.

While *Box Socials* incorporated baseball as just one of its many plotlines, *If Wishes Were Horses* was Kinsella's first novel in which the game served a major role since *The Iowa Baseball Confederacy* a decade earlier. With the complex plot of parallel universes, Kinsella, perhaps more than ever before, blurred the lines between the real and the fantastic. Including Ray Kinsella and Gideon Clarke as characters in the story takes place only because, as John Doyle noted, "they are the only men who might understand what's been happening to Joe McCoy."[48]

Ultimately, Brian Bethune praised the book for its author's use of the game: "The infinite possibilities of baseball is Kinsella's trademark metaphor, and he uses it flawlessly in this tale of love and second chances."[49] Having reached a point where he was "writing for his audience with an instinctive intimacy," Kinsella was now, as Doyle commented, writing "moral fables in which the implausible is implicitly transcendent" with "characters [who] are always wary of moral evasions and deceits," making him "the contemporary inheritor of the 18th-century novel of high feeling and sentiment."[50]

Bill was already preparing a new book in which he would once again weave together material from previously published short stories. And despite the frustrating news he had received from the American publishers, *If Wishes Were Horses* was selling well in Canada and garnered several positive reviews. His productivity had declined somewhat from just a few years earlier, resulting in a poor year financially, but Bill's prospects were buoyed by the end of the year when the film rights for *If Wishes Were Horses* were bought by producer Marvin Worth with a rumour that George Clooney would star in the film. Then, just months later, Barry Levinson and Mark Johnson, who had worked together on *The Natural*, starring Robert Redford in 1984, and *Rain Man*, the 1988 blockbuster starring Tom Cruise and Dustin Hoffman, bought the rights for *Magic Time*, a novel that had yet to be released.

In 1994, TriStar had optioned the titular story from *The Dixon Cornbelt League*, though the film was never made. While the story was in limbo with the studio, Bill had worked on expanding the plot into the novel that would become *Magic Time*. As the option for rights on the short story lapsed, reverting to Kinsella, the unfinished book was purchased with the hope it would see the same commercial success that *Shoeless Joe* had brought him years before. And though the film rights for *Magic Time* had been sold before the book itself was in manuscript form, it was only a few months before the book was under contract with Doubleday Canada, ending Kinsella's longtime relationship with HarperCollins, after the publisher offered him what he thought was an insultingly low amount.

In early 1997, HarperCollins offered Bill a $5,000 advance on *Butterfly Winter*, a novel set in the fictional country of Courteguay. It involved weaving together some of his early stories, and centres on twin brothers who begin playing catch in their mother's womb, eventually working their way to the major leagues. The contract, however, included two stipulations. First, as the book was not yet completed, he had to agree to return half the advance if the publisher chose not to buy the finished manuscript, and second, he would be required to put aside his work on the two projects he was working on concurrently, *The Secret of the Northern Lights* and *Japanese Baseball*. The idea of being only worth $2,500 in Canadian dollars to HarperCollins was insulting to Kinsella, considering he had published eleven books with them. However, they had rejected his most recent collection of Silas stories, so Bill's decision was to take everything he had written elsewhere, believing his fans had always enjoyed his works and would have every reason to want to read these stories as well.

Unlike previous winters, spent in either Palm Springs or Honolulu, this year Bill and Evelyn left for a trip to Cuba where, despite the overwhelming humidity, mosquitoes and frustrations with the local food, Bill was able to write and play Scrabble nearly every day.

Upon returning to Palm Springs, Bill sold the condominium that had been his retreat for so many years, and by late spring he and Ann finally agreed to move beyond the separation stage. Though they had been separated since 1993, Ann indicated she still wanted nothing to do with filing for divorce. In a letter to Bill that spring, after he had taken steps to file a joint petition for divorce rather than one with him as the sole petitioner, she told him, "Such a petition asks me to say something I haven't ever been willing or able to say, that I 'want' our marriage ended." While acknowledging the "abandonment of the honesty that made living together easy and joyful, I haven't been able [to] say I want to be reconciled to you, as a spouse, either."[51] So adamant was she about not having her name as a petitioner for divorce that she offered to pay half of his sole petitioner costs. And though she had reason to harbour resentment towards him for the way he had handled their separation, Ann let him know she felt they had grown and may have even been blessed by it. She closed the letter saying, "I do, and I will, miss 'you.'"

The same week he took the divorce papers to the registry, Bill turned sixty-two. And though Evelyn gave him a gift and took him to dinner, the mood quickly soured by later that evening when she "laid a lot of emotional stuff on [him]," [52] making it, in his own estimation, the worst birthday he had up to that point. By the end of the following month, despite their reconciliation months earlier, Bill became frustrated at her once more when, after drinking through dinner, she "became quite difficult and emotional, causing him to question how much longer their unlikely relationship would last. [53]

In early July, Bill met Barb for lunch before having dinner with Evelyn. Upon returning home, Lau called Bill to inform him that Barb had left a message on her machine. The subsequent fallout effectively ended the tumultuous May–December romance, and within three weeks, Barb was accompanying Bill on a trip to New York City.

By late summer, nearly eighteen years after they were married in Iowa, Bill and Ann were officially divorced. Five weeks later, following years of an on-again-off-again relationship, Bill proposed to Barb and she accepted. An article Evelyn had written for the October issue of *Vancouver* magazine overshadowed the excitement and happiness of the moment, however. Though he had known for several weeks that the article would be published, as a fact-checker from the magazine called to confirm some details, Kinsella found the finished piece to be "in excruciatingly poor taste," and he was, by his own estimation, "trashed by innuendo." [54]

The article, "Me & W.P.," was in an issue guest edited by Douglas Coupland, who had first introduced Kinsella and Lau. Beginning her piece by declaring, "This is the story of a relationship. It is also the story of the older man who leaves his home to try to build a life with a younger woman," Lau went on to describe her own troubled youth living on the streets as a teenager and her introduction to Kinsella's writing while in high school. [55]

In her account of the Christmas party, she recounted discussing her work with Bill while being troubled by Ann's "restless, rather alarming energy." Lau claimed Bill later told her that Ann's erratic behaviour that evening, which indicated Ann was headed towards another manic episode, "marked his decision to leave the marriage, although it would be months before he actually did."

Detailing their relationship, one complicated by Bill's break-up with Ann and the on-again-off-again situation with Barb, Lau admitted she "was embarrassed by his eccentric appearance" and "[p]hysically . . . was not at all attracted to him." Lau went on to provide her analysis of what brought them together in spite of the thirty-six-year age difference and what eventually drove them apart. Ultimately, she recognized they had physical and emotional differences between them that, despite whatever love they may have once shared, "could not be surmounted."

Within days of the magazine appearing on newsstands, author Spider Robinson, who had attended the now infamous Christmas gathering with his wife, Jeanne, had come to Bill's aid, drafting a letter to the magazine's regular editor, Jim Sutherland. Admittedly protective of his friend, Robinson described Lau as "a treacherous cowardly self-centered infantile exploitative vicious hypocritical vindictive unabashedly-amoral shrew."[56]

Kinsella's agent, Carolyn Swayze, who had also attended the party, wrote a letter in which she more calmly but every bit as firmly as Robinson requested that Sutherland and Coupland "Kindly make it known that the friend and mercifully unnamed 'Vancouver writer' who brought Lau to the Christmas party . . . was guest editor Doug Coupland. There is an inherent breach of integrity in Coupland's decision to use Lau to exploit and betray hospitality and friendship, without disclosing his role."[57] Swayze also made the editors aware of numerous factual errors and pointed to Lau's use of a portion of Bill's poem "Broken Dolls" from *Rainbow Warehouse*, which she had never asked for permission to use.

Though he often claimed any publicity was good publicity, Kinsella soon considered filing a lawsuit against Lau, Coupland

and the magazine itself. The following spring, in a cover story in *BC Report*, Bill claimed that while "nothing really bothers me" he was suing because "when you've been wronged, you have to defend yourself."[58] When Lau mentioned to the *Vancouver Sun* that the couple had agreed to allow each other to write about their relationship, Bill maintained, "anything we might have discussed applied only to fiction writing." He had published "Lonesome Polecat in Love" in the winter 1998 issue of *Canadian Author*, but not before he claimed to have sought Lau's approval to do so, as the characters were based on their relationship. His primary complaint following her article was that he felt he had been unfairly portrayed physically, sexually and personally.

Their agreement, dated September 20, 1996, was handwritten and signed by both Kinsella and Lau on a single sheet of paper and simply read, "W.P. Kinsella and Evelyn Lau agree that we will never take legal action against each other on anything we may write or publish."[59] And though the lawsuit would claim the article was a breach of Kinsella's privacy and "[broadcasted] to the public disparaging, demeaning, humiliating, and embarrassing references" to his personal life,[60] the agreement between them made no indication of it extending only to fictional work.

Enduring several weeks of the increasingly public scandal resulting from Lau's article and the impending lawsuit, Bill was grateful for the decision he and Barb made to move in together after returning from a trip they took to New York City. With the concerns that plagued him during his relationship with Lau behind him, he was optimistic that living with Barb would result in a more mature, stable relationship than he had dealt with over the previous two years and was hopeful that their third attempt would prove successful.

Bill hoped to continue publishing at least one book a year, something he had done for several years. *If Wishes Were Horses* was not receiving the commercial reception many of the earlier baseball novels had garnered, but Kinsella was pleased to see its movie option sold, once again ensuring him an income, something that had become increasingly important as the publishing industry shifted and left moderately successful writers like him with shrinking advances. In addition to *If Wishes Were Horses*, Barry Levinson was still trying to get interest in *Magic Time* as a film. Despite the book having not yet been published, the success *Field of Dreams* had generated nearly a decade before continued to create interest in the possibility of another baseball movie based on a Kinsella novel. That fall, Bill continued writing *Butterfly Winter* while revising both *Honk if You Love Willie Nelson* and *Magic Time*.

Then, one Saturday evening, October 11, 1997, he and Barb went for a walk on 20th Avenue, and Kinsella was struck by a car backing the wrong way out of a two-way driveway in front of an apartment building. Kinsella's head struck the rear fender before both his tailbone and head hit the concrete sidewalk. After losing consciousness for several minutes, he awoke, disoriented and with Barb standing over him. Though he had no recollection of the moment of impact or of hitting the ground, Bill was cognizant enough to recall being placed into the ambulance that rushed him to Peace Arch Hospital, where he underwent a battery of tests and x-rays before being released later that night. Diagnosed with a concussion, Bill was awakened every two hours throughout the night to monitor his symptoms in the event they worsened. In addition to the acute head trauma, he suffered several contusions and bruises, a sore neck and severe headaches. Perhaps most alarmingly, he also lost his senses of taste and smell.

The headaches continued, some lasting for several days, and persistent weakness and dizziness kept him in bed much of the time, though both his short- and long-term memory appeared to have suffered no significant loss. He did, however, quickly realize that he did not have the ability to concentrate on reading or writing, describing his thought process at the time as "scrambled."[61] In the ensuing days he felt weak and suffered from bouts of dizziness when he moved very far. Despite the injuries and their lingering effects, just days after the accident he sat down and went through his files, intending to get back into his writing routine, before quickly realizing he was able to concentrate on something for only a few seconds before his mind began wandering. He admitted at the time that even "the idea of creating [made him] feel very tired" and left him wondering about whether or not he should consult a neurologist.[62]

Within two weeks of the initial injuries, Bill began noticing his teeth had shifted out of alignment, further compounding his problems. Not yet three weeks later, however, he began recognizing the effects might last well into the coming months and years with no guarantee of him ever being fully recovered. One day, after being disoriented for over an hour following his afternoon nap, he had to try numerous times to draw blood for his blood sugar reading. He then realized there was no realistic possibility of his being able to work in the immediate future. In the meantime, grateful that he had completed enough material to stay ahead of his publishers, he began reviewing the cache of manuscripts in an attempt to find anything suitable for publication. Included in the material were seven books—*Conflicting Statements; Russian Dolls; Risk Takers; The Secret of the Northern Lights; Magic Time; The Button Box;* and *Butterfly Winter;* two screenplays—*Billy the Kidd* and *The National Passtime;* and several other works in various stages of completion.

Though he had always considered himself "mildly depressive," he claimed the depression never lasted "more than a day or so ever."[63] He had taken Prozac for almost two years at one point, but had stopped nearly three years earlier due to Barb's strong objections to the drug. Although still dealing with his physical injuries and the mental strain of readjusting to life following the accident, Bill avoided succumbing to a major depression in the weeks following his head trauma. Even though he often woke up feeling depressed, the feelings usually dissipated by midday, and looking back, his assessment later on was that within two years of the accident, his mood was back to what it had been before that. Some days, however, the depression was coupled with a growing, oppressive fear he was often unable to explain. Having worried throughout his adult life about financial security, his worries now were mostly about his ability to work.

His physical strength slowly returned in subsequent months, though the troubles with his senses of smell and taste persisted. Most troubling, however, were the changes he noticed in his personality and thoughts. Friends and family noticed he had become more tired and reserved, and he felt lethargic, and lacked the interest and drive that had motivated him to work for so long. Few people, however, were aware of his occasional suicidal thoughts. And despite telling Dr. Anderson, a psychiatrist, that such thoughts were never serious, he did admit that "the thought crosses my mind occasionally," feeling as though "there would be so much less I wouldn't have to face if I was not here."[64] In spite of the feelings of isolation, fear and occasional suicidal thoughts, Bill remained confident in himself and his ability to connect with his readers, noting, "I'm still able to entertain an audience, so that's very affirmative."

Unfortunately, his concentration was so thoroughly diminished that, despite having no shortage of ideas, he could no longer focus enough on his craft to complete anything worthy of publication. Before being struck by the car, he had been working on a screenplay with comedian Chris Farley in mind as the lead. And though he had completed the manuscript in the months following the wreck, the result was "the first half was good and the last half was shit."

Bill's worries began taking their toll on Barb as well. Recognizing that he had "lost the illusion he was in control of things," she became increasingly aware of his fear that he would have a stroke and die. It seemed as though his "cheerful façade" was gone, Barb noticed, and that he had lost some of the confidence he once had, though it started to return within a couple of years.

Unbeknownst to him at the time, Bill's most productive years as a writer were behind him, and he was confronted with the reality that his health would most likely prevent him from reclaiming his position in the Canadian writing community. Yet the accident's lingering physical and psychological effects did afford him an opportunity to step back from his public life while he was still respected as one of the nation's leading writers.

12

The Gin Runs Out

Towards the end of 1997, Bill and Barb bought a large Victorian home in Chilliwack, a community about sixty miles east of Vancouver. And though the house would not be ready for them to live in until later that spring due to the major renovations the 1891 structure required, the project provided some distraction from the continuing lawsuits against Lau, Coupland and *Vancouver* magazine.

Still plagued by the effects from the accident, Bill worked to complete the edits for what would ultimately be his eighth and final collection of Silas stories, *The Secret of the Northern Lights,* due for publication in the spring. Kinsella completed his work on the project the day after getting news from his film agent that the option for *If Wishes Were Horses* would not be renewed, a decision that he estimated would cost him an expected $112,000 for the year and an additional $300,000 he would have received if the film were made. For the first time in several years, his income fell far below what he had expected. And though he was still financially secure, the reality of the impact the accident might have on his long-term earnings was a real concern.

Fortunately, for the short term, publishers had already offered contracts for two books he had completed prior to the accident. With the changes in the publishing world making it increasingly difficult for writers like Kinsella to have the kinds of contracts with major publishers they had enjoyed only a few years earlier, *The Secret of the Northern Lights* was set for an April release with a smaller house, Thistledown Press based in Saskatoon, Saskatchewan. And though no major publishers in the United States made an offer on it, Doubleday Canada released *Magic Time* in June. HarperCollins Canada was also releasing an omnibus of three collections of previously published Hobbema tales, called *The Silas Stories*. Though he had no way of knowing it then, 1998 would prove to be the last time Bill published more than one book in a single year.

Unlike his other baseball novels, Bill set *Magic Time* entirely in the present day—the plot involves no time travel to other periods or parallel dimensions for any of its characters. Its protagonist, Mike Houle, is a former college baseball player whose draft stock plummets when he fails to live up to expectations during his senior year. Going undrafted that year, he takes the only opportunity he has to continue playing the game by moving to Grand Mound, Iowa, where he is assured playing time, a part-time job and a host family. Eventually, however, Houle discovers the team only participates in intrasquad games and doesn't actually belong to a league. In fact, the town perpetually recruits players who fail under pressure, providing a way for them to extend their careers while immersing them in the benefits of small-town American life. The townspeople hope the players will fall in love with their new lives, decide to stay and keep the town from fading away, as similar towns have done in recent years.

While readers had grown accustomed to the rural Iowa landscape and likeable characters in Kinsella's baseball novels, some critics had grown tired of his formula of using short stories as pieces of his plots, essentially offering a collection of largely recycled material. Martin Levin explained, "what we get are short stories [from *The Dixon Cornbelt League*] embedded in a novel," though he acknowledged "these are the book's liveliest parts."[1] And even his use of magic realism was being questioned, with the novel described as having "the occasional flatness of narrative and of prose [that] can be uninspired: The stories lack . . . magic."

Len Gasparini of the *Toronto Star* noted the four previously published stories in the book made for "a patchwork quilt" that became redundant.[2] Despite the criticism of the "mawkishly sentimental" story, Kinsella continued to be praised for "[melding] vernacular and anecdote in the style of Ring Lardner." Still, both of his latest books were criticized, using a baseball reference, for "[showing] signs of overkill, yet attest to the fact that [Kinsella] is loath to retire their numbers." And while the film rights gave him reason to be optimistic, the novel was another in what had become a string of books generating largely mediocre and, at best, mixed reviews.

Though four years had passed since his last book of Silas Ermineskin stories, the criticism of his use of the Indigenous voice in them remained with the release of *The Secret of the Northern Lights*. And in spite of the "engaging stories, likeable characters and an interesting ambiguity about right and wrong, community and self, pragmatism and mysticism," the book was criticized for being "less finely wrought, [and] more casually written than the earlier ones."[3] The glaring problem for one critic was "not so much that Kinsella had appropriated the 'native voice,' . . . [but] that he has treated it rather shabbily in a self-centered and paternalistic way." In short, he argued that Silas "still writes and talks like Tonto."

Not everyone was offended. Colby Cosh argued, "For a modest 15 bucks [Kinsella's] new book of Hobbema Indian stories is a deal hard to beat—whatever you may think of his philosophy, his so-called 'voice appropriation,' or his recent public feud with ex-mistress Evelyn Lau."[4] Looking back on the entire body of the Silas stories, the same reviewer appreciated Bill's willingness to let his characters on the reserve age and, in some ways, mature, declaring "every new book of Hobbema stories is cause for admiration [as] there is no mood which W.P. Kinsella cannot capture, and no aspect of human nature unknown to him."

At this point Bill was uncertain whether he would ever again be able to create anything. But whatever concerns he had regarding his own health and financial issues were pushed aside when Erin, who had been taking care of Olive as her health declined, called that October to inform him of his mother's death. Now sixty-three himself, having watched his father suffer through a painful final struggle with stomach cancer, and seeing his mother's final years overshadowed by her frail body and failing mind, he began to consider his own mortality. Left unspoken was the reality that his creative output, in both quality and quantity, had been in a state of decline for some time. Despite the work he had recently published, Bill considered 1998 to be the worst of at least the past thirty-five years. His productivity had amounted to only slightly more than 200 new pages of material, and he remained discouraged about future prospects for his career. With his senses of taste and smell gone and the vertigo-like symptoms still lingering, he was uncertain when or even if he would return to the health he had once known.

The one aspect of his life he had reason to celebrate was his relationship with Barb. In February 1999, the couple drove from Palm Springs to San Angelo, Texas, where Bill was scheduled for a book event. On the return trip, the couple drove through Nevada's high country, stopping in the old mining town of Pioche to get a marriage licence. On March 2, they were married in the court house in Alamo, Nevada, so that, as Bill jokingly told friends, "We'll be able to say, 'Remember the Alamo!'"[5]

Still unable to produce new fiction, Bill began writing book reviews for *Publishers Weekly* and other periodicals, claiming that he did not "need any magic to review books." Next, Kinsella decided to eliminate another burden, one he had been dealing with for almost as long as his physical injuries. After months of letting his lawsuit against Lau, Coupland and *Vancouver* magazine work its way through legal channels, Bill chose to drop the suit. Realizing he was battling not just the specific parties named in the lawsuit but the insurance company fighting for the magazine, he understood that "their plan was to drag the case out, bury us in paperwork, so we would have to spend huge amounts of money just to bring the case to court." The lawsuit against the driver who hit him, however, continued and would soon end with a modest settlement for damages in Bill's favour.

Now referring to himself as "semi-retired," by the end of 1999 Bill had slowly started writing fiction again. Unsure of its quality, he progressed from the 500 words he completed in a day in early June, his longest effort in a year, to over 1,500 in a single day by the end of December, by far the most productive day of writing since the accident. He was also honoured by his alma mater that year when the University of Victoria established the W.P. Kinsella Scholarship in Fiction to award to a senior writing student in the department each year.

In early 2000, Bill received news from Ann that a biopsy determined she had breast cancer. Unfortunately, it had spread to her lymph nodes. That spring, following an adverse reaction to her chemotherapy, she told her friends and family she did not plan on continuing with it. As it offered only a 10% chance of stopping the disease from spreading and greatly reduced her quality of life, she decided to pursue other avenues of treatment.

Nearly two years had passed since Bill's last book had been published, but now two publishers expressed interest in releasing a new collection of stories. In a two-day period, both Thistledown and Algonquin inquired about *Japanese Baseball*, a collection filled with baseball pieces that incorporated elements of fantasy. Once his agent had secured another contract with Thistledown, plans were made for a fall release. Bill had Barb begin designing the book's cover.

The new collection signalled that Kinsella was not yet fully retired, though it would turn out to be his last new book for more than a decade. Even then, *Japanese Baseball* contained eight previously published stories and two more that had already been accepted for publication before the book went to print. Knowing readers wanted new stories from him, he was eager to get as much of his work in print as possible. But the reality was that he had not been able to come close to regaining even a fraction of his writing pace from before the accident. As he had produced nothing publishable since before his head trauma, the book proved to be more an anthology of his most recent baseball stories than a new collection.

Calling the stories "delightful and imaginative," Peter O'Brien praised them as being "the perfect antidote to all the recent blabber [concerning drug and money stories dominating the game at the time]."[6] And though a review in *Quill & Quire* proclaimed "only four of Kinsella's stories can truly be called home-runs," it noted "but the other seven are anything but strikeouts."[7]

The collection included "The First and Last Annual Six Towns Old-Timers' Game," narrated by Jamie O'Day of *Box Socials* and *The Winter Helen Dropped By*, one of the oldest stories in the book. Though it had been previously included in a collector's edition chap-book published by Coffee House Press in 1991, it had reached a limited audience until now. The other re-released stories had appeared in literary magazines in both Canada and the United States, and one, "Fred Noonan Flying Services," was included in the upcoming *Baseball Fantastic*, an anthology of baseball fantasy tales that Kinsella had edited for publication later in the year.

With stories that were varied in topic and style, some utilizing the game more than others, O'Brien noted the book's greatest strength was that "the stories are no more and no less than exactly what . . . Kinsella wants them to be: thoughtful, charmed stories about the everyday magic of desire."[8] The reviewer for *Quill & Quire* took notice of how Bill's prose had changed, with this collection showing "a new depth and gentleness to [his] storytelling here, a more subtle nuance than his readers may be accustomed to."[9]

Even with the new book and the praise it was receiving, Bill continued telling those closest to him how much he was enjoying retirement, though he was anything but idle. Having played Scrabble recreationally with friends and family for years, he had recently begun entering tournaments to play more competitively. And while he regularly played close to home in places like Victoria and Seattle, he also ventured as far as Reno, Nevada, where he once placed eighth out of twenty-six players in his division. Combining his competitive nature with his love of words, Kinsella had seemingly found the perfect outlet to fill the void his writing had claimed for so many years. Being, by his own account, "essentially retired"[10] now afforded him the oppor-tunity to play regularly with the Chilliwack Scrabble Club, which he had founded two years earlier and that had grown into a flourishing group of regular players. Still holding public readings, he was no longer travelling at the frantic pace he had before. The newly discovered free time allowed him to be more selective towards the projects presented to him.

One such opportunity came late in 2001 when his agent called to inform him of a Japanese publisher that was interested in doing a book on the Seattle Mariners' right fielder Ichiro Suzuki. The most appealing part for Kinsella, who had been a longtime fan of the team and often attended several games a year, was that he would only be obligated to give interviews—someone else would write the book. Knowing that Japanese publishers paid well, he agreed to the project and gave several hours of interviews over a week-long visit from the writers.

On May 9, 2002, Ann Knight died after fighting breast cancer for more than two years. Though they had been separated for nearly a decade and were divorced years earlier, Bill reflected on the impact his ex-wife had not only on his own literary career but on the lives of those who knew her. He privately noted, "she was much loved, [and] had a magnificent singing voice," but he also acknowledged his daughter Shannon's tribute: "Ann took a little piece of all our hearts with her."[11] At some point, both Shannon and Erin had told Ann they "wished she had been their real mother," something Bill noted was "a pretty fine compliment." Beyond the role Ann had played in their lives, Erin recognized the often-overlooked impact she had on Bill's life, saying, "Ann was a force of nature. She was a beautiful person. The whole room lit up when she came in. She could inspire you to great heights. I believe my dad went as far as he did because of Ann."[12]

Ann's loss was followed by Aunt Margaret's death two months later. After Erin, who had stepped in and served as caretaker for Ann and Margaret as their conditions deteriorated, called to inform Bill of her passing the previous night, he wrote, "she was a wonderful, kind, loving little person" and was glad she, unlike his mother, had not suffered in her final years.[13]

Over the coming months, Bill continued travelling around Canada and the United States competing in Scrabble tournaments in

Seattle, Calgary, Reno, San Diego and Portland, where he picked up his second tournament win. Realizing he was unable to consistently compete against the highest-level players, the success he did have was reward enough for the hours he spent playing at home and with the various local clubs.

During this time, Bill started writing a monthly column for *Books in Canada* and kept his name in the public eye. He also began reading unpublished manuscripts of his previous years' work, including *The Button Box*, another novel told through the eyes of Jamie O'Day from *Box Socials* and *The Winter Helen Dropped By*. Finding the story to be "very funny," he was puzzled as to why it had not already been published and it gave him hope that he still had work to offer the public.[14]

In early January a television crew from Bravo visited Bill and Barb for an upcoming documentary on the transformation of *Shoeless Joe* into *Field of Dreams*, in the network's series *Page to Screen*. Despite having answered the same questions about his most recognized book for nearly two decades, Bill still recognized the value of such publicity and what it would undoubtedly mean for interest in and sales of his works.

With their Victorian house restoration project in Chilliwack still not complete, and no sign of it being finished in the near future, by 2003 Bill and Barb had begun looking for a different house with more room for Barb to grow her prized roses. Her current garden was home to more than forty varieties of roses on over ninety bushes, but she soon had an acre of land on which she could develop an even larger garden when they purchased a house in Yale, B.C., overlooking the Fraser River, and soon put the Chilliwack home up for sale. About forty miles east of Chilliwack, Yale had been home to approximately 30,000 people during the height of the gold rush in the late 1850s. By 2004, what remained of the town was slightly fewer than 200 inhabitants, providing the couple the peace and quiet and privacy they craved.

Bill may have been geographically more remote now than during his first ten years on the farm in Darwell, but the internet kept him connected to the outside world and allowed him to play as many as twenty-five different games of Scrabble at any one time, honing his competitive skills. He still travelled to play as many as a half dozen tournaments during any given year. This connection to the world beyond Yale became increasingly important when, following complications from cataract surgery, Bill's sight prevented him from driving the winding roads at night from his home in the Fraser Canyon, ending for the time being his weekly trips to the Scrabble Club in Chilliwack.

In early 2005, nearly three decades after his first book, *Dance Me Outside*, was published, Bill was nominated for the Order of British Columbia. Established in 1989, the award recognizes "those persons who have served with the greatest distinction and excelled in any field of endeavour benefitting the people of the Province or elsewhere."[15] It was open to anyone nominated by another party. Barb nominated Bill, and he nominated his former professor, mentor and longtime friend W.D. Valgardson. Later that summer, Premier Gordon Campbell and Lieutenant-Governor Iona Campagnolo presented Kinsella with the award. Flattered by the recognition, Kinsella felt his evening was diminished only by the fact that Valgardson had not also been chosen as a recipient.

Bill had spent years reading every first novel published in Canada in order to compile the shortlist for the *Books in Canada* First Novel Award. At age seventy, he decided that 2005 would be his final year committed to the task. Whatever free time he might have gained upon relinquishing the role, though, was reduced after he agreed to write a weekly column for the *Vancouver Province* newspaper. Bill viewed the column as the paper's way of giving him free rein to write anything from "button-pushing controversial pieces to little bits of fiction."[16]

During filming for a documentary about his life and work, Bill visited the farm at Darwell in May 2006 for what he suspected would be the last time. Awash in memories from his childhood as he walked the fields where he had played more than sixty years earlier, Bill observed that the old house that had long before fallen into a state of disrepair served as a reminder of time's passing, and that he was the only member of his family who had inhabited the house who was still living. Accompanying the crew to Eastglen High School in Edmonton, Bill was welcomed back by an enthusiastic crowd of students to whom he recounted his days as a student and the advice from the guidance counsellor who had encouraged him to find a proper career and only write as a hobby.

While Scrabble tournaments and online games continued dominating his time, for the first time in nearly a decade, Bill published a new story. His piece, "The Grand Reunion for Anyone Who Ever Attended Fark Schoolhouse, Including George Hewko and the Dubchek Twins," was serialized in the *Globe and Mail*. Even so, he maintained that, other than the weekly newspaper column, he was "pretty much retired from writing."[17] By the spring of the following year, however, he grew annoyed at the newspaper's editors for regularly bumping his column from the final edition, so he chose to stop writing even that, claiming, "I'm much too old to work."[18]

His self-proclaimed retirement proved to be short-lived as he once again picked up the manuscript of *Butterfly Winter* and began revising it. By his own admission, the book had been two-thirds complete when his unexpected hiatus following the 1997 accident took place. By late spring he had completed the draft and sent it to Carolyn Swayze with the hope of having a contract for his first new novel since *Magic Time* in 1998. Almost immediately upon completing that manuscript, he began re-reading *Russian Dolls*.

Just as his writing career was showing new signs of life, and after years of attempting to regulate his blood sugar levels with diet and exercise, he was informed in 2007 that his kidneys were operating well below normal capacity, with one estimate at 30% of their expected levels. Unfortunately, he was not a candidate for a transplant and his kidneys still functioned at levels higher than what the doctors needed to see to put him on dialysis. That summer, confronted with his own mortality, Bill began questioning at what point his quality of life would become such that he would not even consider dialysis.

Perhaps because of the reality that his health had presented him, and reflecting on his life during the filming of the documentary

Curveball, which would air the following January, Bill began researching his family's genealogy, discovering generations of Elliot and Kinsella history far beyond the family stories on which he had relied for so many years.

That fall Alan Twigg arrived at Bill's home in Yale to inform him that he had won the George Woodcock Lifetime Achievement Award, to be officially presented the following summer, in June 2009. Perhaps rejuvenated by the good news, or simply inspired to use the publicity about the award to sell books, Bill began a variety of writing projects, including some of his semi-autobiographical stories told in Jamie O'Day's voice and set on a farm in western Alberta. Tentatively titled *The Grand Review*, the resulting manuscript included a retelling of parts of *Box Socials*, *The Winter Helen Dropped By*, excerpts from *True Crime*, an unpublished project he had been working on for many years, and *The Button Box*. Looking at the disjointed collection of manuscript pages, he privately questioned if he had the ability to piece the fragments together into a novel.

More than ten years had passed since his last novel and nine years since he had released a short story collection, so it seemed appropriate to Bill to travel to Vancouver in early June 2009 to accept the George Woodcock Lifetime Achievement Award for Fiction as his writing career had effectively ended by this time. Kinsella himself joked about its name, telling the media, "I think a lifetime achievement award sounds pretty final, but I'm always happy to see my work recognized."[19] Sponsored by *B.C. Bookworld*, the reception and readings both drew large crowds at the Vancouver Public Library, where a commemorative plaque was placed outside on the Authors' Walk, reminding him of his staying power as one of Canada's most popular writers.

Whether inspired by the event or because he and Barb had begun fighting regularly again, towards the end of 2009, Bill wrote every day for a week, averaging between 1,000 and 2,000 words per day. He had started to realize the burden of his own precarious health situation since his doctor informed him of his chronic kidney disease earlier in the year. When his energy levels became so low he could no longer mow his lawn, he recognized the situation could suddenly turn dire as insulin had become his new routine.

With his financial and literary affairs in order, Bill wrote an essay, "Facing Up to Death," for *The Seattle Review*, in which he explained the only emotion he felt after hearing the news from his doctor was sadness in knowing "that no one else will care for the same things that are precious to me," namely his childhood toys and the dolls he had inherited from his mother. "The next generation," he wrote, "will have no connection to them at all, and they will simply disappear, which makes me infinitely sad."[20]

He took confidence in knowing his daughters were independent and that, though sad, they would not "be devastated by [his] death," and so was not bothered by the prospect of dying. Having been an atheist for most of his life, he believed "religion was created the day the first charlatan met the first fool," and he felt no hope for eternal life or fear in eternal damnation. Reflecting on the out-of-body experience he claimed to have had when his tonsillitis was misdiagnosed and he nearly died from infection in Edmonton as a young boy, and on seeing his uncle die in front of him while sitting at the kitchen table following a game of cribbage, he felt no fear towards the process of dying.

After watching his mother suffer in her final years, he had made the decision that, when his time came, he wanted only to be kept comfortable "while letting nature take its course." Proud of his success and the body of literary work he would leave behind, he claimed to have few regrets, stating bluntly, "I see nothing wrong with leaving the party before the gin runs out."

Bill's health held steady in 2010, and he completed his revisions on a retitled novel he'd finished the summer before, *The Grand Reunion (for anyone who ever attended Fark Schoolhouse in Seven Towns County Alberta)*, and resumed work on *Russian Dolls*. In spite of these efforts, he recognized that his days as a mainstream author were over. To those closest to him, he confided, "The publishing world is in such turmoil what with the unresolved issues of books on the internet, that unless you're Stieg Larsson or Stephen King, or are willing to go with a tiny publisher that will only sell a few copies, the odds of getting a main stream [*sic*] publisher are negligible."[21]

In November, after celebrating seventeen years of living together, Bill and Barb's world was shaken to its core. She had suffered for six months from an unexplained fever that failed to respond to several types of antibiotics before being diagnosed with a carcinoma that was located deep inside her jawbone. With his wife facing surgery, Bill mused, "I can't be 75 anymore, [I] will have to go back to 65 and be there for Barb."[22] Bill had come to the realization that his love for her far outweighed the tensions that arose between them at times.

Soon after the new year, Barb had surgery in Vancouver, at which time the doctors replaced her jaw using bone from her left tibia. And while the medical team felt the procedure had been a success, she had to stay in the hospital for thirty-seven days. Following through on the commitment he'd made to support her through the ordeal, Bill stayed all but one of those nights in a nearby hotel. Reverting to his most productive writing years, he once again used his craft as a means of coping with trouble in his personal life, creating new stories in the anxious days as his wife healed.

Just days after he and Barb returned home to Yale after more than five weeks away, Bill was notified that his latest novel, the unpublished *Butterfly Winter*, had won the Colophon Prize, an award of $5,000 and a contract with Enfield & Wizenty. Slated for a September release, the book, as so many of his novels before, had begun as a short story and had been developed and expanded over the course of several years. In celebration of their twelfth wedding anniversary, Bill dedicated the novel to Barb.

In an attempt to regain a sense of normalcy in his life, Bill continued playing Scrabble at the weekly meeting in Chilliwack, making the hour drive as his health permitted, and at other tournaments as Barb's recovery allowed. The thirty-three days of radiation she endured was physically and emotionally taxing on the couple as it involved a three-hour round-trip drive to Abbotsford, west of Chilliwack. Bill, however, was hopeful the treatment would remove the cancer.

That fall, for the first time since *Magic Time*, he had a new novel on bookshelves, *Butterfly Winter*. Launching the book in Vancouver, where he held a reading with Bill Valgardson, Kinsella enjoyed his return to the spotlight, and he continued touring throughout the fall. While Kinsella's fans eagerly anticipated the book's release, it received mixed reviews from the literary world.

At Larry Kessenich's urging years earlier, Bill had worked off and on to adapt the short story "The Battery," from 1984's *The Thrill of the Grass*, into *Butterfly Winter*. Creating a fictional country to set the story in place, Bill also used two different narrators, one an older wizard and the other a "Gringo journalist," both of whom have a voice reminiscent of Kinsella's. A story of destiny and circumstance, the book follows the lives of twin brothers Julio and Esteban Pimental. One critic remarked, "The novel's light and dark themes don't mesh well, nor do the shifting perspectives and narrative techniques serve the author's grand imagination."[23]

Many compared his current book with his most iconic work. Recognizing *Butterfly Winter* began, like *Shoeless Joe*, "as a short story," Steven Hayward remarked the new book "[lacks] the cohesiveness of a novel," though despite its faults, readers "are reminded of Kinsella's intelligence and verbal facility, and of the particular way his imagination is able to transfigure baseball into transcendence."[24]

After such a long period between novels, many readers were surprised at the changes in his prose. *Butterfly Winter* was not only criticized for being "something of a jumble, lacking the elegance of the game it celebrates," but for its "surprising amount of violence."[25] And its organization, "the apparently random order of the novel's 78 brief chapters," was viewed as a possible "attempt at postmodernism," resulting in a book that ended up "a big, steamy stew of imagination run wild." The economy of words and tightly focused plots of his earlier books had given way to a more avant garde approach that some found not only confusing but distracting.

In spite of the negative reviews, the book later earned Kinsella the Mary Scorer Award for Best Book by a Manitoba Publisher. And with another baseball book in stores, it seemed fitting that Kinsella was recognized for his baseball works when he was awarded the 2011 Jack Graney Award by the Canadian Baseball Hall of Fame. Awarded "for a significant contribution to the game of baseball in Canada through a life's work or for a singular outstanding achievement,"[26] the honour recognized Kinsella's numerous baseball texts, specifically noting the importance of *Shoeless Joe* to baseball literature.

Following the initial tour for *Butterfly Winter*, Bill largely kept to himself at his home in Yale, venturing out to play Scrabble in Chilliwack, now that he was once again able to make the drive, and to participate in occasional quiz nights at the library in Hope, a town just down the road from Yale. He wrote sporadically, beginning a new novel, *Aliases* (soon renamed *The Night That Bandit Mary Died*), in August 2012, sometimes writing more than 1,000 words per day.

In late October 2012, Barb's doctor notified her that the cancer had returned and was inoperable. The physician estimated she might live as little as two months or perhaps as long as eight months. Though they were both in shock at the finality of the diagnosis, Bill was awed by his wife's bravery in the face of the devastating news, attempting to live as normal a life as possible in her remaining time.

The downward turn in Barb's health elevated Bill's own stress levels to the point that his kidney function dropped dangerously low. Upon receiving the news, however, Bill once more used his writing as a means of escape, composing no fewer than 500 words a day, only taking a break on the days when either he or Barb had medical appointments.

Whatever hopes the couple had for Barb outliving the doctor's predictions disappeared in mid-December 2012 when, after nearly dying due to massive hemorrhaging, Barb was transported to a cancer treatment centre in Abbotsford. Following several days of near constant bleeding from her neck, she died around 3:00 a.m. on Christmas Eve. On the day she died, Bill privately noted, "The nicest thing I can say about Barb is if I had to do it over, [I'd] still choose her." Though never religious, he conceded, "if I'm wrong and there is an afterlife, she is the only one I would want to spend it with."[27]

Enduring what he called "probably the most difficult month of my life,"[28] Bill was comforted when Erin and longtime friends Lee and Maggie Harwood arrived to help him deal with Barb's final arrangements and to make plans for the future. Recognizing the potential danger living alone posed to him at nearly seventy-eight years of age, he submitted his name to a waiting list for a retirement community down in Hope.

In an effort to remain as active as possible now that he was, for the time being, living alone, in 2013 Kinsella continued playing Scrabble, driving to Chilliwack every week to meet with the club regulars. And Bill started another club in Hope, providing him yet another outlet for socializing and playing the game that had become his passion. And though he could have easily withdrawn into himself in the house overlooking the Fraser River, he began playing the game on Facebook, which allowed him to stay in contact with friends and family across Canada and the United States. However, he soon began enduring further health troubles, including prostate issues, unexplainable night sweats and chills, and a pulled calf muscle and strained ankle that limited his mobility and forced him to begin using a cane while walking. Even with the mounting physical maladies and still mourning Barb's passing, he reflected positively on his current situation that Thanksgiving, writing, "[I] have most wonderful daughters, good friends, beautiful art work, and passable health to be thankful for."[29]

Early in the summer, Bill was notified that he was next on the list for a space in the retirement centre, but at Christmas he and Erin discussed the possibility of her coming to live with him. Having cared for her grandmother, Aunt Margaret and Ann before their deaths, Erin was no stranger to helping family members in declining health, something for which Bill often praised her. Erin's move to the house in Yale the following February not only provided him the chance to have his daughter near him on a daily basis, but it relieved him of the trouble of moving and gave them both constant Scrabble partners. They played multiple games each day and often competed against each other in tournaments they attended together.

Bill's writing, though nowhere near his old levels of productivity, continued, and he soon began working on short stories like "The Bluebird Café," which were posted directly to his new website. He also returned to unpublished material to see if anything had the potential to be saleable, following the moderate success *Butterfly Winter* had had two years earlier. Hoping to build on its momentum, he spent six months revising *Conflicting Statements*, a novel he had started nearly two decades earlier, before sending it to his agent. Less than a month after it was sent, he picked up *The Night Bandit Mary Died*, the novel he had worked on so furiously during Barb's illness and hospitalization. Though he liked what he read from it, he remembered very little about the creative process—that period had been filled with so much stress due to attending to Barb's needs. And though he likened the experience to reading someone else's work, he continued with the writing, and had two completed manuscripts by the year's end.

On New Year's Day of his eightieth year, Bill started another novel, *My Shoes Keep Walking Back to You*. Ultimately deciding the concept was not working well enough to suit him as there was "not enough material for a novel, [and] too much for a short story,"[30] he thrust himself into editing *Russian Dolls*, the on-again-off-again project that wove together several short stories into the framework of a larger narrative, as he'd done with other novels.

Regardless of whether or not any of the three books he had completed or nearly completed would ever arrive on bookshelves, Kinsella's fans had been eagerly anticipating the release of *The Essential W.P. Kinsella*, published by Tachyon Publications in March 2015. Calling it a "best of the best collection from the hundreds [of stories] I've written in the past 50 years," Kinsella himself helped select the thirty-one stories included in the book. The sampling included a wide range of styles and genres, including several of the Silas Ermineskin stories, his fantasy/science fiction pieces, many of his popular baseball stories, and a few of the quirky Brautigan pieces. And rather than simply being a collection of previously published material, the book included some of the more recent stories he had never before published and some that had only recently been published in literary journals or online.

Unlike his most recent books, which had at best been met by mixed reviews, the career retrospective allowed readers to reconnect with works they had not read in years; more importantly, the book showcased the ways Bill's style, tone and voice had developed over the course of his career, from *Dance Me Outside* in 1977 to the stories published for the first time in this collection. Described as "eclectic, dark, and comedic by turns," the book was praised as being "a living tribute to an extraordinary writer."[31]

Though his health prevented him from travelling long distances, eliminating any hope of a U.S. book tour, Bill was rejuvenated by the book's publicity and attended a variety of readings, panels and festivals in Canada. Shortly before one such event in Chilliwack, he reflected on his career to a reporter and what it meant for him to read his own work after so many years as a writer. "I've always liked my work. I laugh out loud when I read it," he said. And he expressed his frustration towards those people who only spoke of writing without committing themselves to the process as he had done when selling his restaurant and going to the University of Victoria for a writing degree. "I get very exasperated with people who say 'I'm going to write a novel some day but I don't have the time.' If you're really interested you'll make the time. You'll get up at 5 a.m. and write for two hours, throw hot water on your hands and then go off to some awful job."[32]

As a result of the book's success, Bill was more in demand for public readings than he had been in several years. The appearances ranged from intimate gatherings of twenty-five people in some bookstores to an audience of nearly 250 at the always popular Word on the Street festival in Saskatoon. Bill had returned to the place where he felt the most comfortable—reading his stories to eager audiences.

On the weekend of his eightieth birthday, the day after another successful book event in Vancouver, longtime friend and literary agent Carolyn Swayze hosted a birthday party for Bill at her home in Surrey. His daughters Shannon and Erin, Mickey's daughter Lyndsey Callander, and Barb's daughter Scarlet Gaffney, attended, as did two of Bill's grandsons and several of his closest friends. Surrounded by those who had known him for decades, Bill spent the afternoon visiting and reminiscing with the crowd as *Field of Dreams* played in the background. Enjoying the company of those celebrating his life and career, Bill confided in his best friend of more than forty-five years, Lee Harwood, that he did not want to live to be eighty-two, as his mounting health problems were becoming too much to deal with while maintaining his dignity.[33]

Perhaps even more than the milestone birthday and having another successful book selling well in Canada, Bill enjoyed the success of his Scrabble efforts that fall when he and Erin participated in the five-day Canadian Open Scrabble Championship. Though he'd slowed down in recent years, he remained as competitive as ever. Finishing the tournament with a 17–4 record, Bill won the event, laying claim to the title of Canadian Open Scrabble Champion for Division Three. He called it "my most prestigious win in about 25 years of play."[34] Pleased by what had been his busiest and most successful year in recent memory, in his annual letter for 2015 Bill lamented his declining health and mobility, though he acknowledged, "I've probably done more than most 80 year olds this year."

The health issues he had tried for so long to keep at bay caught up to him early the following year. He no longer felt inclined to travel much, preferring instead to stay at home playing Scrabble on his iPad and watching *Jeopardy!* in the evenings. *The Essential W. P. Kinsella* was selling well and still garnering positive reviews, so he gave occasional interviews but began declining requests for his time for book ideas or research projects related to his life and work. As was often the case in the early months of a new year, especially as baseball teams travelled to spring training, he entertained inquiries from fans and the media as to what team he thought would be the one to beat in the upcoming season.

Over the preceding three seasons, the Chicago Cubs, a team that had not won a World Series title since 1908, had developed into a serious threat. Though he had a deep appreciation for and understanding of baseball's history and tradition, having incorporated much of it into his fiction for many years, Bill was not one to grow sentimental about the Cubs making the 2016 playoffs, or perhaps even winning the World Series.

In 2003, the last time the Cubs had made the playoffs, the Boston Red Sox were attempting to win their first championship in eighty-five years. Unmoved by the possibility of witnessing history that year, as both teams desperately fought to break their respective droughts, Bill admitted he was rooting against both teams since they would both be "better as loveable losers. If they ever won what would they have to look forward to?"[35] He was, however, intrigued as he watched Boston lose the opportunity to advance to the World Series when their manager made an ill-advised decision that cost them the American League pennant, as it so closely mirrored one of his most famous baseball pieces, written many years before. "It is interesting that the scenario of my story 'The Last Pennant Before Armageddon' came to pass with Boston instead of the Cubs. When Grady Little walked to the mound and left his tired ace in to lose rather than bring in a reliever, life was imitating art."

As the summer drew to a close, it looked more likely that the Cubs would in fact earn a place in the postseason and at least make if not win the World Series. Ever the pragmatist, Bill began thinking of ways to encourage the publisher to reissue his story in an effort to make more sales on the heels of the Cubs' success.

Sadly, however, his longtime kidney problems had resurfaced, this time with a dismal outlook. Following Barb's death, Bill had become more concerned with his health than perhaps ever before. Though he had various ailments dating back to his time on the farm as a boy, his daughter Erin, who had been living with him for more than two years, had noticed his obsession with researching online various symptoms he had or felt he was dealing with. The longer she lived with him, the more she noticed the change in her father's attitude, but by the end of the summer, it had begun to seriously affect his life.

After years of telling his friends and family that he never wanted to go on dialysis, Bill was presented with that as his only option for living. Spending four hours a day in one-hour increments on dialysis was, Erin later lamented, a full-time job for Bill and "the beginning of the end."[36] Rather than providing relief, however, the dialysis caused Bill to develop a peritoneal leak, causing his scrotum to swell to the size of a football, a side effect he was informed would most likely be with him for the rest of his life. Additionally, he began having to urinate every fifteen minutes, until the urges came so frequently that he was unable to leave the bathroom.

The discomfort and bladder problems soon became so overwhelming that Erin concluded her father needed to get to the hospital; however, as he needed to urinate every five minutes by this point, she knew they would need to have assistance transporting him. After he was taken by ambulance to the hospital in Hope, on September 2, Bill's pain continued and he complained to Erin that the doctors and nurses had only told him of the benefits dialysis might bring, saying "They lied to me." After he was transferred to Abbotsford, doctors were unable to bring any relief to Bill, as by this point he was unable to keep down any solid food or liquid.

Watching her father suffer unbearable pain and thinking how unfair it was for anyone to live like that, Erin desperately hoped for some relief for her dad. She and Bill soon began considering invoking Bill C-14, Canada's new assisted dying legislation, which had passed just that past June. With no reasonable solution to alleviate his pain and provide any real quality of life, Bill had no desire to prolong his suffering. Headstrong to the very end, Bill also wanted to forgo the two-week waiting period and petitioned for an expedited process.

Once Bill had made, what seemed to Erin, an easy decision, considering his intense pain and low quality of life over the past several weeks, he was transferred back to Hope where the paperwork was pushed through, allowing Bill to end his life four days later. Not wanting many visitors, Bill only notified Shannon and her husband, Barb's daughter Scarlet, and his best friends Lee and Maggie Harwood, all of whom came to Hope to see him in his last days.

Once the paperwork was expedited, securing the date for his death, Bill spent his remaining days getting his affairs in order and visiting with friends and family. At peace with his decision to utilize the new law, and never one to shy away from controversy, Bill made it clear to his agent, who was out of the country at the time, and those close to him that his decision to end his life had to be included in the press release following his death. In the nights leading up to his final day, his longtime friend Maggie Harwood stayed with him, reminiscing about his life and the times they shared through the years. She also read Bill his favourite book, Richard Brautigan's *In Watermelon Sugar*, one last time. Like Brautigan, Bill was opting to leave the world on his terms rather than letting things run their natural course.

As they sat together talking through the memories, Bill often providing commentary on events and people he knew in his life, the discussion turned to his legacy. When Maggie asked what he'd like the world to hear as his epitaph, something perhaps to be posted on social media, he didn't hesitate. Bill quoted poet Hilaire Belloc, as he had many times in the past, who wrote, "When I am dead, I hope it may be said: 'His sins were scarlet, but his books were read.'"[37]

On Friday, September 16, 2016, at 12:05 p.m., two weeks after he left his house for the last time, Bill Kinsella died peacefully, surrounded by his family, friends and the necessary medical personnel just hours after the Cubs clinched the National League Central title and secured a place in the playoffs. Seven weeks later, for the first time since 1908, the Chicago Cubs won the World Series.

Epilogue

One month after Bill's death, his daughter Erin, Barb's daughter Scarlet, and Lee and Maggie Harwood returned to the house in Yale to scatter Bill's and Barb's ashes among the ten flower beds on the property. The event was unplanned and simply happened to coincide with them all being at the house at the same time, fitting with Bill's wishes that there be no formal memorial service and no funeral. No eulogies were given and no tributes were planned, as Bill would have wanted.

Despite my knowing he had chosen to invoke the provisions of Bill C-14 a few days in advance of his death, the hours following Bill's death left me with a feeling of emptiness. I had known him personally for not quite four years, and most of our relationship was through telephone calls and emails. Yet I had been familiar with his work since that summer day in 1989 when I went into a theatre by myself because the idea of a man building a baseball field on his farm had me hooked.

Through the years as I first read, then researched and wrote about his work, I was amazed by the people who, though they may not have immediately recognized W.P. Kinsella by name, certainly were aware of his writing. On my first trip to meet Bill at his home in 2013,

I was crossing the Canadian border when the guard asked if my trip was for business or pleasure. I informed him that it was business and that I was coming to Canada to research a book I was going to write. Somewhat intrigued, the guard asked if I had written anything he had read, and I told him that was highly unlikely. When asked about the book I was researching, I told him, "I'm writing the biography of W.P. Kinsella, the writer." As the guard squinted his eyes as if trying to recall where he had heard the name, I began rattling off titles, "He's the guy who wrote *Shoeless Joe, Born Indian, Dance Me Outside. . .*" The guard began nodding.

Bill spent just five years teaching at Desolate U., but I have spent my professional career as an academic. And in a world where people are often judged by the projects they are working on, I often received blank stares when I informed those who asked what I'd been researching: "Oh, I'm writing W.P. Kinsella's biography." But once I said, "He's the writer whose novel *Shoeless Joe* was turned into *Field of Dreams*," they almost always responded with positive comments about how much they loved the story and how, even though they weren't baseball fans, they enjoyed the emotions that came as Ray Kinsella had a catch with his dad as the credits began rolling.

Seven weeks after Bill's death, I awoke one Saturday morning to a phone call from my brother informing me that my own father had collapsed and was being flown to a much larger, more equipped hospital than the small county hospital in my hometown. Two days later, having been informed that the damage was far too great for any likely recovery, we said goodbye to Dad.

The characters in Bill's baseball stories often have a father who is absent, due to estrangement, death or some other circumstance beyond their control. Ray Kinsella is able to reunite with his father on the ball field at his farm, simultaneously allowing his twin brother, Richard, the chance to reconcile with their dad after running away from home as a teenager. And when Gideon Clarke goes back in time and watches the Iowa Baseball Confederacy All-Stars prove their worth against the 1908 Chicago Cubs he fulfills the quest his father started as a graduate student years before.

But I am no Kinsella character and my relationship with my father had no unresolved issues. Just weeks before Dad's death, I made a trip up to Ohio to visit my parents and got to spend time with him, just the two of us, going to a farm festival and talking about things he did as a boy growing up in West Virginia. To me, it was an unremarkable day, not unlike dozens of others we had over the years. Yet, as I sat there in the hospital room knowing he was drawing his last breaths, I couldn't help but reflect on that day and my favourite line in all of Bill's works.

When Ray Kinsella slips back in time and gets to visit with Dr. Archibald "Moonlight" Graham, he asks the old ballplayer what it was like playing in that one game for the Giants, never getting an at-bat. Ray, as a man in his late thirties, sees the game as a lost opportunity, one that must certainly haunt the old man in front of him. After pressing Doc Graham to explain what it was like "to brush against fame like a stranger hurrying past in a crowd," Ray sits and listens as Doc responds. "I didn't think much of it at the time. Hardly anybody recognizes the most significant moments of their life at the time they happen. I figured there'd be plenty more days."[1]

I didn't realize the significance of that last weekend with Dad at the time it was happening any more than I realized the significance of leaving the group to watch *Field of Dreams* rather than the newest Indiana Jones movie more than twenty-seven years earlier.

In *Shoeless Joe*, Ray Kinsella is given three commands by the disembodied voice. The first, "If you build it, he will come,"[2] typifies Bill's own approach to writing. When teaching summer workshops or speaking to audiences about his work, Bill would tell those interested in his craft that much of his work was based on the simple question of "what if?" His first Silas story, "Illiana Comes Home," was his own unique take on the movie *Guess Who's Coming to Dinner*, except Bill wondered, "What if the story took place on a reservation and the dominant culture was a group of Cree and the minority was white?" In his most famous novel, he once again asked "what if," but this time it was: "What if Shoeless Joe Jackson came back from the dead to play baseball in Iowa?"

The second command, "Ease his pain,"[3] is the one that sends Ray on his quest to find J.D. Salinger and take him to a game at Fenway Park. For many, the appeal of Bill's fiction is that it affords them an escape from the reality in which they live, transporting them to a place where anything is possible. The dead can be brought back to life, broken relationships can be mended, time and distance mean nothing when dealing with love, and, yes, the Chicago Cubs can win the World Series. In his remaining days, the physical pain Bill had endured for so long had gotten to the point where he no longer wanted to endure it. In our last emails, despite his pain, he remained pleased with the way his life had turned out, having become the writer he had known he could be since high school and having raised two independent, successful daughters.

The last instruction the voice gives Ray is "Go the distance," though it also tells Salinger to "Fulfill the dream."[4] Whenever Bill signed a letter to a fan, something he did with surprising regularity even after his fame took off following the release of *Field of Dreams*, or when he would inscribe a book to someone, he often signed, "Go the distance" before his name. As a teacher, he would tell students the most difficult part of being a writer is committing to putting pen to paper every day and adhering to a strict schedule—to go the distance. Having spent far too many years in his early adulthood working at jobs he loathed and for people he despised, Bill encouraged students to follow their dreams and passions until they too were able to see them realized—to go the distance.

Just days before he died, Bill Kinsella responded to the last round of questions I had for him. Dictating the answers to his daughter Erin from his hospital bed in Hope, Bill's last response was to my question about how he thought people would remember him. Though friends and family would remember him as stubborn, complicated, curmudgeonly, honest, loyal and a host of other adjectives, Bill answered, "I'm a story teller [and] my greatest satisfaction comes from leaving [while] making people laugh and also leaving them with a tear in the corner of their eye."[5]

Four days later, Canada and the rest of the world mourned the loss of Bill Kinsella. But both the laughter and the tears remain.

Acknowledgments

Perhaps the most difficult task of this entire project is simply acknowledging all the people who have helped me over the years since Bill first contacted me about the idea of writing his biography. While I fear, with some legitimate reasons, I will forget a name or two (or more), I would be remiss if I didn't attempt to acknowledge the many individuals who have helped in some capacity along the way.

My wife, Heather, the most important person in my life, and the best wife, mother for our girls, friend and editor I could ever hope to have. I love you.

My daughters, Molly and Marianne. I hope seeing me pursue my passions inspires you to pursue your own.

My parents, John and Linda Steele. Dad, your memory will always sustain me. Mom, your strength and commitment to your family shouldn't amaze me, yet it does every day.

My family: J.L., Lisa, Jessie and Destiny; Eddie, Anita, Austin and Morgan; and Priscilla. Your support and encouragement in all aspects of this project have helped make it what it has become.

Kelly and Debbie Barker, with much love and appreciation for your unwavering support, even when we moved. Again.

Todd and Melissa Scaramucci and Brent and Abby Clark. Extended family is still family, and I'm thankful you are part of mine.

Carolyn Swayze, my literary agent. Working with you has been a true pleasure. Thank you for your wisdom, insight and encouragement. Bill was right—you are the best. Many thanks to Kris Rothstein for your work during this process as well. Your help has been invaluable.

Al and Ev Trabant. I'm so glad you got the ball rolling on this project and am appreciative of your help with my research, for filling out my library with Kinsella books, and, most importantly, for your friendship. Special thanks to Christina Klassen for your help in getting the material from Burnaby sent my way.

Shannon and Erin Kinsella. Thanks for sharing your dad with me and helping me better understand who he was.

Phil Robinson, whose film is really what got this started in the summer of 1989.

Lawrence Kessenich. I'm glad you had the foresight to write Bill a letter telling him you knew his story would make a great novel. Good call.

To the many people who provided their insight and reflections on Bill Kinsella, including Derk Wynand, Bill Valgardson, Lee Harwood, Maggie Harwood, Kay Harper and Bill Swank.

Special thanks to Ann Knight, whose detailed observations and thorough bibliography of Bill's work and reviews of his work made this entire process much smoother and far more substantive than it would have otherwise been. Everyone who knew you had only good things to say, and my greatest regret while researching this book was that I never got to meet you myself.

To the fine staff at Library and Archives Canada, specifically Catherine Hobbs, Martin Lanthier and Susanne Sulzberger, for all your help in locating material, helping me access files and always having an answer when the questions arose.

To Jack and Barbara Rowe, for the Rowe Distinguished Scholar Award. Your generosity allowed me to complete much of the research found in these pages.

To my friends and former colleagues at Oklahoma Christian University who were so supportive as this project began—Scott

LaMascus, David Lowry, Cami Agan, Tina Ware Walters, Frances Sawyer, Gail Nash, Gary Lindsey, John Maple, Matt McCook, Bailey McBride, Jim Dvorak and Bill Arbuckle. A special thanks to the librarians at the Beam Library who helped with my research and interlibrary loans: Tamie Willis, J.J. Compton, Chris Rosser, Dara Tinius, Connie Maple and Kathy Fuller.

Thank you to Becky Briley for all your help with the research in Ottawa. There is no one else with whom I'd rather spend a night or two in jail.

Thank you to Saul Gonor and Leah Garven, curator of the Allen Sapp Gallery.

To Lipscomb University for their generosity with the faculty Summer Grant, allowing me to finally complete this manuscript. Special thanks to Craig Bledsoe, Norma Burgess, Kim Reed, Matt Hearn, Steve Prewitt, Lynn Griffith, Kent Johnson, Lin Garner, Al Austelle, John Lewis and Kim Chaudoin.

Thanks to Shawn Jones, Darren Williamson and Gary Tandy for your constant encouragement and what is still the most fun I've ever had teaching.

To the folks at the Cooperstown Symposium on Baseball and American Culture, who provide the best forum for baseball scholarship and allowed me to first present on Kinsella's fiction. Many thanks go to Jim Gates, Bill Simons, Tim Wiles and Matt Rothenberg.

To my friends at *NINE*, who have been among the most supportive and enthusiastic group along the way. I look forward to many more conferences and more field research. Thank you to Trey Strecker, Jean Hastings Ardell, Dan Ardell, Steve Gietschier, Geri Strecker, David Pegram, Rob Bellamy, Anna Newton, Gary Mitchem and Lee Lowenfish.

Thanks to Tom Wolf, Patricia Bryan, Paul Hensler, Bob Cullen, Bob Harden, John Ross, Charles DeMotte, Keith Spalding Robbins and the staff at the Doubleday Café for keeping me on task over many years.

Thanks for Julie Sinclair and Lynne McCarthy Williams with Pyramid Productions. Your *Curveball: W.P. Kinsella* is a tremendous asset to any Kinsella fan, particularly this one.

Many thanks to Kate Kennedy, Anna Comfort O'Keeffe, Pam Robertson, Peter Robson and Emma Skagen for helping bring this project to completion. Your ideas and insight down the homestretch only helped make this a better book.

No project of this magnitude is ever completed without good friends to support, motivate, counsel and, when needed, provide the right words at the right time. Thanks to Robert Hicks, James Carr, Ryan Lynch, Chad Wise, Jason Cost, Axel Spens, Clay Nicks, Jason Butcher, Josh Jackson and Chip Jenkins. Thanks as well to Christa Hill for helping us figure out formatting issues late at night.

And thank you Karen Cramer, the first person to show me that baseball can work well in teaching. You made learning fun.

I have made every effort to verify dates, quotes and chronology. Bill Kinsella's generosity in letting me have his notes, personal diaries and unlimited access to him via phone and email allowed me to clarify most of these things. His friends and family helped fill gaps in the months following his death. The archival material in Ottawa and Burnaby was overwhelming, but Bill's refusal to throw anything away provided additional necessary details. The things that are correct are because of the resources and people already mentioned. Whatever errors there may be are my own and make me appreciate even more Bill's comment to me: "If I need the facts, I'll make them up."

Notes

Chapter One: Six Hundred Miles from Anywhere
1.   W.P. Kinsella. Unpublished notes.
2.   W.P. Kinsella.". . . Several Unnamed Dwarfs." *Contemporary Authors Autobiography Series*. Volume 7. Chicago: Gale Research, 1991. p. 98.
3.   W.P. Kinsella. Unpublished notes.
4.   W.P. Kinsella. *Box Socials*. New York: Ballantine, 1991. p. 139.
5.   W.P. Kinsella. Unpublished notes.
6.   W.P. Kinsella. ". . . Several Unnamed Dwarfs." *Contemporary Authors Autobiography Series*, Volume 7. Chicago: Gale Research, 1991. p. 99.
7.   Library and Archives Canada, W.P. Kinsella fonds, LMS 0107 1998-08, Mrs. E.J. Satermo letter to Mary Olive Kinsella. June 25, 1943.
8.   W.P. Kinsella. Unpublished notes.
9.   Library and Archives Canada, W.P. Kinsella fonds, LMS 0107 1998-08, Billy Kinsella letter to Margaret Elliot. Undated.

Chapter Two: Edmonton
1.   W.P. Kinsella. Unpublished notes.
2.   W.P. Kinsella. "Nursie." *The Thrill of the Grass*. Toronto: Penguin, 1984. p. 80.
3.   W.P. Kinsella. Unpublished notes.
4.   W.P. Kinsella. Personal interview. August 12, 2013.
5.   W.P. Kinsella. Unpublished notes.
6.   In compiling her comprehensive bibliography of Kinsella's work, Ann Knight discovered the clippings of his earliest published pieces often had dates missing.
7.   W.P. Kinsella. Unpublished notes.

Chapter Three: The Lost Years
1. W.P. Kinsella. Unpublished notes.
2. Suzanne Zwarun. "Who's On First." *Quest*, September 1983. pp. 51–58. Qtd. in *W.P. Kinsella: A Bibliography, 1953–1992*. Ann Knight. Iowa City: A-Cross, 1992. p. 186.
3. W.P. Kinsella. Unpublished notes.

Chapter Four: Back to School
1. W.P. Kinsella. Unpublished notes.
2 W.P. Kinsella quoted in *W.P. Kinsella: A Partially-Annotated Bibliographic Checklist (1953–1983)*. Compiled by Ann Knight. White Rock, BC: A-Cross Publications, 1983. p. 6.
3. W.P. Kinsella. Unpublished notes.
4. Quoted in Kinsella's comments, *W.P. Kinsella: A Partially-Annotated Bibliographic Checklist (1953–1983)*. Compiled by Ann Knight. White Rock, BC: A-Cross Publications, 1983. pp. 5–11.
5. Library and Archives Canada. W.P. Kinsella fonds, LMS 0107 1992-09 Box 2, "Real Writers Write." *The Calgary Herald*. December 5, 1989.
6. W.P. Kinsella. Unpublished notes.

Chapter Five: Iowa
1. W.P. Kinsella. Unpublished notes.
2. Library and Archives Canada. W.P. Kinsella fonds, Therapist notes. January 19, 1978.
3. Jim Hill. "Kinsella's Indians." *The Daily Iowan*. October 6, 1977. p. 6B.
4. Library and Archives Canada. W.P. Kinsella fonds, LMS 0107 1984-08 Box 31, Reid Powell. "Dance Me Outside." *The Ontarioan*.
5. Patricia Morley. "An inside out view from the reservation." *The Ottawa Journal*. May 21, 1977. Qtd. in *W.P. Kinsella: A Partially-Annotated Bibliographic Checklist (1953–1983)*. Compiled by Ann Knight. White Rock, BC: A-Cross Publications, 1983. p. 38.
6. Nancy L. Russell. "Rare gift for telling story." Accent on Books, *Saskatoon Star Phoenix*. Undated. p. 18. Qtd. in *W.P. Kinsella: A Partially-Annotated Bibliographic Checklist (1953–1983)*. Compiled by Ann Knight. White Rock, BC: A-Cross Publications, 1983. p. 38.
7. Brian E. Burtch. "W.P. Kinsella." A review of *Dance Me Outside* and *Scars*. *Canadian Journal of Sociology* 5, no. 1 (Winter 1980). pp. 80–82. Qtd. in *W.P. Kinsella: A Partially-Annotated Bibliographic Checklist (1953–1983)*. Compiled by Ann Knight. White Rock, BC: A-Cross Publications, 1983. p. 38.
8. Reg Silvester. "Look back, but not in anger." *The Edmonton Journal*. July 11, 1977. p. 12. Qtd. in *W.P. Kinsella: A Partially-Annotated Bibliographic Checklist (1953–1983)*. Compiled by Ann Knight. White Rock, BC: A-Cross Publications, 1983. p. 38.

9.   W.P. Kinsella. Unpublished notes.

Chapter Six: Desolate U.

1.   W.P. Kinsella. Unpublished notes.
2.   Reg Silvester. "Writing at the precipice." *Edmonton Journal.*
December 30, 1978. p. H4.
3.   Library and Archives Canada. W.P. Kinsella fonds, LMS 0107 1988-11
Box 27, Alan Ricketts. "Reservations are for Writers." *NeWest ReView.*
4.   Library and Archives Canada. W.P. Kinsella fonds, LMS 0107 1988-11
Box 27, Steve Weatherbe and Rick Spence. "Vignettes from Hobbema; By a man
who *wasn't* there." *Saint John's Calgary Report.* December 18, 1978. p. 34.
5.   Library and Archives Canada. W.P. Kinsella fonds, LMS 0107 1988-11
Box 27, Alan Ricketts. "Reservations are for Writers." *NeWest ReView.*
6.   Library and Archives Canada. W.P. Kinsella fonds, LMS 0107 1988-11
Box 27, Walt Kellythorne. "Indians, but People First." *Victoria Times.*
7.   W.P. Kinsella. Unpublished notes.

Chapter Seven: "If You Build It. . ."

1.   Library and Archives Canada. W.P. Kinsella fonds, LMS-0107 1988-11
Box 9, Personal letter, Lawrence Kessenich to W.P. Kinsella. December 7, 1979.
2.   Doug Holder. "Lawrence Kessenich: Behind the Scenes at Houghton
Mifflin." November 14, 2008. http://dougholder.blogspot.com/2008/11/lawrence-
kessenich-behind-scenes-at.html.
3.   Kessenich to W.P. Kinsella, December 7, 1979.
4.   Library and Archives Canada. W.P. Kinsella fonds, LMS-0107 1988-11
Box 9, Personal letter, W.P. Kinsella to Kessenich. January 4, 1980.
5.   Library and Archives Canada. W.P. Kinsella fonds, LMS-0107 1988-11
Box 9, Personal letter, Kessenich to W.P. Kinsella. January 29, 1980.
6.   Doug Holder. "Lawrence Kessenich: Behind the Scenes at Houghton
Mifflin." November 14, 2008. http://dougholder.blogspot.com/2008/11/lawrence-
kessenich-behind-scenes-at.html.
7.   Kessenich to W.P. Kinsella. January 29, 1980.
8.   Library and Archives Canada. W.P. Kinsella fonds, LMS-0107 1988-11
Box 9, Personal letter, W.P. Kinsella to Kessenich. February 8, 1980.
9.   W.P. Kinsella. Personal Diary. February 19, 1980.
10.   Library and Archives Canada. W.P. Kinsella fonds, LMS-0107 1988-11
Box 9, Personal letter, W.P. Kinsella to Kessenich. March 11, 1980.
11.   Library and Archives Canada. W.P. Kinsella fonds, LMS-0107 1988-11
Box 9, Personal letter, Kessenich to W.P. Kinsella. March 24, 1980.
12.   Library and Archives Canada. W.P. Kinsella fonds, LMS-0107 1988-11
Box 9, Personal letter, Kessenich to W.P. Kinsella. April 30, 1980.
13.   Library and Archives Canada. W.P. Kinsella fonds, LMS-0107 1984-08
Box 22, Unpublished interview notebook, Ann Knight. 1980.

14. Edwin McDowell. "Publishing: Canadian Gets Houghton Mifflin Prize." *The New York Times.* January 15, 1982.

15. Ann Knight. Annotated notes. *W.P. Kinsella: A Partially-Annotated Bibliographic Checklist (1953–1983).* 2nd printing. Iowa City: A-Cross, 1983. p. 44.

16. Library and Archives Canada. W.P. Kinsella fonds, LMS 0107 1988-11 Box 27, William French. "Author breaks loose with magical tales." *The Globe and Mail.* May 29, 1980.

17. Library and Archives Canada. W.P. Kinsella fonds, LMS 0107 1988-11 Box 10, Anthony Bukoski. "Shoeless Joe Jackson Comes to Iowa" book review. *The Fiddlehead.* Issue 129. pp. 126–27.

18. Library and Archives Canada. W.P. Kinsella fonds, LMS 0107 1988-11 Box 10, Ken Adachi. "Author's second love is baseball."

19. Library and Archives Canada. W.P. Kinsella fonds, LMS 0107 1988-11 Box 10, Jon Whyte. "Where Man and Mountain Meet." *Banff Crag and Canyon.* October 1, 1980.

20. Jerry Wasserman. "Fantasy Lives." Reviewed with *Cry Evil* by Leon Rooke. *Canadian Literature.* Winter 1981. pp. 106–9.

21. W.P. Kinsella. Personal Diary. September 3, 1980.

22. W.P. Kinsella. Unpublished notes.

23. W.P. Kinsella. Personal Diary. November 11, 1980.

24. W.P. Kinsella. Unpublished notes.

25. W.P. Kinsella. Personal Diary. December 30, 1980.

26. W.P. Kinsella. Unpublished notes.

27. John Cook. "New Books: Born Indian." *Queen's Quarterly* 90 (Spring 1983). pp. 243–44. Qtd. in Ann Knight's *W.P. Kinsella: A Bibliography, 1953–1992, with unpublished notes and annotation.* Iowa City: A-Cross, 1992. p. 107.

28. Erling Frus-Baastad. "Red and White and bleak all over." *Books in Canada* 10 (October 1981). pp. 15–16. Qtd. in Ann Knight's *W.P. Kinsella: A Bibliography, 1953–1992, with unpublished notes and annotation.* Iowa City: A-Cross, 1992. p. 107.

29. W.P. Kinsella. Unpublished notes.

30. Mark Czarnecki. "Schemers and Redeemers." *Maclean's.* May 11, 1981. pp. 58, 61.

31. Library and Archives Canada. W.P. Kinsella fonds, LMS 0107 1988-11 Box 27, Mike Walton. "Kinsella's Indian tales are getting tired and tiresome." *Toronto Star.* April 11, 1981.

32. Library and Archives Canada. W.P. Kinsella fonds, LMS 0107 1988-11 Box 27, Judith Russell. "Indian life as she is lived." *Kingston* [Ontario] *Whig-Standard.* June 20, 1981.

33. Library and Archives Canada. W.P. Kinsella fonds, LMS 0107 1988-11 Box 27, Ian B. McLatchie. "Subversive Form." Reviewed with books by Margaret Craven and Steve Luxon. *Canadian Literature.* Summer 1982. pp. 145–47.

34.   James King. *Jack, A Life With Writers: The Story of Jack McClelland*. Toronto: Knopf Canada, 1999.

35.   W.P. Kinsella. Unpublished notes.

36.   W.P. Kinsella. Personal Diary. April 16, 1981.

37.   W.P. Kinsella. Unpublished notes.

38.   Mike Shannon. *Baseball: The Writer's Game*. Brassey's: Washington D.C., 2002. p. 158.

39.   W.P. Kinsella. Unpublished notes.

40.   W.P. Kinsella. *Shoeless Joe*. New York: Houghton Mifflin. 1982. p. 26.

41.   W.P. Kinsella. Unpublished notes.

42.   W.P. Kinsella. Personal diary. August 27, 1981.

43.   W.P. Kinsella. Unpublished notes.

44.   W.P. Kinsella. Personal Diary. December 31, 1981.

45.   Charles Gordon. "Kinsella's dreams and nostalgia could be the year's best writing." *The Ottawa Citizen*. March 27, 1982. p. 37.

46.   Qtd. in *W.P. Kinsella: A Bibliography, 1953–1992, with unpublished notes and annotation*. By Ann Knight. Iowa City: A-Cross Publications, 1992. p. 135.

47.   Qtd. in *W.P. Kinsella: A Bibliography, 1953–1992, with unpublished notes and annotation*. By Ann Knight. Iowa City: A-Cross Publications, 1992. p. 137.

48.   Michael J. Francis. "'Shoeless Joe' . . . and friends return to play ghostly baseball games." *Southland Tribune*. May 16, 1982. Qtd. in *W.P. Kinsella: A Bibliography, 1953–1992, with unpublished notes and annotation*. By Ann Knight. Iowa City: A-Cross Publications, 1992. p. 138.

49.   KCCK. National Public Radio. Cedar Rapids. May 28, 1982. Qtd. in *W.P. Kinsella: A Bibliography, 1953-1992, with unpublished notes and annotation*. By Ann Knight. Iowa City: A-Cross Publications, 1992. p. 139.

50.   Library and Archives Canada. W.P. Kinsella fonds, LMS 0107 1988-11 Box 10, Ann Knight travel diary. March 30, 1982.

51.   Library and Archives Canada. W.P. Kinsella fonds, LMS 0107 1988-11 Box 10, Ann Knight travel diary. April 13, 1982.

52.   Library and Archives Canada. W.P. Kinsella fonds, LMS 0107 1988-11 Box 10, Ann Knight travel diary. April 13, 1982.

53.   Library and Archives Canada. W.P. Kinsella fonds, LMS 0107 1988-11 Box 10, Ann Knight notes.

54.   W.P. Kinsella. Personal Diary. April 30, 1982.

55.   Library and Archives Canada. W.P. Kinsella fonds, LMS 0107 1988-11 Box 10, Ann Knight travel diary. May 3, 1982.

56.   Library and Archives Canada. W.P. Kinsella fonds, LMS 0107 1988-11 Box 10, Ann Knight travel diary. May 5, 1982.

57.   Library and Archives Canada. W.P. Kinsella fonds, LMS 0107 1988-11 Box 10, Ann Knight travel diary. May 10, 1982.

58.   Library and Archives Canada. W.P. Kinsella fonds, LMS 0107 1988-11 Box 10, Ann Knight travel diary. May 21, 1982.

59. W.P. Kinsella. Personal Diary. June 21, 1982.

60. W.P. Kinsella. Personal Diary. June 29, 1982.

Chapter Eight: Goodbye, Desolate U.

1. W.P. Kinsella. Personal Diary. August 29, 1982.

2. Library and Archives Canada. W.P. Kinsella fonds, LMS 2001520751 Box 6, Letter from Elliot L. Hoffman, Esq. to W.P. Kinsella & Houghton Mifflin. August 18, 1982.

3. W.P. Kinsella. Personal Diary. August 30, 1982.

4. W.P. Kinsella. Personal Diary. September 14, 1982.

5. W.P. Kinsella. Personal Diary. September 27, 1982.

6. W.P. Kinsella. Personal Diary. October 18, 1982.

7. Library and Archives Canada. W.P. Kinsella fonds, LMS 2001520751 Box 6, Letter from Michael Macklem to W.P. Kinsella. August 22, 1982.

8. Library and Archives Canada. W.P. Kinsella fonds, LMS 2001520751 Box 6, Letter from W.P. Kinsella to Michael Macklem. August 31, 1982.

9. Library and Archives Canada. W.P. Kinsella fonds, LMS 2001520751 Box 6, Letter from Nicholas Macklem to W.P. Kinsella. September 13, 1982.

10. W.P. Kinsella. Personal Diary. April 23, 1983.

11. W.P. Kinsella private files. Draft of personal appearance expectations. Undated. Yale, British Columbia.

12. W.P. Kinsella. Personal Diary. May 4, 1983.

13. W.P. Kinsella. Unpublished notes.

14. James Black. *The Calgary Herald*. May 19, 1983, p. A6. Qtd. in *W.P. Kinsella: A Partially-Annotated Bibliographic Checklist (1953–1983)*. By Ann Knight. Iowa City: A-Cross, 1983. p. 60.

15. W.P. Kinsella. "Letter to the Editor." *The Calgary Herald*. June 20, 1983, p. A6. Qtd. in *W.P. Kinsella: A Partially-Annotated Bibliographic Checklist (1953–1983)*. By Ann Knight. Iowa City: A-Cross, 1983. p. 61.

16. W.P. Kinsella. "Strings." *The Moccasin Telegraph*. Toronto: Penguin, 1983. pp. 13–14.

17. Don Murray. *The Fiction of W.P. Kinsella: Tall Tales in Various Voices*. Fredericton, NB: York Press, 1987. p. 22.

18. "The Moccasin Telegraph." *Publishers Weekly*. Vol. 225. May 18, 1984. p. 142. Qtd. in *W.P. Kinsella: A Partially-Annotated Bibliographic Checklist (1953–1983)*. By Ann Knight. Iowa City: A-Cross, 1983. p. 112.

19. Jay Carr. "Humor & outrage with no reservations." *The Detroit News*. August 26, 1984. p. 2K. *W.P. Kinsella: A Partially-Annotated Bibliographic Checklist (1953–1983)*. By Ann Knight. Iowa City: A-Cross, 1983. p. 112.

20. Linda E. Leppanen. "Stories Focus on the Plight of Indians." *Sunday Telegram* (Worcester, MA). September 23, 1984. p. 12D.

21. Wendy Roy. "Communities define short story characters." *Western People*. June 16, 1983. p. 13.

22.   Library and Archives Canada. W.P. Kinsella fonds, LMS 0107 1988-11 Box 27, Barbara Rose. "No fun to be Indian." *The Edmonton Journal*. June 18, 1983.

23.   Qtd. in Alan Hustak. "A call for repentance." *Alberta Report*. June 20, 1983. p. 46.

24.   Library and Archives Canada. W.P. Kinsella fonds, LMS 0107 1988-11 Box 27, Paul Pintarich. "Humor, Pathos With an American Indian Flavor." *Sunday Oregonian Magazine*. September 23, 1984.

25.   W.P. Kinsella. "Introduction." *The Thrill of the Grass*. Toronto: Penguin Canada, 1984. p. x.

26.   John E. Smelcer. "'The Mining of Gold': A Conversation with W.P. Kinsella." *Rosebud* Undated.

27.   W.P. Kinsella. "The Thrill of the Grass." *The Thrill of the Grass*. Toronto: Penguin Canada, 1984. p. 189.

28.   W.P. Kinsella. "The Last Pennant Before Armageddon." *The Thrill of the Grass*. Toronto: Penguin Canada, 1984. p. 4.

29.   Library and Archives Canada. W.P. Kinsella fonds, LMS 0107 1988-11 Box 27, Paul McKay. "Life down on the farm." *The Whig-Standard Magazine*. August 8, 1984. p. 21.

30.   Library and Archives Canada. W.P. Kinsella fonds, LMS 0107 1988-11 Box 27, Ken Adachi. "W.P. Kinsella hits a home run." *Sunday Star*. July 8, 1984.

31.   Library and Archives Canada. W.P. Kinsella fonds, LMS 0107 1988-11 Box 27, Greg Hickmore. "Love, loss, despair and lots of baseball." *Edmonton Journal*.

32.   Larry Kusch. "Try Kinsella for baseball yarns." *Western People*. October 18, 1984. p. 13.

33.   Library and Archives Canada. W.P. Kinsella fonds, LMS 0107 1988-11 Box 27, Elliot Krieger. "Baseball books: a couple of hits." *Providence (R.I.) Journal*.

34.   Library and Archives Canada. W.P. Kinsella fonds, LMS 0107 1988-11 Box 27, Alan Twigg. "Baseball diamonds are forever." *Vancouver Province*. August 26, 1984.

35.   Library and Archives Canada. W.P. Kinsella fonds, LMS 0107 1988-11 Box 27, John Keres. "Kinsella bunts." *Alberta Report*. August 20, 1984.

36.   Library and Archives Canada. W.P. Kinsella fonds, LMS 0107 1988-11 Box 27, Susan Monsky. "Short Tales: 'The Thrill of the Grass.'" *Boston Globe*. May 5, 1985.

37.   Elliot Krieger. "Baseball books: a couple of hits." *Providence (R.I.) Journal*.

38.   Library and Archives Canada. W.P. Kinsella fonds, LMS 0107 1988-11 Box 27, Gail Hand. "W.P. Kinsella's book on baseball is very funny, stands on its own." *Grand Forks Herald*. October 12, 1984.

39.   W.P. Kinsella. Personal Diary. September 23, 1984.

40.   W.P. Kinsella. Telephone interview. July 17, 2016.

41.   W.P. Kinsella. Personal Diary. December 12, 1984.

42.   W.P. Kinsella. Personal Diary. January 24, 1985.

43.   Mike Shannon. *Baseball: The Writer's Game*. Washington, DC: Brassey's, 2002. pp. 163–64.

44.   W.P. Kinsella. Personal Diary. April 6, 1985.

45.   W.P. Kinsella. Personal Diary. August 18–19, 1985.

46.   W.P. Kinsella. "Introduction." *The Alligator Report*. Coffee House Press: Minneapolis, 1985. p. 5.

47.   Library and Archives Canada. W.P. Kinsella fonds, LMS 0107 1988-11 Box 27, William French. "Gators, jugglers and the gerbil that ate L.A." *The Globe and Mail*. February 19, 1987.

48.   Library and Archives Canada. W.P. Kinsella fonds, LMS 0107 1988-11 Box 27, Paul Craig. "Kinsella: An original worth a look." *The Sacramento Bee*. December 22, 1986.

49.   Library and Archives Canada. W.P. Kinsella fonds, LMS 0107 1988-11 Box 27, William French. "Gators, jugglers and the gerbil that ate L.A." *The Globe and Mail*. February 19, 1987.

50.   Library and Archives Canada. W.P. Kinsella fonds, LMS 0107 1988-11 Box 27, Cary Fagan. Review of *The Alligator Report*.

51.   Bronwen Wallace. "Flattering by imitating." *The Whig Standard*. April 4, 1987. p. 23.

52.   Thomas S. Woods. "Alligator pulls Kinsella off track." *The Vancouver Sun*. February 28, 1987. p. E4.

53.   W.P. Kinsella. Personal Diary. December 31, 1985.

Chapter Nine: Trouble on the Reserve

1.   Kenneth McGoogan. "Edmonton-born writer embraces magic, baseball." *Calgary Herald*. April 5, 1986. p. F9.

2.   Eric Gerber. "This turn at bat, Kinsella and his 'Confederacy' just don't have it." *The Houston Post*. June 1, 1986.

3.   Patrick Ercolono. "Fantasy about 40-day ball game tries too many plays." *The Baltimore Sun*. May 11, 1986.

4.   John Gayton. "Baseball and Blue Quills." *Briarpatch*. July/August 1986. p. 26.

5.   Bob McKelvey. "Books and Authors: Baseball lover weaves fantasy into the game." *Detroit Free Press*. May 4, 1986.

6.   Bob McCoy. "Keeping Score: The Confederacy Rises." *The Sporting News*. June 16, 1986.

7.   Chris Farlekas. "Books to watch the Series by." *Orlando Sentinel Record*. October 1988. Qtd. in *W.P. Kinsella: A Bibliography, 1953–1992*. By Ann Knight. Iowa City: A-Cross Publications, 1992. p. 158.

8.   Michael J. Bandler. "Play Ball." *American Way*. May 18, 1986. pp. 76–77. Qtd. in *W.P. Kinsella: A Bibliography, 1953–1992*. By Ann Knight. Iowa City: A-Cross Publications, 1992. p. 156.

9. Roger Kahn. "The Iowa Baseball Confederacy." *Los Angeles Times/The Book Review.* July 6, 1986. p. 1. Qtd. in *W.P. Kinsella: A Bibliography, 1953–1992.* By Ann Knight. Iowa City: A-Cross Publications, 1992. p. 160.

10. Bruce Levett. "Fresh shenanigans from a band of Indian scallywags." *The Vancouver Sun.* November 15, 1986.

11. Jim Spencer. "Heap big humor that's right on the edge." *Tribune.* September 10, 1987.

12. Fred Liddle. "Kinsella Leaves the Big Leagues." *The Tampa Tribune.* September 20, 1987.

13. W.P. Kinsella "The Fencepost Chronicles." *Kirkus.* July 15, 1987.

14. William French. "The whimsical spinner of tales." *The Globe and Mail.* November 15, 1987. p. E3.

15. Jim Spencer. "Heap big humor that's right on the edge." *Tribune.* September 10, 1987.

16. Frank Moher. "The good ole braves." *Alberta Report.* December 29, 1986.

17. Michael Dorris. "Collection of Indian stories engrossing, but leaves a nagging doubt." *Minneapolis Star Tribune.* September 27, 1987.

18. William French. "The whimsical spinner of tales." *The Globe and Mail.* November 15, 1987. p. E3.

19. Paul Pintarich. "Ermineskin and Fencepost Again." *Northwest Magazine.* October 18, 1987. p. 29.

20. Fred Liddle. "Kinsella Leaves the Big Leagues." *The Tampa Tribune.* September 20, 1987.

21. Norbert Blei. "A funny visit with the Crees." *Milwaukee Journal.* October 11, 1987.

22. W.P. Kinsella. "Introduction." *Red Wolf, Red Wolf.* Toronto: Collins, 1987. p. ii.

23. Kenneth McGoogan. "Kinsella displays new range." *Calgary Herald.* August 30, 1987. p. E4.

24. Thomas Woods. "Silly at times, but Kinsella can't miss with these tales." *The Vancouver Sun.* September 26, 1987. p. H4.

25. Jerry Rogers. "Kinsella probes loneliness." *The Spectator.* October 3, 1987. p. D2.

26. Ken Adachi. "Kinsella finds the pathos in ordinary lives." *Sunday Star.* September 6, 1987.

27. Mary Walters Riskin. "More pizzazz expected from Kinsella collection." *The Edmonton Journal.* September 12, 1987.

28. Burt Heward. "Five Canadians excel in varied fiction forms." *The Ottawa Citizen.* October 31, 1987. p. H4.

29. William French. "Kinsella focuses on the middle class." *The Globe and Mail.* September 3, 1987. p. A10.

30. W.P. Kinsella. Personal Diary. March 9, 1987.

31. W.P. Kinsella. Personal Diary. March 13, 1987.

32. W.P. Kinsella. Personal Diary. April 2, 1987.

33. W.P. Kinsella. Personal Diary. April 24, 1987.

34. W.P. Kinsella. Personal Diary. July 8, 1987.

35. Laura Leake. "Leaving it all behind, ex-exec gains what he always wanted." *The Ring*. April 7, 1976. p. 6.

Chapter Ten: "... He Will Come"

1. W.P. Kinsella. Personal Diary. February 10, 1988.

2. Roger Angell to W.P. Kinsella. November 9, 1978. Private collection, W.P. Kinsella.

3. Ken Adachi. "W.P. Kinsella: Writer on a hitting streak." *Toronto Star*. May 14, 1983. p. F10.

4. Denny Boyd. "Baseball is just a platform for Bill's enchanting plays." *The Vancouver Sun*. April 4, 1986. p. B2.

5. W.P. Kinsella. Personal Diary. May 24, 1988.

6. Library and Archives Canada. W.P. Kinsella fonds, LMS 0107 1992-09 W.E.L. *Kliatt*. June 1988. p. 3.

7. Bill Ott. "Quick Bibs: New and recent books on a timely topic." *American Libraries*. April 1988.

8. Morton Ritts. "The Mystery of Baseball." *Maclean's*. May 30, 1988.

9. Marylaine Block. "Book Review." *Library Journal*. June 1, 1988. p. 142.

10. Morton Ritts. "The Mystery of Baseball." *Maclean's*. May 30, 1988.

11. Review of *The Further Adventures of Slugger McBatt*, by W.P. Kinsella. *Kirkus*. April 1, 1988.

12. *Publishers Weekly*. April 8, 1988.

13. Qtd. in W.P. Kinsella. Personal Diary. June 2, 1988.

14. W.P. Kinsella. Personal Diary. August 5, 1988.

15. W.P. Kinsella. Personal Diary. September 30, 1988.

16. W.P. Kinsella. Annual Letter. December 28, 1988. Private files. Yale, BC.

17. Shannon Kinsella. Telephone interview. November 13, 2014.

18. Greg Heaton. "Me storyteller, you Tonto." *Western Report*. December 11, 1989. p. 37.

19. Sarah Harvey. "Old formula, new sensibilities." *Globe and Mail*. January 27, 1990. Qtd. in *W.P. Kinsella: A Bibliography, 1953–1992*. By Ann Knight. Iowa City: A-Cross Publications, 1992. p. 128.

20. Joan Donaldson. "Kinsella tales tell of trials." *Calgary Herald*. December 26, 1989. p. 10. Qtd. in *W.P. Kinsella: A Bibliography, 1953–1992*. By Ann Knight. Iowa City: A-Cross Publications, 1992. p. 128.

21. Byron Rempel. "Flak and Fiction." *Western Report*. December 25, 1989. p. 33.

22. W.P. Kinsella. Personal Diary. December 7, 1989.

23. Qtd. in Byron Rempel. "Flak and Fiction." *Western Report*. December 25, 1989.

24. Graham Hicks. "The defence of Kinsella." *The Edmonton Sun.* December 6, 1989. p. 86.

25. Library and Archives Canada. W.P. Kinsella fonds, LMS 0107 1992-09 Box 11, John Holman. "'Hobbema Pageant' hits us in the heart."

26. Qtd. in Byron Rempel. "Flak and Fiction." *Western Report.* December 25, 1989.

Chapter Eleven: "Nowhere To Go But Down"

1. W.P. Kinsella. Personal Diary. January 8, 1990.

2. W.P. Kinsella. Annual Letter. 1990.

3. W.P. Kinsella. Personal Diary. March 29, 1990.

4. W.P. Kinsella. Personal Diary. July 25, 1990.

5. W.P. Kinsella. Personal Diary. December 31, 1990/January 1, 1991.

6. W.P. Kinsella. Personal Diary. April 14, 1991.

7. W.P. Kinsella. Annual Letter. 1991. Private files. Yale, BC.

8. W.P. Kinsella. Personal Diary. May 29, 1991.

9. V. Dwyer. "Patchwork Prose." *Maclean's* (1991). p. 90.

10. James C. Roberts. "Baseball writer hits double in 'Social'." *The Washington Times.* May 18, 1992. p. D2.

11. Library and Archives Canada. W.P. Kinsella fonds, LMS 0107 1992-09 Box 1, W.P. Kinsella conference brochure.

12. W.P. Kinsella. Annual Letter. 1992. Private files. Yale, BC.

13. W.P. Kinsella. Personal Diary. February 23, 1993.

14. W.P. Kinsella. Personal Diary. May 1, 1993.

15. W.P. Kinsella. Personal Diary. September 22, 1993.

16. Richard Warnica. "W.P. Kinsella is still at bat (for baseball fans and mid list authors." *National Post.* March 30, 2015.

17. Araminta Wordsworth. "Ball Park Ghosts: Kinsella again evokes the spirits of baseball." *The Financial Post* (Toronto)." July 31, 1993. Section 4. p. 57.

18. Ken Belson. *The Daily Yomiuri.* May 14, 1995. p. 17.

19. Bob Minzesheimer. "Kinsella's nine storied innings/Mystical tales are all over the field." *USA Today.* February 14, 1995. p. 4D.

20. Philip Marchand. "Conjuring up the spirits of baseball." *The Toronto Star.* July 19, 1993. p. G12.

21. Jay Stone. "Kinsella deserves early trip to the showers." *The Ottawa Citizen.* July 24, 1993. p. B7.

22. W.P. Kinsella. Personal Diary. November 18, 1993.

23. W.P. Kinsella. Personal Diary. January 26, 1994.

24. W.P. Kinsella. Personal Diary. February 12, 1994.

25. "Order of Canada." The Governor General of Canada His Excellency the Right Honourable David Johnston. gg.ca.

26. W.P. Kinsella. Personal Diary. February 17, 1994.

27. W.P. Kinsella. Personal Diary. February 28, 1994.

28. W.P. Kinsella. Personal Diary. March 27, 1994.

29. Virginia Byfield. "Endearing Stereotypes." *Alberta Report/Newsmagazine.* 22, no. 11 (1995). p. 37.

30. Stephen Rouse. "A poor swan song for Silas." *The Ottawa Citizen.* August 14, 1994. p. B3.

31. W.P. Kinsella. Personal Diary. March 31, 1995.

32. W.P. Kinsella. Personal Diary. April 1, 1995.

33. W.P. Kinsella. Personal Diary. December 30, 1995.

34. W.P. Kinsella. Personal Diary. December 31, 1995/January 1, 1996.

35. John Doyle. "Kinsella still has his fastball." *The Globe and Mail.* August 19, 1995.

36. Colby Cosh. "Helen's No Shoeless Joe." *Alberta Report/Newsmagazine.* 22, no. 36 (1995). p. 34.

37. W.P. Kinsella. *The Winter Helen Dropped By.* Toronto: HarperPerennial, 1996. p. 1.

38. Nancy Baele. "The broad brushstrokes of W.P. Kinsella's storytelling." *The Ottawa Citizen.* July 30, 1995. p. C3.

39. W.P. Kinsella. *The Winter Helen Dropped By.* Toronto: HarperPerennial, 1996. p. 81.

40. Lee Harwood. Telephone interview. July 29, 2017.

41. W.P. Kinsella. Personal Diary. March 17, 1996.

42. W.P. Kinsella. Personal Diary. March 25, 1996.

43. W.P. Kinsella. "The quiet scourge of Invisible Writers Syndrome." *The Globe and Mail.* March 30, 1996.

44. W.P. Kinsella. Personal Diary. May 14, 1996.

45. W.P. Kinsella. Personal Diary. May 23, 1996.

46. Library and Archives Canada, W.P. Kinsella fonds, LMS 0107 1998-08 Box 6, Letter from Larry Kessenich to W.P. Kinsella. June 5, 1987.

47. Library and Archives Canada, W.P. Kinsella fonds, LMS 0107 1998-08 Box 6, Letter from W.P. Kinsella to Larry Kessenich. June 13, 1987.

48. John Doyle. "Grand propaganda for living in dreams, readers must suspend their cynicism to take W.P. Kinsella's exquisitely sentimental journey." *The Globe and Mail.* October 5, 1996. p. D15.

49. Brian Bethune. "Diamonds are Forever." *Maclean's* (1996). p. 69.

50. John Doyle. "Grand propaganda for living in dreams, readers must suspend their cynicism to take W.P. Kinsella's exquisitely sentimental journey." *The Globe and Mail.* October 5, 1996. p. D15.

51. Library and Archives Canada, W.P. Kinsella fonds, LMS 0107 1998-08 Box 6, Letter from Ann Knight to W.P. Kinsella. May 6, 1997.

52. W.P. Kinsella. Personal Diary. May 25, 1997.

53. W.P. Kinsella. Personal Diary. June 29, 1997.

54. W.P. Kinsella. Personal Diary. October 1, 1997.

55. Evelyn Lau. "Me & W.P." *Vancouver.* 30, no. 6 (October 1997). pp. 82–97.

56.   Spider Robinson email letter to Jim Sutherland. October 1, 1997. Private files of Carolyn Swayze.

57.   Carolyn Swayze letter to Jim Sutherland and Douglas Coupland. October 9, 1997. Private files of Carolyn Swayze.

58.   Shafer Parker, Jr. "He said, she said, he sued." *BC Report*. 9, no. 23 (March 23, 1998). p. 24.

59.   Library and Archives Canada. Burnaby, British Columbia. Handwritten agreement between W.P. Kinsella and Evelyn Lau. September 20, 1996.

60.   Library and Archives Canada. Burnaby, British Columbia. Statement of Claim. William Patrick Kinsella against Evelyn Lau, Telemedia Communications Inc., Douglas Coupland, and Jim Sutherland.

61.   W.P. Kinsella. Personal Diary. October 13, 1997.

62.   Library and Archives Canada. Burnaby, British Columbia. W.P. Kinsella private notes. p. 2.

63.   Library and Archives Canada. Burnaby, British Columbia. Dr. Stephen D. Anderson notes. October 18, 1999. pp. 7–15.

Chapter Twelve: The Gin Runs Out

1.   Martin Levin. "Several stories in search of a novel." *The Globe and Mail*. August 1, 1998. p. D13.

2.   Len Gasparini. "Kinsella's two-trick pony." *The Toronto Star*. June 6, 1998. p. M19.

3.   H.J. Kirchhoff. "It up to you." *The Globe and Mail*. August 1, 1998. p. D13.

4.   Colby Cosh. "Frank and Silas are Older, but Not Yet Wiser." *Alberta Report*. 25, no. 26 (1998). p. 38.

5.   W.P. Kinsella. Annual Letter. December 1999.

6.   Peter O'Brien. "Kinsella hits one deep." *The Globe and Mail*. January 27, 2001. p. D11.

7.   *Japanese Baseball and Other Stories*. Review. *Quill & Quire*. Undated.

8.   Peter O'Brien. "Kinsella hits one deep." *The Globe and Mail*. January 27, 2001. p. D11.

9.   *Japanese Baseball and Other Stories*. Review. *Quill & Quire*. Undated.

10.   W.P. Kinsella. Annual Letter. December 1999.

11.   W.P. Kinsella. Personal Diary. May 9, 2002.

12.   Erin Kinsella. Telephone interview. February 19, 2017.

13.   W.P. Kinsella. Personal Diary. July 16, 2002.

14.   W.P. Kinsella. Personal Diary. November 23, 2002.

15.   Order of British Columbia. Website. orderofbc.gov.bc.ca.

16.   W.P. Kinsella. Annual Letter. December 2005.

17.   W.P. Kinsella. Annual Letter. December 2006.

18.   W.P. Kinsella. Personal Diary. April 23, 2007.

19. "B.C. writer W.P. Kinsella wins lifetime achievement award." *CBCNews*. June 10, 2009. http://www.cbc.ca/news/entertainment/b-c-writer-w-p-kinsella-wins-lifetime-achievement-award-1.842143.

20. W.P. Kinsella. "Facing up to Death." *The Seattle Review*, Issues with Death, (2010). 169. pp. 167–70.

21. W.P. Kinsella. Annual Letter. December 2010.

22. W.P. Kinsella. Personal Diary. November 23, 2010.

23. *Butterfly Winter*. Review. *Publishers Weekly*. Undated.

24. Steven Hayward. *Butterfly Winter*. Review. *The Globe and Mail*. November 8, 2011.

25. *Butterfly Winter*. Review. *Quill & Quire*. Undated.

26. "Author W.P. Kinsella Named Jack Graney Award Winner." The Canadian Baseball Hall of Fame and Museum. https://baseballhalloffame.ca.

27. W.P. Kinsella. Personal Diary. December 23, 2012.

28. W.P. Kinsella. Annual Letter. December 2013.

29. W.P. Kinsella. Personal Diary. October 14, 2013.

30. W.P. Kinsella. Annual Letter. December 2015.

31. *The Essential W.P. Kinsella*. Review. Buffalo & Erie County Public Library. Review by *Booklist Review*. Website. www.booklistonline.com/The-Essential-W-P-Kinsella-Kinsella-W-P/pid=7299303.

32. Jessica Peters. "WP Kinsella to read to Chilliwack audience." *Chilliwack Progress*. September 11, 2015.

33. Lee Harwood. Telephone interview. July 29, 2017.

34. W.P. Kinsella. Annual Letter. December 2015.

35. W.P. Kinsella. Annual Letter. December 2003.

36. Erin Kinsella. Telephone interview. February 19, 2017.

37. Maggie Harwood. Telephone interview. July 29, 2017.

Epilogue

1. W.P. Kinsella. *Shoeless Joe*. Boston: Houghton Mifflin, 1982. p. 146.

2. W.P. Kinsella. *Shoeless Joe*. Boston: Houghton Mifflin, 1982. p. 1.

3. W.P. Kinsella. *Shoeless Joe*. Boston: Houghton Mifflin, 1982. p. 31.

4. W.P. Kinsella. *Shoeless Joe*. Boston: Houghton Mifflin, 1982. p. 105.

5. Email Interview. September 13, 2016.

Index

Page numbers in **bold** refer to photographs